'WATER, WATER EVERYWHERE': THE GREAT WESTERN FALLACY

HISTORY OF WATER IN THE WEST AND ITS FUTURE

GENIA GALLAGHER

Dedication

This book is dedicated to the two men in my life: Gary, who gave me the time and freedom to pursue my passion, and Bailey, who never complained about all the walks he missed.

Contents

Dedication iii

CHAPTER 1

"For What It's Worth" – Introduction 1

CHAPTER 2

Who Would Want to Live There? – Prehistory & Water 23

CHAPTER 3

"Build It And They Will Come" – Recorded History.................51

CHAPTER 4

Taming the Wild River – Colorado River History 71

CHAPTER 5

'California Dreamin'[1] – California Today 107

CHAPTER 6

"Drought Does Not Equal a Water Shortage"[1]
– Arizona Today 133

CHAPTER 7

"What Happens in Vegas Does NOT Stay in Vegas"
– Las Vegas Today...147

CHAPTER 8

"The Trouble I'm In"[1] – Colorado River Today.......................159

CHAPTER 9

    What Do You Pay for Water? – Price of Water.........................189

CHAPTER 10

    "Teach Your Children Well" – Lessons Learned
    From Other Countries 207

CHAPTER 11

    "Something's Gotta Give" – A New Water Ethic 237

CHAPTER 12

    "Whiskey is for drinking and water is for fighting."
    – The Future 247

Notes 261

Bibliography...331

Acknowledgements...371

Index..373

Chapter 1

"For What It's Worth" – Introduction

CATASTROPHE MOVIES OVER THE PAST fifty years have depicted earthquakes, tsunamis, volcanic eruptions and bird attacks in California, but as of 2016, a water crisis has not appeared on the big screen. In an Op Ed in *the L.A. Times* Jay Famiglietti stated.

> *Imagine a disaster movie in which 22 million people are told that they have only 12 to 18 months of water left. Unless Southern Californians pull together, we will be making that movie.[2]*

Unfortunately, Mr. Famiglietti is not a Hollywood producer with the next great idea for a disaster movie but is instead the Senior Water Scientist at the NASA Jet Propulsion Laboratory and a professor at UC Irvine. His comments are a result of both research and working in the field for twenty-five years, making him a leading expert, especially as it relates to ground water. In spite of his dire prediction and Governor Brown issuing a State of Emergency in January 2014, water usage in Southern California increased by 2.8% as of February of 2015.[3]

Famiglietti's movie is not just occurring in California. In 2015, water levels dropped to below 50% capacity at both Lake Mead and

Lake Powell, the major storage facilities for the Colorado River. Arizona warned farmers they might not receive water to irrigate their fields as early as 2016. In addition, Las Vegas completed a third intake pipe to draw water from Lake Mead as their other two intake pipes were in danger of "sucking air" if the water level dropped another seventy-five feet. This is pretty scary stuff! But certainly conditions will change and everything will be all right as soon as the rains return. So, why is Famiglietti waving such a huge red flag? Isn't El Niño bringing water to California and the mountains of Colorado?

Oh, if it were that simple! But first, we need to slow down and make sure we understand some basics before delving into this highly complicated and confusing issue of water. Remember elementary school and the water cycle? Recall how your crayon drawings showed raindrops watering plants and feeding streams and the sun heating the puddles of water and evaporating and reemerging, or condensing in the form of clouds that led to more rain? How many of your 2nd grade classmates made the connection that this movement of water was constantly occurring and happened everywhere on the planet and not just in their small world? How many understood that because of this hydrological cycle the water they got out of the tap was the same water the dinosaurs drank and eliminated?

I remember winning third place in a science fair when I was in the 4th grade for depicting the water cycle by placing a plant and a light under a plastic cover. Mrs. Sorenson, my science teacher, clearly taught how the water cycle worked and in all probability made the connections as to how this cycle related to farmers, but I cannot recall nor did I understand how the water cycle related to where the water I drank originated nor how it related to the many droughts that Texas experienced. (I lived in Dallas until I was 13)

Another concept I was not taught was infiltration, which involves precipitation not directly entering a river or stream by surface runoff, but seeping or percolating into the soil. This water enters the roots of plants and then through evapotranspiration (another term I did not learn), returns to the atmosphere. In fairness, these terms may have been covered, but I did not grasp their significance and thus did not learn them. I now understand the infiltration process also entails water sinking deeper into the ground where it "recharges" aquifers, or underground natural storage. Infiltrated water could be stored in the ground for varying lengths of time: days, months, years and in many cases, centuries.

I am also fairly confident that I did not learn that some aquifers, called alluvial, ultimately "discharged" or returned this infiltrated water into nearby rivers and streams. Thus, surface runoff or water not absorbed into the roots of plants from precipitation or irrigation, through return flow, reentered the surface water system. With groundwater depletion in California constantly in the news today an understanding of this aspect of the water cycle is critical as this return of water to rivers and streams is an important part of the total amount of water that ultimately flows into major reservoirs like Lake Mead.

A striking example of the impact on how groundwater depletion affects the amount flowing into a river is the Santa Cruz River in Tucson, Arizona. This once perennial flowing river on which a prehistoric culture depended for centuries is now dry except during the spring, sporadically during the monsoonal season in mid-summer or when Tucson's wastewater treatment plant releases some effluent.

Why did the Santa Cruz become a dry river? In *Water Follies: Groundwater Pumping and the Fate of America's Fresh Waters,* Robert Glennon claimed that it was due to groundwater pumping that provided water for municipal, agricultural and mining purposes. Over a sixty-year period, groundwater pumping increased from 40,000 acre-feet each year (over 13 billion gallons) to over 330,000 acre-feet (over 107 billion gallons).[4]

One acre-foot equals 325,851 gallons and is a term used to quantify the amount of water in a body of freshwater. Initially, I had a hard time grasping how much water this actually meant until someone told me to picture a football field covered with a foot of water. That is an acre-foot.

Thus, over a sixty-year period pumping of the Santa Cruz River increased by 290,000 football fields covered with a foot of water.

Prior to this increase in pumping, the aquifer discharged into the local river. Today, "Groundwater pumping literally sucks the water out of the Santa Cruz River."[5] Thus, man destroyed the flow of the Santa Cruz by circumventing this naturally occurring exchange between surface and ground water—a basic part of the water cycle.

Hopefully, 4th graders are being taught about alluvial aquifers today and how they provide water to the streams and rivers in the West. This symbiotic relationship between alluvial aquifers and rivers and streams becomes critical when discussing groundwater depletion as well as understanding how water used to irrigate fields returns to a water source for a use further downstream by percolating into or infiltrating the soil.

Another aspect of the water cycle that I also did not understand was that this massive amount of water movement involved time delays. It is estimated that as water evaporates and enters the earth's atmosphere, it remains water vapor for up to ten days. So, water stored in Lake Mead located behind Hoover Dam, which loses more than 260 billion gallons or 800,000 acre-feet (again, one acre-foot is 325,851 gallons) each year to evaporation reverts to its liquid form as either rain or snow over the Midwest, East Coast, Atlantic Ocean or possibly Europe.[6] Imagine how much more will evaporate as the temperature continues to increase. Given the time delay of water turning into rain or snow, couldn't this make arid and semi-arid climates even dryer? But, we are getting ahead of ourselves.

I never understood the magnitude of this hydrological cycle, nor did I even begin to comprehend how it all related to the water each of us MUST consume each day. I am sure I was no different from the "Average Josephine" as I just turned on the tap for my drinking water to brush my teeth or take a shower and did not give a second thought as to where the water came from nor the influence the water or hydrological cycle had on my daily life. I completely took water for granted.

So, as I look out my window at the lofty altitude of 9,752 feet in Colorado, I finally realize that water that evaporated in Fiji, Hawaii or somewhere over the Pacific Ocean actually reemerges as snow and provides perfect skiing conditions. As the snow melts it joins the Colorado River that begins in Rocky Mountain National Park and winds its way over 1,450 miles into Mexico.

I also believed water to be "mine" as do most Americans and in fact, in many state constitutions water is considered a usufructuary right or a claim on a resource without a legal contract to prove ownership. Water like air is a basic necessity of life and everyone is entitled to access to both resources. However, when there is not enough to go around, as is the existing situation in California, a process is needed to determine who should or should not have the right of access to the water. Without such a system, chaos prevails. This scenario could be the crux of Famiglietti's movie not dissimilar from *Atlas Shrugged* by Ayn Rand[7] or the recent book *Water Knife* by Paolo Bacigalupi[8], which could actually be the story line behind Famiglietti's movie.

Another elementary school flashback involved learning that over 70% of the earth's surface is covered with water, thereby earning our nickname, the "water planet."

FIGURE 1 – Where Is Earth's Water

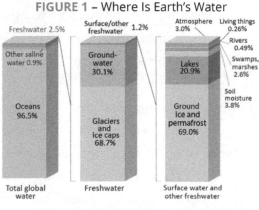

Source: Igor Shiklomanov's chapter "World fresh water resources" in Peter H. Gleick (editor), 1993, Water in Crisis: A Guide to the World's Fresh Water Resources.
NOTE: Numbers are rounded, so percent summations may not add to 100.

Retrieved from: http://water.usgs.gov/edu/earthwherewater.html[10]

To summarize Figure 1, of the estimated 358 million trillion gallons on earth, over 97.5% is found in oceans or other saline water; in other words, the salinity is too high for human, animal and most plant consumption. To further complicate matters, of the remaining 2.5% considered freshwater, or what is available for irrigation, drinking, bathing, etc., around 69% is frozen solid in glaciers or ice caps leaving around 30% of the 2.5% in groundwater (water below the surface of the earth) and 1.2% in surface water (lakes, rivers, reservoirs, streams, etc.)[9] It is not surprising people do not think about where they get their water, there are just too many numbers! Hopefully, Figure 1 makes it easier to comprehend.

In the western United States, most of the water consumed by humans and animals comes from surface water, which is .009 of 1% of the total amount of water on earth. But even though surface water is just a miniscule amount, there is still almost 2.3 million trillion gallons in rivers, lakes, and soil moisture. That is a lot of water so it is no mystery why Americans turn on the tap without giving it a second thought.

So if there is so much water, why is Jay Famiglietti painting a doomsday picture and indicating that California only has 12 months of water left? Why did Governor Brown issue an Executive Order on April 1, 2015 that stipulated a mandatory reduction of 25% on potable, or drinkable, urban usage by February 2016 and also prohibited the use of potable water on public street medians, or newly constructed buildings not irrigated by drip or micro-spray systems? Additionally, why are water managers concerned with the declining water levels in Lake Mead and Lake Powell? What is going on that requires such alarmist measures? Could Famiglietti's movie idea actually be gaining some sense of reality?

Perhaps our first clue comes in a statement found in the seminal book on water in the West by Marc Reisner, *Cadillac Desert: The American West and its Disappearing Water.*

> *Los Angeles is drier than Beirut: Sacramento is as dry as the Sahel [...] California, which fools visitors into believing it is "lush," is a beautiful fraud.* [11]

How can California be a "fraud"? Aren't the lush lawns and swimming pools part of the American Dream? After all, Disneyland is where "all your dreams come true." How could California be considered a fraud when one enters the magic of Fantasyland or Tomorrowland? Furthermore, as of 2014, the state generated $54 billion in revenue producing over 400 crops.[12] There does seem to be a disconnect between how we envision sunny California with its swimming pools and manicured lawns and year round flowers with Reisner's view.

The current uproar due to the drought in California has many water managers in the western states rejoicing in the fact that red flags are finally being waved and some action at long last is materializing in the Golden State. Is this problem of drought and lack of water bigger than just an issue that California faces? Perhaps Mikhail Gorbachev says it best.

> *Water, like religion and ideology, has the power to move millions of people. Since the very birth of human civilization, people have moved to settle close to it. People move when there is too little of it. People move when there is too much of it. People journey down it. People write, sing and dance about it. People fight over it. And all people, everywhere and every day, need it.*[13]

Returning to basics: even though there is certainly a lot of water, remember our source of drinking and irrigation water comes mainly from rivers, lakes, streams, reservoirs and groundwater. Figure 2 shows the major rivers in the United States. One is struck with the realization that apart from the northwestern part of the West, there are precious few major rivers west of the 100th meridian, or for the sake of simplicity, anything west of the Texas Panhandle, west of the Kansas/Colorado border, west of the Nebraska/Wyoming border and west of the border between North and South Dakota and Montana.

FIGURE 2 – Major Rivers in United States

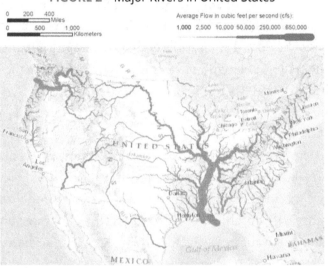

Source: Adapted from Challenges of the Colorado River Basin Presentation, October 16, 2013[14]

Clearly, this map reveals that although there are some rivers west of the 100th meridian, most are concentrated east of the Mississippi River. If the Southwest and California expect to continue the explosive growth seen in the last fifty years, where will newcomers get their water? Will farmers and ranchers be expected to give up the water that provides their livelihood?

Another elementary school lesson I remember was that the world's earliest civilizations formed around rivers. This makes sense, as water is a necessity for life. Although it is not clear when the alluvial lands of modern-day Iraq were initially settled, it is believed to have started on a mound of silt in the Euphrates Valley. The Sumerian civilization began in a land called Mesopotamia between the Euphrates and Tigris around

3000 BCE. In fact, Mesopotamia means the "land between rivers." Simultaneously, the Egyptian civilization started next to the Nile. Also, around the same time, the Lungshan culture developed in China along the Yangtze River. Later, Rome began its civilization along the Tiber River.[15] Thus from ancient times, these rivers allowed cultures to exist and controlled the fate of those living next to them.

United States recorded history mirrors this also as first settlements by Europeans proved successful on the East Coast near rivers and where water was readily available and accessible. However, as the Spanish started their missions in the Southwest and California, they found the arid and semi-arid climate dictated adaptation and manipulation of the landscape.

Perhaps a brief overview of the climatic and environmental conditions in the West is in order. When one thinks of the West, an image of a hot, arid, barren landscape comes to mind. The fact is the West is actually a region of extremes ranging from high mountain ranges that receive heavy snowfall during the winter to the hot desolate deserts. The snow in the mountains provides the annually renewable water source for the entire region; except for a brief monsoonal flow during mid-summer. Aside from this brief period of moisture and the snow in the mountains, precipitation in the majority of the region is minimal, ranging in totals of 3 to 12 inches per year. With the exception of snowpack run-off occurring in May and June and two weeks of the monsoonal flow, there is very little precipitation during the growing season when temperatures climb to over 100 degrees in many areas. Due to the high temperatures and arid conditions, evaporation rates are quite high and in fact, the evaporation rate is often greater than the amount of precipitation. As a result, during the 18th and 19th century, the area west of the Mississippi River to the coastal ranges of California was called the Great American Desert.[16]

Stages of Man's Relationship with Water

Just as in Mesopotamia and Egypt, water was a driving force behind the history of the United States. An examination of the history and pre-history west of the Mississippi River reflected water clearly influenced the rise and fall of numerous cultures as well as the settlement of the West by Anglo-Americans. This development of the West occurred over several thousand years with an evolving relationship between humans and nature that consisted of three stages. These stages are human's dependence on water, human's manipulation and mutuality with water, and finally, human's "taming" or controlling water. If one reviews both pre-historic as well as recorded history in the West, aside from several examples where man just depended on the abundance of what water provided, the old adage "don't fool with Mother Nature" holds true. With climate change and the drought in the Colorado River Basin since 2000, the Grand Old Lady may be flexing her muscles again showing who is really in control.

The first stage of the relationship between man and water reflected an almost total dependence on water for survival as revealed by those who lived along the Columbia River near the Long Narrows located on the current border of Oregon and Washington. From circa 10,000 B.C.E. until 1855, these indigenous folks lived along the banks of Wauna or the Columbia River. Kennewick Man, found further up the river dated back to around 7300 B.C.E., confirmed prehistoric human habitation in the area. The lifestyle along Wauna consisted of multi-family long houses or smaller groups that moved seasonally with the greatest fishing around the Long Narrows. These native people sustained their way of life by fishing, hunting and gathering plants that were in abundance along the river for over a thousand years until the Treaty of 1855 moved the descendants of these ancient people to reservations in a more desolate setting.[17]

Clearly, along the Columbia River, Native Americans depended on the ecosystem for over several millennia and survived on the bounty of the river. They existed on what the river provided without manipulating or changing nature. Given this, Mother Nature looked favorably on the Columbia River people where they lived until forced to relocate by other human beings in the late 1800s.

Another example that reflected man's dependence on water involved the nomadic Plains Indians of the Great Plains or the Great American Desert. As Anglo-Americans began to settle the West, they found an assortment of nomadic tribes that lived in this arid region. It had not been that way for long! For thousands of years prehistoric Native Americans hunted and lived along lakes and streams fueled by the Wisconsin Glacier to the north. As the glacier disappeared the area gradually dried up and by 1000 C.E. some prehistoric Indians settled in semi-permanent villages along perennial flowing rivers and streams. These ancient people supplemented their subsistence by hunting, gathering and planting corn, beans and squash.[18]

Over the centuries, variable precipitation led to a wide variety of grasses that adapted to local conditions and remained totally dependent on the sparse rainfall on the Plains. Additionally, localized and seasonal water flows resulted in the grasses peaking at different points during the spring and summer. This variation in timing ultimately led the bison to roam the Plains in search of the most nutritious fodder, both annual and perennial. All of this was determined by Mother Nature and where and when she provided water. Although bison became a part of the way of life of prehistoric Native Americans by 9000 B.C.E., their relatively semi-permanent riparian life style continued until the 13th or 14th century when bison hunting became a key element of their subsistence.[19]

With the introduction of horses by the Spanish in the 16th century, the Great Plains Native American's life style changed dramatically. The larger semi-permanent villages located along riverbanks were abandoned and a nomadic existence of smaller bands penetrated into the heart of the North American continent in search of the bison.[20] This coincided with the Anglo-Americans beginning their westward movement.

Following the bison, the Great Plains Native Americans adopted a distinct migration cycle that mirrored this large and rugged animal. In the summer, the bison moved in large herds in search of food and water fed by spring snowmelt as well as the limited rainfall. Likewise, during the summer, the Great Plains people congregated in large groups following the herds. With the approach of winter, the bison dispersed as fodder was not as plentiful. Similarly, the Native Americans broke into smaller bands. These ancient people developed a migratory lifestyle that tracked the bison on which they depended for survival.[21]

Both the bison and these Great Plains people understood that the land provided their sustenance as long as its ability was not stretched beyond its carrying capacity, or the maximum number of individuals the available food, water and habitat supported. Instead of attempting to change their environment, some prehistoric Native Americans on the Great Plains adapted their way of life to blend with the vagaries of Mother Nature.

Thus, the living patterns of the Plains Indians were totally dependent on water over the centuries. Whether they lived by the rivers and streams that were fed by the Wisconsin Glacier in prehistoric times, or they evolved into a nomadic existence to follow the buffalo, water drove their lifestyle. Living along the streams an abundance of plants and animals provided their sustenance. Pursuing the American buffalo, the Native Americans also essentially followed water that produced the grasses and plants necessary for the bison's survival. This total dependence on the availability of water to feed the grasslands or nourish the riparian existence resulted in increased vulnerability on the Plains given its extreme climatic variability. However, they adjusted their lifestyle and survived based on an understanding and acceptance of their dependence on the availability of water.

As Anglo-Americans intruded upon the Great Plains people that followed the bison and the Columbia people who lived off the bounty of the river for centuries, man's relationship with water started to change and demands started to exceed available supply. With this, the carrying capacity of the land and the water that nourished so many became strained. Given the harsh conditions as well as the inability to control their destiny, new comers had no choice but to modify their surroundings in order to create a permanent homestead and stabilize their existence to some degree. This led to the next stage in water informing history.

In *Cadillac Desert*, Marc Reisner described the area west of the 100th meridian and east of the Sierra Nevada Mountains similarly to that of the early explorers and mountain men of the west. He furthered indicated:

> *Everything depends on the manipulation of water [...]*
> *Confronted by the desert, the first thing Americans wanted*
> *to do was change it.*[22]

In *Collapse: How Societies Choose to Fail or Succeed*, Jared Diamond wrote that the "fragile and marginal environment for agriculture" in the Southwest required organization and changing the environment via some form of water management to provide sufficient food for the new social/economic structures.[23] Living in the arid and semi-arid Southwest required significant adaptation, which was not necessary along the Columbia River nor required for the Great Plains people to survive.

This manipulation of the desert landscape began long before settlement of the American West started. It was seen in pre-historic cultures in Chaco Canyon and Mesa Verde with the Anasazi, or Ancient Puebloans, and in between the Gila and Salt Rivers with the Hohokam. Likewise, in the arid and semi-arid regions of the Central Valley and Southern California, adaptations emerged.

As we look at prehistory, water sustained and organized these cultures but when the various southwestern civilizations tried to maximize the available water, Mother Nature inevitably stepped in and the carrying capacity of the land was surpassed. In the end, this dictated the decline of these cultures. Jared Diamond indicated in *Collapse: How Societies Choose to Fail or Succeed*:

Despite these varying proximate causes of abandonments, all were ultimately due to the same fundamental challenge: people living in fragile and difficult environments, adopting solutions that were brilliantly successful and understandable in the "short run," but that failed or else created fatal problems in the long run, when people became confronted with external environmental changes or human-caused environmental changes that societies without written histories and without archaeologists could not have anticipated...... Over the course of six centuries the human population of Chaco Canyon grew, its demands on the environment grew, its environmental resources declined and people came to be living increasingly close to the margin of what the environment could support.[24]

It is only in recorded history that the third stage of man's relationship with water emerged. Increasingly it was acknowledged that settlement of the West, seen as a "safety valve" to the increased immigration and growing urban issues in the Eastern United States and slavery in the South was impeded by the inability to deal with the climatic variability and lack of dependable water sources. The recognition of this situation coupled with advancements in technology led to the next stage of the relationship between man and water or controlling the water in the West.

Given the massive influx of Eastern and Southern European immigration during the 19th century, the need to protect the vast expanse of land obtained with the Louisiana Purchase and the Mexican War and opportunities for the disillusioned gold miners that increased the population in California and Colorado, settling the West became a national priority.

Initially as settlers moved west, the Mormons proved highly successful in developing communal irrigation to improve agricultural productivity, which allowed for the aggregation of people into communities. Building on prehistoric traditions, this provided a solution to settlement in the West. But, by the turn of the century, most farmers in the West had progressed as far as they could. Frederick Jackson Turner, the noted historian and author of the "Frontier Thesis" maintained that although the frontier made American democracy possible, the irrigation required to develop the West was too expensive for the Jefferson's idealized yeoman farmer.[25]

Thus, given the capital investment needed to accomplish the task, the prerequisite to controlling water in the West required participation by the federal government. With this, the age-old question of the constitutionality of internal improvements was laid to rest. The first step occurred in 1902 with the Newlands Reclamation Act and its major dam building period that lasted well into the twentieth century and provided storage of water for irrigation to supplement the meager precipitation in this arid region. These dams also provided hydroelectric power and storage of water for the increasing populations of the large sprawling cities like Los Angeles and San Diego. All of this occurred in areas that were essentially deserts.

The Reclamation Act also provided water to the Valley of the Dead in Southern California, known today as the Imperial Valley, which currently provides 70% of the nation's winter vegetables. Prior to 1905, this area, which received less than 3 inches of rainfall each year, was a desert. Additional water was only available when the Colorado River changed its course due to increased stream flow. Ultimately, by controlling water California became the leading agricultural producer in the country and allowed many other areas in the Southwest to turn millions of acres of desert into productive farmland and ranches.

All of this became possible given the American tradition of innovation, independence, creativity and a reliance on technology. With the formation of the Bureau of Reclamation (USBR) and an investment of over $7 billion and the technology it provided, man's dominion over most of the rivers in the West occurred. Technical expertise allowed the

West to truly "tame" the wild rivers of the West, resulting in the belief that through technology water supply would not be an issue, even with sustained droughts and natural conditions of the region.

Colorado River Basin

A re-examination of the map showing the major rivers in the United States shows only two sizable waterways that flow in the Southwest, the Rio Grande and the Colorado. Both start in the Rocky Mountains of Colorado with the Rio Grande River flowing southeast for 1800 miles into the Gulf of Mexico and the Colorado River flowing west and south into the Gulf of California. Although both of these rivers allowed humans to exist in prehistory, as well as today, a focus on the Colorado River Basin will serve to illustrate the demands and issues of water in the West.

The Colorado River and its 246,000-square mile drainage basin witnessed the rise and fall of various ancient societies and today contains some of the fastest growing urban populations in the country. Figure 3 outlines the Colorado River Basin, which also includes the USBR 20th century technology and provides an appreciation of the reach of the river.

The major source of water for the Colorado River comes from snow melting in the mountains, some exceeding elevations of 14,000 feet, all feeding the river and its

FIGURE 3 – Colorado River Basin

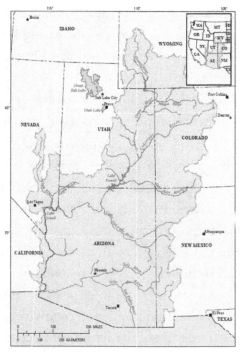

Source: USGS: Colorado River Basin Area Study[26]

16

tributaries. This once wild and flowing river, that few dared to enter, courses through some of the most arid regions in the country. Through technology, man tamed this tempestuous river to where it is overused with almost the entire annual flow destined to flow through a tap for drinking or the irrigation of crops. Interestingly, even though the Colorado River does not flow through California, the state has become the single largest user of its water.

So, *"For What It's Worth"* by reviewing what has happened over several thousand years to what has become one of the most overused and overworked and, quite frankly, abused water sources in the world as well as man's relationship with this river over time, there may be some lessons that need to be taught in elementary school in order for those living in the West to begin to accept the hydrological realities of the region and change how water is viewed.

The voyage of discovering about water in the Colorado River Basin and Southern California begins with exploring how prehistoric man survived in this harsh environment. Next, a review of recorded history will provide background on how technology and the American Dream allowed the desert to bloom. Then, the history of the Colorado River and its 246,000 square mile basin that now supports around 40,000,000 people will hopefully provide an appreciation as to why the river has become so controversial over the years. This, of course, requires an understanding of the current conditions in those states that depend on this once wild and flowing river. With this, perhaps we will understand the need for some changed behaviors by all those who live in this land that provides such beauty and a wonderful lifestyle.

The Southwest, and more specifically the Colorado River Basin, which has been in a drought since the beginning of the 21st century, as well as California's parched circumstances places the entire region at a crossroads that requires immediate action. Maintaining the traditional manner of managing water in a region that continues its explosive growth, depleting of groundwater, adhering to water law established in the late 1800s and avoiding some difficult decisions by "kicking the can down the road" will only lead to a future crisis where many currently existing options may no longer be available.

The belief in water's abundance in an arid environment due to technology making it so readily available needs to change. If this does not happen, Famiglietti's disaster movie will become a reality. Cynthia Barnett's *Blue Revolution: Unmaking America's Water Crisis* calls for a new water ethic that looks at the reality of this natural resource.[27] By developing a set of guidelines and values that allows us to stop depleting this life sustaining natural resource, perhaps we can avoid the likes of Catherine Case in Bacigalupi's *Water Knife*.

Some Basic Water Terms

Before we delve into the past as well as the current situation, some basic water terminology could be helpful.

- Acre-feet (af) – A volumetric measurement of water stored in reservoirs and lakes, etc. One acre-foot equals 325,851 gallons. Imagine a football field covered with one foot of water. As reservoirs hold a large amount of water, the term million acre-feet (maf) is used often. This would be 325,851,000,000 gallons.
- Aquifer – An underground reservoir for groundwater. The two most common types are confined and unconfined.
  - A confined aquifer is one that has impermeable rock above and below it where water is stored. Refilling or recharging this type of aquifer occurs over a long period of time and water must enter it at a point where the impermeable rock is absent. This can be many miles away.
  - An unconfined aquifer has no confining or impermeable layer between the water table and the ground above it. This type of aquifer is recharged through infiltration of

precipitation, or water sources submerged beneath the land. As it is unconfined, it can also return to a water source.

- Basin - A basin is an area of land where snowmelt or rainfall collects and drains into a common body of water, such as a stream or a river.

- Consumptive use versus demand – Consumptive use is the amount of water used and not returned to a water source. Demand is the total amount of water needed or withdrawn from a water source.

- Cubic feet per second (cfs) – A volumetric measurement of flowing water sources, such as rivers, streams, creeks, etc. One cfs equals 448.83 gallons each minute.

- Depletion - Depletion is the amount of water lost to a river system or aquifer when water is diverted, pumped or evaporates.

- Diversion – Moving water from its natural course or location. This normally involves some form of technology or land manipulation.

- Groundwater – Water that exists beneath the earth's surface.

- Groundwater recharge – The flow of water into an aquifer. Recharge occurs naturally or through human manipulation by constructing seepage ponds or the re-injecting water into the ground.

- Hydrologic cycle – The hydrologic cycle or the water cycle is the circulation of water from the earth's surface to its atmosphere and back to earth again through evaporation, evapotranspiration, condensation, precipitation, and infiltration. The earth has a constant amount of water present, which is in constant motion, moving from place to place in its different forms.

- Land use – The development and utilization of land for different human or economic purposes. Typical categories include environmental, industrial, recreational, residential, and transportation.

- Reservoir – A manmade body of water impounded by a dam. Purposes of reservoirs include storage, recreation, and hydroelectric power
- Return flow – Water that returns to streams and rivers after it has been used. For example, water used for irrigation will flow over the land and return to a water source or seep into the ground finding its way into the stream or groundwater.
- Salinity – The amount of salts dissolved in water. This occurs naturally as well as through human manipulation by irrigation run-off. High salinity levels may be toxic to fresh water fish, harm vegetation and impact irrigated agriculture.
- Surface water – Any water that is above ground in lakes, rivers, streams, reservoirs, etc. Its source is snowmelt and rainwater. Surface water is a renewable but due to the hydrological cycle is highly variable in amounts.
- Watershed – Watersheds are areas of land that catch precipitation and drain into a body of water. Watersheds can refer to either small collection areas that feed into streams or small bodies of water or they can refer to large areas such as river basins.

Law of the River and Water Rights terms

- Law of the River – A body of federal laws, compacts, court decision, regulatory guidelines, contracts and decrees, that collectively regulate the use, allocation and management of the Colorado River.
- Water right – A water right is a private property right in most states in the West that establishes the priority someone may use water for a beneficial purpose. This right is granted by water courts and allows diversion of a certain amount of water, in a specified order among other water users, from a certain point along a body of water and for a specified purpose. Throughout

the West, the older, or more senior water right receives water before those rights that are adjudicated as junior.

- Abandonment – Abandonment is the loss of all or part of a water right due to non-use or the failure to prove diligence on a conditional water right.
- Adjudication – A judicial process confirming a water right that is given a priority date determining it seniority when there is not enough water to meet the needs of all users.
- Beneficial use – Beneficial use is required to allow diversions of water from surface and groundwater supplies. Purposes allowed are economic, social, recreational, domestic, industrial and agricultural.
- Compact – An interstate agreement, approved by Congress, thus Federal oversight is inherent. River compacts establish the allocation of interstate rivers.
- Over-appropriation – When a stream or river does not have sufficient water to meet the needs of all the adjudicated water rights.
- Priority date – A priority date is the date assigned to a water right by the water court, reflecting the earliest time water was put to beneficial use. Also called the appropriation date.
- Prior appropriation – Prior appropriation is the basis for most of the laws that allocates water in the West. The first person to put water to a beneficial use has a senior right to a specified water source when it is insufficient to meet the needs of all water users. Those using water beneficially at a later date are subordinate to those with more senior adjudicated dates. Under prior appropriation, a water right is considered private property, thus can be bought, sold, inherited, traded, exchanged or donated. Currently the transfer of any water right requires an extensive approval process and steep legal fees.
- Riparian – Bordering a natural watercourse.

- Riparian doctrine – Riparian law allows one residing on property that borders a water way to divert as much water as they need with the caveat that they do not injure users downstream.
- Trans-basin/trans-mountain diversion – The transfer of water from one river basin to another. A form of trans-basin diversions is a trans-mountain diversion (TMD) that removes and transports water across the Continental Divide. This diversion must be used to extinction as none of the water from the diversion can return to the basin of origin as return flow.
- Unappropriated – Water not yet claimed by an existing water right.
- "Use it or lose it" – The requirement to beneficially use a specified amount of water from a specified source or risk losing the right. This provides the state the ability to declare water rights that have fallen into disuse as abandoned.

Chapter 2

Who Would Want to Live There? – Prehistory & Water

PRIOR TO 1900, IT WAS little wonder that only the very brave of heart ventured west of the Mississippi River. The descriptions provided by early expeditions were certainly not inviting. However, with the technology of the 20th century such as air conditioning, turbine engines and the construction of massive dams with their vast reservoirs storing billions of gallons of water, the Valley of the Dead in the California Desert south of modern day San Diego turned into the Imperial Valley. Today this region produces 70% of the nation's winter vegetables. In addition, these marvels of engineering created the sprawling megalopolis of Los Angeles and ultimately a population boom in cities like Las Vegas and Phoenix where a temperature of 105^0 F on any given summer day was not unusual. In both cities, and throughout the Colorado River Basin, lush green lawns and swimming pools proliferated. Clearly, the arid and barren landscape Mother Nature created would not be where most Americans would choose to live today without these creature comforts technology provided.

There were several cultures that flourished for centuries in the arid and semi-arid Southwest as well as the deserts of Southern California without the aid of modern technology. The different environments these societies inhabited required various strategies learned over the centuries allowing these prehistoric people to adapt to the harsh and arid environment and actually succeed in raising crops. The Ancestral Puebloans of the Four Corners region, the Hohokam of central and southern Arizona, the Chumash along the southern California coast and the Paiute of Owens Valley, California adapted quite well for almost a thousand years and handled the vagaries of Mother Nature by manipulating their environment, to different extents. And, the Old Lady allowed them to thrive, at least for a while. From time to time, she would throw a curve ball and they adapted yet again and continued to do so until the European invasion and diseases essentially decimated most of the descendants of these ancient people.

Prehistoric Hydrological and Environmental Conditions[1]

Perhaps an understanding of the climate that existed while these ancient people built thriving communities is in order before we review each of these cultures and their relationship with water. Although as in much of prehistory in the West disagreements as to what occurred and specific dates or time periods still remain unresolved, there is a general consensus that during the period between C.E. 800 to 1350, climate created significant stress on the inhabitants of California and the Southwest.

Over fifty years ago, Hubert Lamb, an early paleo-climatologist, identified a warm period that began in the 11th century in many regions of the world. Subsequently, Scott Stine named this warm period the Medieval Climatic Anomaly. Although specific dates are still debated, there is a general consensus of severe droughts occurring for fifty years in the mid 11th century and also between C.E. 1250 to 1330 throughout the West and Southwest. Furthermore, a group of paleo-climatologists determined that the reconstructed mean annual average flows over a twenty-five-year period of the Colorado River at Lee Ferry fell by 15% during the mid-1100s. These extended droughts and decline in river flow had a dramatic impact on the Ancestral Puebloans and Hohokam.

Another phenomenon also present in the Medieval Climate Anomaly was the climate's variability throughout the West. For example, the same mega-drought that had major implications on the prehistoric people in the Colorado River Basin for almost half of the 11th century was not as devastating to the ancient peoples of Central and Southern California. This inconsistency in climate continues to exist today.

Also, in the mid 13th century cooler temperatures prevailed due to a major volcanic eruption thought to have occurred in Indonesia.[2] This cool period coincided with the long extended drought that existed throughout the west having devastating economic, political and social consequences. This cooling shortened the growing seasons and made farming at higher elevations quite precarious.

How the Ancestral Puebloans, the Hohokam, the Paiute or the Chumash societies altered their environments in order to survive in this arid and semi-arid land and what they did to survive as Mother Nature challenged them provides insights that may apply many centuries later. But first, Figure 4 shows where these prehistoric people lived and the geographic extent of their cultures.

Figure 4 – Location of Prehistoric Man

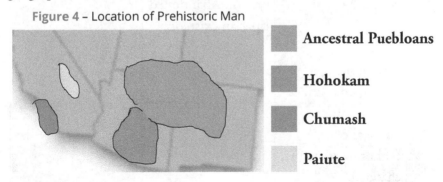

Ancestral Puebloans

Hohokam

Chumash

Paiute

A Summary Before We Start

Attempting to relate and correlate the adaptations of these prehistoric societies to the environmental conditions befuddles even those familiar with this period. With the caveat that distortions and gross generalizations occur when histories are summarized, a very brief review of the major changes in climate and the adaptations by these ancient people is shown in Chart 1. Even though a summary, it is clear that the scarcity of water

CHART 1

Environmental Impact in the Southwest and Southern California

	Drought Combined* 1020-1070	Wet SW** 1045-1130	Drought Combined 1130-1177	
Ancestral Puebloans	Dispersed population	Chaco expands 1020-1125. Mesa Verde & Aztec start around 1100	Construction in Chaco stops around 1125 & empty by 1150	
Hohokam	Riparian existence. More flooding concerns. Consolidation began.	Consolidation into larger autonomous villages and expansion of canal system. Abandoned riparian existence	Snaketown disperses	
Chumash	Settlement disruption. Aggregated near reliable sources. Political & economic structure changed.			
Paiute	Dispersed into different bands during this dry period. Arrived in Owens Valley	Remained hunter/gatherer existence. Did not exceed carrying capacity		

cannot be eliminated as a root cause of the changes in each of these societies.

Wet Combined 1170-1250(S)	Drought Combined 1250-1330 Drought SW 1273-1300	Wet period So. AZ 1350-1380
Mesa Verde & Aztec expand. In 1200 aggregation, cliff dwellings and violence emerge	Four Corners disperses to other regions by 1300	Four Corners region empty
Consolidation into larger autonomous villages and expansion of canal system	Migration into territory. Platform mounds replace ball courts. Walled compounds Emerge	Defensive structures emerge. Dispersal out of region begins
Population increased as did density of settlements	Settlement disruption into smaller units. Substantial violence and health deterioration	
	In-migration increased. Supplemented with seasonal manipulation of land.	

*Combined – includes SW and California**SW - SW only

Ancestral Puebloans (Anasazi) on the Colorado Plateau[3]

Reverting once again to my elementary school days, I remember learning of an ancient people known for their cliff dwellings that remained well preserved in a very arid environment. The main fact that remained with me for years involved the Anasazi's mysterious disappearance. Of course, it was close to the last Little Ice Age when I learned from my 3rd grade teacher about this culture's vanishing act. Since then, research by archaeologists, anthropologists, dendro-climatologists, paleo-climatologists, and many more 13-letter words, contributed a vast amount of research data that revealed a different story than just a people disappearing. As is the case of most prehistory, where no written records exist, there is no way to actually prove some of these new theories; however, there seems to be a growing agreement around how and why the Anasazi appeared to have abandoned their cliff dwellings in Mesa Verde. Today's 3rd graders could learn a great deal from these ancient people and perhaps teach their parents why a new way of looking at water is necessary.

To begin, the people who populated the Four Corners in the Southwest, I learned were called Anasazi. In the past twenty years, this has changed as Anasazi in the Navajo language meant "ancestors of my enemies." Although still debated, the Navajo most likely did not arrive in the region until sometime in the 15th century, in other words, after the Anasazi's unexplained disappearance. As it has been determined that the Navajo were not descendants of the Anasazi, many believed a Navajo word for this ancient group was inappropriate. On the other hand, the Hopi referred to the people who inhabited Mesa Verde as Hisatsinom, which meant Ancient Ones. Most felt a Hopi word for a culture believed to also be the ancestors to the Zuni and the Acoma was not accurate either. The term Ancestral Puebloans increasingly gained favor.

To complicate this even further, many archaeologists still refer to the Anasazi as an archaeological typology that characterized the people who built Chaco and Mesa Verde. Between C.E. 600 and 1110 in archaeological jargon, Anasazi represents stone masonry pueblos, pit houses, kivas, black-on-white decorated pottery and dryland farming.[4] Thus, when you see the term Anasazi determine if it is about the Ancient Puebloans or an archaeological description of a group of people that inhabited the Four Corners of the Colorado Plateau. In this book, I refer to these ancient people as Ancestral Puebloans.

The Ancestral Puebloans inhabited a large region on the Colorado Plateau concentrated in the Four Corners area, extending along most of the southern boundary of Utah and Colorado and the northern boundary of Arizona and New Mexico. This region consisted largely of high desert and limited forest areas. Between A.D. 400 to 750, the Four Corners area was sparsely populated with around one hundred small settlements, called outliers, consisting of one or two families, located along streams and rivers. Given the vagaries of the water flow in the Colorado Plateau, these ancient people moved to different locations each generation along other streams and rivers as the water conditions changed.

Beginning around C.E. 900, in the middle of nowhere and miles from any dependable water source, construction began on the Great Houses in Chaco Canyon. It is still debated as to whether these Great Houses were only part of a ceremonial center that those living in the outliers scattered throughout the entire Colorado Plateau visited or palaces in which the Ancestral Puebloan leaders or elite lived. In either case, Chaco Canyon was the largest site in the Colorado Plateau from C.E. 900 to around 1150. In the beginning of the 12th century the architecture in Chaco Canyon expanded considerably. One of the better known Great Houses, Pueblo Bonita is depicted in Figure 5. This Great

FIGURE 5 – Pueblo Bonita

Source: https://en.wikipedia.org/wiki/Pueblo_Bonito [5]

29

House was constructed in stages between 850 and 1150. It ultimately was five stories high and had 650 rooms.

The environment the Ancestral Puebloans selected was inhospitable and considered by most archaeologists as an agriculturally marginal area that had an erratic growing season, poor soil, and annual precipitation less than 9 inches. Today, the consensus of most archeologists is that food was imported from the outliers with some suggesting that Chaco Canyon served as a food bank for these ancient people.[6]

How was this possible with no reliable water source nearby? It is conjectured that these industrious people exploited the water run-off from the northern rim of the canyon by constructing small diversion dams and ditches to channel the water to the crops. What was more significant, as Chaco grew in importance in the Ancient Puebloan world, the Southwest also experienced an unusually wet period. This increased the carrying capacity of the land and also resulted in a higher density. Ultimately, Mother Nature brought back the normal arid conditions in Chaco Canyon and started a long-term drought around C.E. 1130. When normal arid conditions returned the ability to produce sufficient food declined and the carrying capacity was surpassed. At this point, Chaco began its decline. Within twenty-five years, this amazing place with its Great Houses was essentially empty.

If you ever visit Chaco, you will find it a very barren land that makes it difficult to comprehend how or why people ever chose to live there. Spend some time amongst the ruins that are minimally restored and you will be transported to a different time. Let your imagination run wild and you will actually see the Ancient Puebloans bringing their maize into Chaco via the North Road constructed over a thousand years ago; which still exists. Imagine how you would have survived in such a barren land.

Unfortunately, just as the ancient people could not exist in a dream world, neither can we, so back to reality and the history of these people. Just as Chaco appeared to be abandoned, an interesting increase in population occurred in the Northern San Juan region, eighty miles northwest of this special place, most notably Mesa Verde and Aztec.

Mesa Verde and Aztec (ruins mistakenly attributed to Aztecs by early Euro-American settlers) initially existed as "outliers" to Chaco Canyon where population increased and decreased as family units moved to areas where water was more readily available. Most of these outliers moved locations every generation, reflecting the variability of precipitation prevalent throughout the Southwest as well as an agriculturally marginal land.

When water became scarce during the 12th and 13th centuries, the nomadic existence of small outliers that endured for over 400 years started to change. There is evidence of small groups living in the Mesa Verde area prior to C.E. 700 and growing in size in the 11th century but shrinking again. Early in the 12th century, this began to change where both Aztec and Mesa Verde experienced considerable growth and a significant transformation in architecture and life style. This, of course, raises the question as to why such major changes occurred.

As an aside, until recently I was totally unaware of Aztec and still relied on my earlier understanding that the ruins of Mesa Verde represented a stand-alone society. Although the Ancestral Puebloans sporadically inhabited the Four Corners region for centuries, the cliff dwellings of Mesa Verde that I learned about in elementary school were actually short-lived. Likewise, Aztec was constructed and vacated within one century.

Although only sixty-seven miles apart, both Aztec and Mesa Verde are in two different eco-zones. Mesa Verde is located in southwestern Colorado at an elevation ranging from 6000 to 8572 feet. Given the naturally created north to south slope of the land and due to wind and water erosion, fertile soil was abundant. In addition, this semi-arid region received an average annual precipitation of around eighteen inches. With fertile soil and sufficient annual precipitation, those living in Mesa Verde survived using dryland farming with check dams, terraces and small reservoirs.

Dry-land farming is used throughout the world and permits agricultural production in regions where water is not readily available and irrigation not used. This involves being more efficient with the available water by increasing the moisture in the soil through various techniques such as terracing or deep tillage. Although dry-land farming does not require major manipulation of the environment, it is very susceptible to the vagaries of Mother Nature. Even during wet periods, yield is substantially less than irrigated farming and during droughts, dry-land farming has an extremely high risk of crop failure.[7] One does not have to be a rocket scientist to understand why the Ancestral Puebloans were constantly on the move.

Aztec was the other region that developed as Chaco declined. In fact, Steve Lekson believes that Aztec replaced Chaco as the center of the Ancestral Puebloan world and included Mesa Verde as part of its realm.[8]

Aztec's elevation ranged from 5630 to 5820 feet and received an average annual precipitation of 10.5 inches. However, unlike Mesa Verde, Aztec was bordered by the perennially flowing Animas River with its headwaters north of Telluride. The inhabitants of Aztec were also dry-land farmers but manipulated their environment to a greater degree by using small ditches to divert water from the Animas River to their crops.

Why did the Ancient Puebloans transform their lifestyle and move away from the dispersed outliers that prevailed during the Chaco Canyon era? It may have started as some of the leaders of Chaco relocated north. But in both Mesa Verde and Aztec, the Ancestral Puebloans started to aggregate and settle in concentrated locations fifty years after Chaco was essentially empty. It is believed that this concentration was possible in areas of scant surface water due to the wet periods that existed at the time.[9]

Another major change in settlement practices that occurred simultaneously with the concentration of people in Aztec and Mesa

Verde involved the choice of where they lived. At this point, the Ancient Puebloans began building large cluster dwellings in the cliffs that were very difficult to access. Researchers increasingly believe that the intensification of hostility among the Ancient Puebloans, absent in preceding generations, led to this dramatic change in lifestyle. This raises the question as to why violence began in a traditionally peaceful culture?

When our family first visited Mesa Verde in the early 1970s, this violence was thought to be external in nature; however, current research indicates that this aggression was internal. Thus, the tradition of dispersed and short-lived settlements that existed for centuries disappeared and the appearance of denser and more permanent living structures started in the early part of the 13th century. Violence within and between the various settlements increased at the same time.

Once again, water may have played a major role. As the population of both Aztec and Mesa Verde grew, the Southwest experienced one of Stine's wet periods. However, with the expanding populations, the water that serviced the smaller outliers for centuries may have been stretched beyond its ability to produce sufficient food. Reliance on dry-land farming, also contributed to exceeding the carrying capacity of the land. While the smaller outliers of the past just relocated, the larger community with the more permanent dwellings made it more difficult for those living in the Four Corners to just pick up and leave. When another dry period started in the mid-13th century, the resulting reduction in food production led to violence within each community. Evidence of cannibalism has also been uncovered.

Although explanations for these changes in the manner the Ancestral Puebloans lived and the escalating violence continues uncertain; by the mid 1290s, the infamous and mysterious disappearance I learned about in grade school occurred and the Four Corners essentially emptied.

What I never learned, as it was not understood at the time, was these ancient people did not just disappear but continued their long-lived tradition of mobility. In this instance they moved to other areas in the lower San Juan Basin, for example Sand Canyon and the Kayenta region. But the majority settled in the Rio Grande Valley, the Zuni Mesa and along the Little Colorado River, which are areas where modern day Puebloans still live. It is now believed that this practice of mobility was the method the Ancestral Puebloans used to adapt to declining environmental conditions, especially drought.

Ultimately, Sand Canyon and Kayenta also emptied given the sudden onset of the Great Drought of 1277-1300 with most of the inhabitants of these locations believed to relocate to the Rio Grande Basin or central Arizona where abundant game and a more dependable environment for agriculture existed. It is at this point historians eliminated the term Ancient Puebloans and referred to these people as just Puebloans. This tradition of movement continued with population expanding in both dispersed as well as aggregated settlements, which continued until the Spanish arrived and disease wreaked havoc on this ancient culture.

With the caveat that this trajectory of isolated settlements, to Chaco Canyon, to the upper San Juan Basin in Mesa Verde and then to the Rio Grande Valley and central Arizona cannot be proven with 100% accuracy, one has to agree that there is a logical progression. This explains, at least in part, this mystical "abandonment" or disappearance about which the early Baby Boomers learned. But why were these ancient people so mobile, why did they change the mode in which they lived and why did inter-community violence emerge in a people that had existed peacefully for centuries? Perhaps, at the risk of being branded an environmental determinist, water and its availability sheds some light on this.

Using Stine's identified "perfect droughts" and "wet periods" and MacDonald's regional conditions in the Southwest, where the Ancestral Puebloans lived, it is clear these people made choices of where and how to live based on what Mother Nature decided to throw their way. Prior to the 11th century, population was dispersed into small groups that moved almost every generation. The construction of the Great Houses in Chaco Canyon occurred during a wet period. Then with the regional mega-drought of the mid 12th century when the Colorado River flow reduced significantly, those living in Chaco Canyon dispersed north into areas with more rainfall, more fertile soil and for Aztec, next to the perennial Animas River. It has also been suggested that some migrated into Central Arizona along the Salt and Gila rivers. During the next wet period in both Aztec and Mesa Verde, a transition to larger above ground masonry structures began the tendency to aggregate into specific locations. This again made sense as during this wet period agriculture productivity intensified that increased the carrying capacity of the land and allowed people to live in denser settlements.

It is imminently logical that a people with a tradition of mobility would continue this practice, but with the onset of another mega-drought in the mid-13th century, the Ancestral Puebloans adapted once again. This is when the remote cliff dwellings appeared simultaneously as inter-community violence escalated. What had worked at Chaco, during a relatively wet period did not ultimately work at Aztec and Mesa Verde as another dry period stressed their resources. These new areas of concentration for the Ancient Puebloans perhaps grew beyond the carrying capacity of the land and ultimately they were "unable to keep the peace or to bring the rain as Chaco had done."[9]

Although there does not seem to be a problem with water until the mid to late 13th century according to paleo-climatologists, perhaps the increased population density that occurred during the wet period stretched the resources in both Mesa Verde and Aztec, which led to the mass migration when an eighty-year drought began in 1250. This heightened strain on resources led to an increased conflict between the water "have and have-nots" within the region. The dry period beginning in 1250 became the "final nail in the coffin" for settlement in the Four Corners. Thus, the vanishing act I learned about when I was 10 years old occurred.

Inter-community conflict over water probably led to increased hostilities that resulted in further aggregation, for defensive reasons, thus placing additional strain on the carrying capacity of the land. This could explain why defensive structures such as the cliff dwellings in Mesa Verde or other defensible locations in canyons with wells dug in the central plaza appeared. Then with the Great Drought of 1273-1300 the carrying capacity was truly surpassed resulting in increased violence and most of those living in the Four Corners reverted to their historical roots of mobility and relocated.

Hohokam of Central Arizona[10]

Although I learned in elementary school that early civilizations began in Mesopotamia and Egypt along rivers as well as about the "disappearance" of the "Anasazi," I learned nothing about the Hohokam, an amazing culture that lived in the southern Arizona desert for almost 1500 years. Their name, derived from the Tohono O'Odham, believed to be the descendants of the Hohokam, meant "those that have gone." This seems to be a continual theme regarding cultures in the Colorado River Basin. In this case, the ability of the Hohokam to survive such arid conditions for such a long period stemmed from the use of a vast irrigation system with canals that "became the most impressive 'public works' project undertaken in arid North America until the early 20th century reclamation boom. Hohokam canals were bigger than any in ancient Mesoamerica."[11]

Initially canals were modest and built along the moderately flowing Santa Cruz River as early as 1500 BCE.[11] However, with a constantly shifting channel and floodplain these prehistoric farmers needed to adapt to their ever-changing hydrological conditions. Given the nature of the river, these small clusters of semi-permanent huts represented the early Hohokam riparian lifestyle that dictated where they lived and for how long. Around C.E. 450 the Hohokam moved to the confluence of the Salt and Gila rivers near modern day Phoenix where a large complex of canals linked to irrigated fields appeared.

Between C.E. 750 and 1150 the Hohokam culture was characterized by numerous small villages, hamlets, and farms found next or near the Salt and Gila rivers. Population peaked in the larger villages during this period. Most prominent was Snaketown, located southeast of Phoenix with an estimated population between 1,000 and 3,000.

The location of these dispersed villages required construction of a water system that required extensive labor as well as cooperation. Some have maintained this water system existed as a network between groups of small, autonomous villages located along specific canals. This riparian lifestyle supplemented by canals continued for several centuries. In the early to mid-13th century, substantial down cutting or erosion due to extensive flooding deepened and widened the streambeds, thus destroying many of the existing canals, causing crops to fail. Most probably, production reduced. With this, the riparian existence adjacent to the Salt and Gila rivers changed, as did the Hohokam way of life. Clearly, with the impact of too much water destroying the canal system the Hohokam decided to try different strategies to cope with Mother Nature.

By 1100, this enterprising group of agriculturalists expanded their canal infrastructure and the Hohokam moved away from the riverbanks and many of these villages developed into larger communities. With this, the Hohokam became more sedentary. This change in how the Hohokam lived occurred during a wet period.

Initially, each of the larger villages consisted of a ball court, similar to that of the Mayans and Aztecs and also included outlying smaller settlements on the canal system surrounded by a large expanse of cultivated farmland. Although the purpose of ball courts is not known, it is believed they served as a means of connecting the entire Hohokam world, which covered most of central and southern Arizona. According to most archaeologists, the wet period that lasted from A.D 1045 to 1130 was the expansionary period of this ancient people.

Just as the Ancestral Puebloans were constructing the Great Houses in Chaco Canyon, the Hohokam concentrated into larger communities and expanded their canal infrastructure. In both situations, these changes in lifestyle occurred during one of Stine's identified wet periods. Likewise, during the extended drought of the 11th century, which witnessed the demise of Chaco Canyon, one of the larger Hohokam communities, Snaketown, dispersed. It was also during this prolonged drought that archaeologists uncovered significant changes in the Hohokam culture that continued for the next 250 years.

These changes included the replacement of the sunken, unifying ball courts, integral to the Hohokam culture in the past, with raised platform mounds, an aggregation of the population into walled compounds and an expansion and consolidation of the formerly autonomous canal and irrigation systems. The effect of this consolidation resulted in irrigation communities. It is believed that these irrigation communities became the administrative centers that regulated the allocation of water and managed the maintenance and construction of the canal system for that particular area. However, the jury is still out as to whether an elite class developed.

Some archaeologists feel the replacement of the ball courts with the raised platform mounds, signified the beginnings of an elite or leader class. The sunken playing fields were readily accessible to everyone and believed to unite the Hohokam world. The elevated platform mounds represented a dramatic change in the culture. Aside from the disappearance of the ball courts and the replacement with the platform mounds, there is no archaeological evidence to support a leadership elite.[12] Even though a ruling class did not exist, some researchers believe this extensive canal system led to the beginnings of a localized bureaucracy reflecting some social stratification that had not existed before.[13]

Who became the leaders of these villages? Perhaps, the farmers with the largest landholding or some suggest that as of the mid 1100s, the Chaco elite were looking for opportunities to rule. As Chaco was dispersing, there is a possibility that some of their elite moved south and not just north to Aztec.

Why did these changes occur in the Hohokam world after almost a thousand years of working just fine? It is understandable that the flooding between C.E. 1020 and 1060 and the destruction of the smaller canal systems strained a system that worked for over a millennium, and led the Hohokam to consolidate and leave their riparian existence. This consolidation resulted in the expansion of the canal system with a more centralized labor force and allowed this culture to withstand the extended drought of the 12th century due to increasing agricultural productivity.

These ancient people significantly manipulated their environment even though they lacked the aid of modern technology. Without the aid of bull dozers and using just a wooden digging stick, the Hohokam dug canals that averaged 10 feet deep, up to 30 yards wide and fifteen-miles long. These canals were also perfectly calibrated to drop 2.5 meters/ mile to control erosion and maintain stream flow.[14] In addition, this industrious society developed silt fields during periods of flooding that were almost three-feet deep to improve crop productivity.[15] All of this basic engineering increased agricultural productivity; and thus, the carrying capacity of the land in a very harsh environment.

In the Salt and Gila River Valleys, the Hohokam were better situated than the Ancestral Puebloans to manipulate the landscape with extensive use of check dams and terraces fed by an expanded canal system. The construction of large silt fields further increased productivity, increasing water retention and enhancing soil quality.[15] At its height, there were over 500 miles of canals that irrigated almost 70,000 acres and fed up to 80,000 people. This expansive irrigation infrastructure allowed the Hohokam who inhabited the Tucson and Phoenix Basins to withstand prolonged droughts that the dry-land farming techniques of their contemporary Ancestral Puebloans could not.

After 1300, those living in the Four Corners dispersed throughout the Southwest with many going to the Rio Grande Valley; however, there is some indications that some also migrated into Hohokam territory. Archaeologists indicated this might be the case as Anasazi architecture appears in some Great Houses, such as Casa Grande, located south of Phoenix. This three story structure was constructed in the early to mid 13th century. The lure of the Hohokam environment was a more continuous and dependable water source from the Salt and Gila rivers, even during droughts.

In the latter part of the 14th century, numerous massive floods occurred in the Phoenix and Tucson basins resulting in the destruction of many of the canals. Research has indicated that a flood in 1382 was double anything that occurred in the previous five centuries.[16] The 1382 flood devastated the intricate canal systems constructed over the centuries by the Hohokam. Unlike the Ancestral Puebloans' strategy of packing their belongings and moving to "greener pastures" the Hohokam with their canal infrastructure were stuck. They had to rebuild if their lifestyle was to remain the same. Following these disastrous floods of 1382 and 1383, the region experienced a decade-long drought. Thus, following the Ancestral Puebloan strategy of mobility, by 1450 the Hohokam changed their way of life again and dispersed into small isolated riparian settlements.

Why did the Hohokam return to their segregated and remote lifestyle along rivers and streams or the way they had lived 400 years previously? One factor to be considered involved the increased salinity of the soil, a by-product of irrigation. As plants absorbed water or it evaporated into the atmosphere, salt remained in the soil. That ever-present water cycle was just another trick Mother Nature pulled from her bag of goodies to show who was boss. Over time, the salinity level in the soil significantly reduced the productivity of the land. Given the sedentary nature of the Hohokam over an extended period of time, increased salinity must be considered a factor in the changes in their society.

Archaeologists and paleo-climatologists have speculated that a damaged canal system (due to extreme flooding), a severe extended drought and the increased salinity in the soil contributed to the significant alteration of the Hohokam existence. Thus, water sustained and organized both the Hohokam and the Ancient Puebloans. But when both of these southwestern civilizations attempted to maximize the impact of the available water, Mother Nature inevitably stepped in to show her power. Also, when the carrying capacity of the land was surpassed the dispersal of these cultures became necessary.

Chumash of Southern California

And then there is California that ranges from semi-arid coastal environments to extremely arid deserts in the center and far southern part of the state. Scientist believe that southern California's Mediterranean climate developed around 4,000 years ago, even though, there is evidence that groups settled along the coast and inland drainages over 10,000 years ago. The Chumash settled into the coastal inland region and Channel Islands between what is Santa Barbara and Los Angeles today. On Santa Rosa Island in the northern Channel Islands, there is support that habitation occurred over 13,000 years ago with evidence on mainland sites around 10,000 BCE. As to be expected, the protein diet of the ancient people living on Santa Rosa Island was comprised of fish (50%) where as the mainland ancestors of the Chumash survived on shellfish (80%) for their protein.[18] Very early it was clear that this prehistoric group understood the natural world by beginning seed production and minor manipulation of the land. The ancient Chumash were not considered agriculturalists but were thought to be advanced hunter-gatherers that were semi-sedentary. They returned to the same seasonal sites for centuries. However, just as in the Southwest, the paleo-environment and the scarcity of water led the ancient Chumash to adopt different survival strategies.[19]

Various paleo-climatologists have presented different time periods for droughts in California with a general consensus that there were significant mega-droughts during the Medieval Climate Anomaly that mirrored that of the Southwest; however, some believe these dry periods started earlier and lasted longer in California. Using Stine's research on radiocarbon dated stumps, prolonged droughts occurred in California from C.E. 900 to 1100 as well as C.E. 1220 to 1350. These dry periods correlated with changes within the culture in the area.

Beginning in the mid-11th century and for the next one hundred years, there was a sharp residential shift on many of the Channel Islands to sites with more reliable and perennial fresh water sources such as artesian wells, and springs. Likewise, the Chumash living in the inland areas moved to areas along perennial flowing rivers and streams located close to the coast to cope with the reduced water availability during these droughts. As the dry period continued, an increased reliance on marine protein occurred as local wildlife became scarce. In addition, inter-community and possibly intra-community violence escalated during this time period.[20] Researchers attributed this change in diet and increased violence to the persistent drought. Fortunately, the proximity to the ocean allowed the Chumash to substitute marine sources as access to other protein sources reduced.

Correlation with population density that occurred in the Southwest is not as apparent in California. This is possibly attributed to the fact that the size of the settlement concentration patterns depended on the amount of water available in the specific locations selected by the Chumash. As accomplished hunter-gatherers, they understood very well the carrying capacity of the land that allowed them to more readily adapt to the vagaries of Mother Nature.[21] The Chumash remained essentially hunter-gatherers and did not rely on manipulation of the land to any great extent. They were more mobile and like the Ancestral Puebloans adapted by dispersing when conditions changed.

The political and economic structures of the Channel Island Chumash changed during a dry period or subsequent to it with the establishment of chiefdoms.[22] Also, between C.E. 1150 and 1200, craft specialization and the production of beads increased greatly. This explains their name meaning "bead maker" or "seashell people." It is believed the beads were used for trade with the coastal and inland Chumash as a strategy to obtain more food from the mainland.

However, as the Chumash became more dependent on the readily available fresh water sources, they became a bit more sedentary and the population increased as did the density. With the onset of the next extended drought that lasted for 150 years (C.E. 1200-1350) another "disruption in settlement" occurred.[23] Interestingly what Southwestern archaeologists refer to as abandonment or dispersal, California archaeologists use the term disruption of settlement.

As in the earlier dry period, violence increased substantially as evidenced by mass graves dating to this period. In addition, health deteriorated rapidly with osteological research showing severe signs of anemia, especially in children.[24] During this disruption of settlement, smaller populations in less dense settlements developed close to reliable water sources, retaining the chiefdom political structure and the traditional hunter-gather and marine subsistence. This way of life continued until the Spanish entered the various settlements the Chumash inhabited for centuries.

Thus, just as with the Ancestral Puebloans and the Hohokam the prehistoric Chumash developed their political, economic and social structures based on accessibility of water that required adaptations as the hydrological conditions changed. As the Chumash used minimal manipulation of the environment and adapted to Mother Nature's stunts, they continued to exist with essentially the same lifestyle—with some adaptations during dry periods—until the Spanish arrived.

Central California

Although receiving little water from the Colorado River, the Central Valley and Owens Valley are areas that have a dramatic impact on today's water situation with both in the news consistently given the drought and groundwater depletion. A brief review of the prehistory in these two areas present other strategies for surviving in an arid or semi-arid climate.

Central Valley[25]

The Central Valley, located in the center part of California, runs almost 450 miles, north to south, and is between 40 to 60 miles wide. Bordered by three mountain ranges to the east and the California Coast Range to the west, the Central Valley accounts for around 14% of the land in the state. Two major drainages, the Sacramento in the north and the San Joaquin in the south deliver snowmelt to their respective rivers and valleys.

In prehistoric time, most of the Tulare Basin was covered with water that ultimately flowed into the Pacific Ocean through what is today's San Francisco Bay. Tulare Lake existed in ancient times and was the largest surface lake west of the Mississippi River. During heavy snow melts several other lakes, the Kern and Buena Vista combined, filling much of the Tulare Basin. Sadly, none of these lakes exist today. Overtime the water either evaporated or infiltrated the aquifers. These are the aquifers that currently are being depleted at an alarming rate.

Although very little is known about the people who originally occupied this land, artifacts dated to B.C.E. 9500 have been found. Around 4,000 years ago, water flowed from the mountains to the Sacramento and San Joaquin valleys allowing the prehistoric people to live and flourish in a riparian existence in moderate sized sedentary villages. Even with the extended drought of the 11th century that resulted in the disruption of settlements for the Chumash, the ancestors of the modern day Yokuts remained stable as the Sacramento and San Joaquin rivers continued to provide sufficient food to thrive and grow. It is estimated the Yokuts had a population of around 18,000 by the time the Spanish arrived. With the abundance of water the snowmelt provided, wild life, fish and local plants supplied enough food where agriculture was not needed. Thus, the Yokuts and their ancestors, just as the Columbia River people, had little need to manipulate the land to access water and continued to live and thrive for centuries.

Today, the Central Valley that the ancestors of the Yokuts inhabited is one of the world's most productive agricultural regions. It accounts for around 20% of the nation's total irrigated acres and represents 8% of the nation's agricultural production. All of this irrigated acreage has developed over the past 150 years.

It goes without saying how significant this change is from the prehistoric period when Tulare Lake dominated the area and the Yokuts' ancestors lived without needing to divert, manipulate or irrigate anything.

Paiutes of Owens Valley

One mountain range to the east of the Central Valley is Owens Valley. The Owens basin is seventy-five miles long and only six to ten miles wide, lying between the Sierra Nevada on the west and the White-Inyo Range to the east. Annual precipitation in this area is less than six inches, thus as in the Central Valley, snowmelt provided water during prehistoric times. The Paiute moved into the southwestern area prior to C.E. 1000 where they dispersed into Northern, Southern and Owens Valley bands. Initially the Owens Valley Paiute remained hunter-gathers; however, at some undetermined point in the past these ancient people abandoned their nomadic ways and settled into a more sedentary life style.

During the 12th or 13th century, basic irrigation ditches and a small dam on Bishop Creek serviced two large plots that were used alternatively on a bi-yearly basis to increase yield. For the Owens Valley Paiute, irrigation was a communal endeavor and their small diversion ditches were merely seasonal with the dams destroyed each fall allowing the water to flow to the main channel.[26] In other words, the Paiute borrowed water as they needed it, understanding the continued flow of the river supported the health of the entire watershed.

Why did the Owens Valley Paiute begin irrigation when, like the Central Valley, there was certainly enough wildlife and plants to sustain them? It is believed that a massive migration increased the size of the population and agriculture emerged to supplement the bounty of the land. As the Ancestral Puebloans dispersed by 1300, perhaps some of them ventured into the Owens Valley. When the Spanish arrived, there were 30 permanent villages scattered along the various rivers and streams in the valley.

In the case of the Paiute, although they manipulated the land to support the communal living that expanded in the 13th century, they did so in a manner that respected the environment. Even though extended drought had a negative impact on their lifestyle, to date there is little evidence of major disruptions in the way they lived or any increase in violence.

Owens Valley today would have these ancient Paiutes turning in their graves. With most of the water in the valley piped 250 miles to Los Angeles, the landscape became dry and dusty and the land returned to desert in most areas. Owens Lake, which dried up in the 1920s, resembles a moonscape where dust storms are continual. Mother Nature is clearly letting us know she is not pleased.

Prehistory Revisited

This is just a brief synopsis of how the prehistoric people of the Southwest and Southern California existed for centuries in a harsh environment where Mother Nature constantly reminded them who was in control. As Norris Hundley, Jr. indicated in *The Great Thirst: Californians and Water: A History*, just as in Sumeria and Egypt, the "location and quantity of water, influenced the settlement patterns, material culture, and lifestyles of the native peoples," but he also emphasized that they made thoughtful decisions and did not just submit to environmental determinism.[27] In other words, they lived and adapted their worldview according to the cards Mother Nature dealt by practicing resource management. Although, Hundley's comments focused on the prehistoric people of California, these sentiments clearly applied to the Ancient Puebloans and Hohokam. The practice of natural-resource management required constant evaluation, re-evaluation and adaptation as conditions changed in this difficult environment. What ultimately determined where they lived and how many people lived there was the amount of food the land could provide to sustain them. Water clearly controlled this. Thus, when any of these prehistoric people were unable to produce sufficient food for the population, they adapted.

Paul E. Minnis, Professor of Anthropology at University of Oklahoma, in "Social Adaptation to Food Stress" indicated that there are common responses to food stress with the easiest to implement adopted first. The more permanent or harder to execute actions were employed only as the more short-lived options did not solve the problem or the climatic fluctuation of either drought or flooding persisted for an extended period.[28] Some of the adaption responses Minnis identified included: diversification of activities (ex. changing the location of the field to a nearby location or changing the crop); storage of food (ex. most of the Southwestern ancient people stored food for approximately three years); conversion of surplus into tradable commodity (ex. beadmaking by the Chumash); cultivation of other regions to expand food sources (ex. Chaco Canyon serving as a food bank); population dispersal into temporary foraging or smaller farming groups (ex. the Ancient Puebloan mode of existence in the 10th and 11th centuries); raiding and warfare; and aggregation or consolidation as the agricultural environment was destroyed (ex. the Hohokam consolidating their canal system after floods destroyed the riparian environment).

In the end, even with all of these adaptations and different manipulations of the landscape that varied in intensity, Mother Nature triumphed and left most ancient populations scattered throughout the Southwest and Southern California with only the descendants of the Ancient Puebloans, possibly some Hohokam living in Pueblos along the Rio Grande and Hopi and Zuni mesas and the Paiute in Owens Valley and the Yokuts in the Central Valley dispersed into small groups. In smaller villages/hamlets, these various groups survived along perennial flowing water sources where they did not exceed the carrying capacity of the land. If necessary, they reverted to the tradition of the Ancestral Puebloans and moved to another riparian site where access to water was more reliable.

Although droughts occurred prior to the arrival of the Europeans, that placed stress on these dispersed clusters of Native Americans, none of them compared to those that occurred during the Medieval Climate Anomaly. When the Spanish arrived in the 16th century, the descendants of these prehistoric cultures lived as they had for centuries, using the water that Mother Nature provided for their crops, with minimal manipulation of the land, such as check dams and small irrigation ditches. In the end, the descendants of each of these prehistoric societies learned they had to adapt to Mother Nature, as she would not change for them. Adaptation was required as water became scarce or too abundant. When any of these prehistoric cultures surpassed the ability of the land to provide their sustenance, they retreated and dispersed.

> *Among these ancient civilizations there was a remarkably similar pattern of straining the limits of water. Populations grew to a point that too many people depended on a fickle water supply, or inequitable distribution led to conflict and violence, or excessive water use ruined the land. The consequences of overuse, misuse, and denial of use to some for the benefit of others were hard learned [...] The Modern world should be able to build on these and many other lessons.[29]*

The question remains, are we learning from the past or will history repeat itself?

Of course, none of these groups had the benefit of the Industrial Revolution and all of the technology that it spawned. One has to wonder, if today's know-how was available to those living in Aztec or in the Phoenix Basin in the 14th century, would they have used it to control Mother Nature? Or, would they have continued to respect and understand that a symbiotic relationship was the most they could expect from Mother Earth?

Chapter 3

"Build It And They Will Come" –
Recorded History

WITH THE ARRIVAL OF THE Spanish in Mexico in 1519, life as the Hohokam, the Ancient Puebloan descendants, the Paiute and the Chumash knew it changed and continued to dramatically do so for the next three centuries. The Native Americans that survived the onslaught of European diseases found their lives concentrated around missions that exerted more control over the their livelihood as well as their water. The Puebloans, no longer called Ancient, continued their riparian existence along rivers and streams using their check dams and ditches to irrigate their small fields. One of the many changes the Spanish implemented was administrative control over the irrigation system the Puebloans used for centuries, now called acequias, meaning "one that brings water" or "barmaid". The control of these ditches was a concept derived from a Middle Eastern practice, and involved a community-managed stream, supervised by a "mayordomo" who allocated the water, and oversaw the continued maintenance required of the ditches. During dry periods, which occurred frequently in an area that received little rainfall, the mayordomo ensured that those at the head of a ditch left enough water for those downstream.[1]

One wonders if this in fact was the manner by which the Puebloans managed the ditches prior to the Spanish invasion, to which the Spanish provided a name and more than likely became the mayordomo. This local and community driven system still exists today in Northeastern New Mexico and parts of Southeastern Colorado. It allows the Puebloans along the Rio Grande and others that have settled in this area to maintain a subsistence in this arid environment without exceeding the carrying capacity of the land. However, for the rest of the Southwest and particularly Southern California, the expansion of the newly formed United States would start the real transformation of the western United States.

Although parts of the West had been inhabited for thousands of years, written accounts did not exist until after the Louisiana Purchase and the expeditions of Lewis and Clark, Zebulon Pike, Stephen Long and a few mountain men. Both Pike and Long focused their expeditions on the Great American Desert; the land west of the Mississippi River extending to the deserts east of the California coastal regions. All of these initial trailblazers found it unsuitable for settlement. By 1830, many believed that the Louisiana Purchase was a waste of money.[2] Zebulon Pike equated the land to "the sandy deserts of Africa"[3] Edwin James (1823), the botanist and geologist on Stephen Long's expedition of 1819-1820 more graphically described the area between the Mississippi and Rocky Mountains.

> *In regard to this extensive section of the country, I do not hesitate in giving the opinion, that it is almost wholly unfit for cultivation, and of course uninhabitable by a people depending upon agriculture for their subsistence. Although tracts of fertile land considerably extensive are occasionally to be met with, yet the scarcity of wood and water almost uniformly prevalent will prove an insuperable obstacle in the way of settling the country.[4]*

Furthermore, the arduous and treacherous journey described by Lewis and Clark's northern route led many to believe the Northwest not accessible. Although the Lewis and Clark's journals, finally published in 1814, described the diverse geography, temperature, precipitation and water availability in detail, Long's concept of the Great American Desert persisted.[5]

John Wesley Powell, the one-armed Civil War hero and the second Director of the U.S. Geological Survey distinguished between these different regions with the "Humid Columbia," the "Sub-Humid located between the Mississippi River and 100th meridian" and the "Arid Region west of the 100th meridian to California" in his 1879 "Report on the Lands of the Arid Region of the United States."[6] It is Powell's "Arid Region west of the 100th meridian" that included the Colorado River Basin where precipitation was limited.

In fact, tree ring studies have indicated that since 1539, the Great Plains suffered 160 years of drought.[8] Thus, drought existed in excess of one-third of the time during a 435-year period. From 1975 to the present, although interspersed with some very wet years, droughts were present for around two-thirds of the past four decades in the Colorado River Basin. Since 1999, except for three years of above average flow the Colorado River Basin has faced a sustained drought.[9] Of course, what Long, Pike and others did not know at that time was that underneath the grasses of the Great Plains was the Ogallala Aquifer and its vast water resources that had accumulated over a million years. Figure 6 shows the Great Plains part of the Great American Desert with the 100th meridian inserted.

FIGURE 6 – Map Showing 100th Meridian and the Great Plains

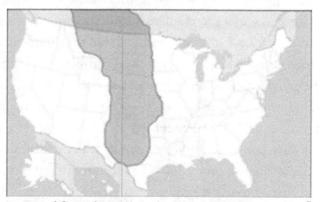

Retrieved from: https://enwikipedia.org/wiki/Great Plains[7]

Powell's report highlighted the cyclicality, seasonality, and variability of precipitation and also indicated that this "Arid Region" encompassed four-tenths of the country; but unlike Pike and Long, he believed irrigation could reclaim some of this land.

> *But westward the amount of aqueous precipitation diminishes in a general way until at last a region is reached where the climate is so arid that agriculture is not successful without irrigation.*[10]

Powell also stipulated that the amount of land suitable for irrigation was a small percentage based on the proximity to streams and smaller tributaries. In 1874, the amount Powell mentioned was between 1% and 3%, later increased to 12%.[11] Interestingly, in a lecture in 1977, Thadis Box, a professor at Utah State University indicated that the earlier estimation was more accurate as "only slightly more than 2% of the region's area has ever been irrigated at a given time."[12] With modern technology, as water was delivered from hundreds of miles away, this percentage has increased more in line with the latter estimation. In the end, Powell's opinion that most of the West did not favor agriculture was discounted and largely ignored.

Over time, it became increasingly clear that water was key in determining how humans lived in the West and how they could survive. With the passage of the Homestead Act in 1860 and many disillusioned gold miners from California and Colorado, settlement began in earnest in Powell's 'Arid lands'. Fortunately, or unfortunately, these adventurous people arrived during several extremely wet years.[13] Both the abundant rainfall during this period and the "Garden Myth" or "moisture follows the plow" increased settlement in the Great American Desert. Just like the nursery rhyme "London Bridge," it all came tumbling down with the extended drought of the 1890s. To survive, farmers either moved further west or turned to dry-farming.

As previously mentioned, dry-farming was used extensively by the Ancient Puebloans on the Colorado Plateau where precipitation averaged between 9 and 20 inches a year. This form of farming did not require irrigation and endeavored to increase the soil moisture that provided water to roots during dry periods. Techniques such as terracing, deep seed planting, and deep tillage of the soil were used. Ditch irrigation and shallow wells powered by windmills were further adaptations that Plains farmers used to ensure continued flow of water. However, just as with the Puebloan cultures, the struggle of maintaining a dependable source of water remained elusive and dry farming was not always successful.[14]

The farmers of the Plains did not surpass the carrying capacity of the land, as did the Anasazi and Hohokam, given how dispersed homesteads were. But, due to the manipulation and adaptation of the landscape there was an unintended consequence. The dry-farming technique used by many of the farmers resulted in a deterioration of the soil that left the area vulnerable to wind erosion. This, combined with drought in the mid-1930s, resulted in the Dust Bowl.[15]

The difficulties encountered by farmers of the Great Plains who continued to scratch out an existence were totally dependent on the vagaries of Mother Nature providing sufficient rainfall.[16] This was also true of farming within the Colorado River Basin and Southern California. Lack of rainfall, temperature extremes, and wind erosion were the tools the Old Lady used to show her superiority. Very quickly, it was acknowledged that settlement of the West, which was a "safety valve" to increased immigration, slavery, and growing urban issues, was impeded by the inability to deal with the climatic variability and lack of dependable water sources.

Fortunately, the Mormons, building on the Hohokam tradition, began a more systematic and community driven irrigation scheme in Utah and by 1890, supported over 200,000 people with 263,473 acres under irrigation. More importantly, productivity increased substantially with wheat yield increasing by 1500%.[17] These results were far superior to the acequia method and established the idea that the desert could be conquered.

Likewise, in California, as the economy shifted from mining to farming the realization that irrigation was necessary to supplement the insufficient rainfall emerged. The San Joaquin & King's River Canal & Irrigation Company, established in 1871, built a 40-mile canal from Fresno to the San Joaquin River, in the Central Valley, to irrigate 16,000 acres.[18] Thus began California's journey into intensive agriculture.

It was quickly realized that the expense of building irrigation systems that brought water to small farms dispersed throughout the Sacramento and San Joaquin valleys was well beyond their means. In addition, the larger landowners did not wish to absorb such large expenditures. The recognition of this situation coupled with the irrigation successes of the Mormon communities and the advancements in technology led to the next stage of water development, which was controlling or "taming" the water in the West. Given the huge capital investment required to accomplish the task, the prerequisite to gaining control of the water in the West involved participation by the federal government.

As the 20th century commenced, President Theodore Roosevelt indicated in his 1st Annual Message to Congress,

> *Great storage works are necessary to equalize the flow of streams and to save the floodwaters. Their construction has been conclusively shown to be an undertaking too vast for private effort. Nor can it be best accomplished by the individual States acting alone. Far-reaching interstate problems are involved; and the resources of single States would often be inadequate. It is properly a national function, at least in some of its features. It is as right for the National Government to make the streams and rivers of the arid region useful by engineering works for water storage as*

to make useful the rivers and harbors of the humid region by engineering works of another kind.[19]

Echoing this, the noted historian Frederick Jackson Turner advocated the need for funding irrigation to continue the development of the West. Interestingly, neither he nor Roosevelt alluded to urban or industrial demands and the related power requirements that also developed.

But when the arid lands and the mineral resources of the far West were reached, no conquest was possible by the old individual methods. Here expensive irrigation works must be constructed, cooperative activity was demanded in utilization of the water supply, capital beyond the reach of the small farmer was required.[20]

To this end, Congress passed the Newlands Act in 1902 that formed the Reclamation Service, later renamed the Bureau of Reclamation, in 1924. The Bureau of Reclamation (USBR) was charged with selling public land in the West with the stated purpose of "[…] Construction and maintenance of irrigation works for the storage, diversion and development of waters for the reclamation of arid and semi-arid lands."[21]

One of the first dams to be constructed by the Reclamation Service was on the Salt River in Arizona. This is the area the Hohokam inhabited for a millennium. The project, begun in 1905, built the Roosevelt Dam and started the tendency of the Reclamation Service to support existing private property and not the intended targets, Jefferson's yeoman farmers. Original intentions of the Newlands Act were to facilitate homesteading, or small farming, on public lands with the goal of increasing settlement in the West. However, the facts indicated large private property received a majority of the benefits. Even though the Newlands Act stipulated only families owning 160 acres could receive water from any of the federal projects, almost fifty years after the Salt River Project was completed there were 134 farmers that used water from the Salt River Project even though they all held well over 160 acres.[22]

The same occurred in California, but on a grander scale. It was found that in the five water districts of the San Joaquin Valley, over half of the 479 farms held 160 acres, which accounted for less than one-third of the total acreage. The remaining irrigated acres were controlled by eight concerns. These companies were Chevron, USA, Getty, Shell, Prudential Insurance, Tenneco, the Blackwell Land Company and the Chandler family, owners of the *LA Times*. Although this concentration grew significantly over the years, the precedent started during the early stages of controlling the water in the West. While Congress, the Bureau of Reclamation and the Corps of Engineers characterized these huge projects as supporting small-scale agriculture or Jefferson yeoman farmer, in actuality the benefits of the subsidized and abundant water produced by these projects for irrigation accrued mostly to large corporate landowners. While the industrialists and financiers were amassing both political and financial power back East, the same thing occurred in the West with the taming and controlling of water. Thus, controlling or taming water continued the destruction of the agrarian myth on which this country was formed.

Very quickly, it was determined that land sales would not cover the cost of these projects; however, the commitment to expand the development of western land continued. As the years passed it became apparent the projects that provided irrigation to develop the 160 acres designated in the Reclamation Act, were not economically viable. Increasingly, most projects focused on massive dams, called "cash register" dams that provided hydroelectricity. The revenues from the sale of power generated by these immense projects, such as Hoover Dam, provided the government with the repayment for the construction of large storage facilities and canals that delivered water to urban areas and farmers.[23] With this, the massive reclamation projects began establishing enormous subsidies to farmers that were unable to cover the costs of such massive projects.[24] Thus, the government was repaid for providing water to develop the arid and semi-arid West through electric bills. More importantly, everyone got used to not paying for water or the massive infrastructures that made it all possible.

Los Angeles—From Backwater to Metropolis

An additional consequence of controlling water led to the creation of the sprawling cities in the West. The clearest example of this is Los Angeles. For the last couple of decades of the 19th century, Los Angeles remained essentially a "back-water" town of around 5,000. The Southern Pacific Railroad connected the town to San Francisco in 1867 and to the east coast in 1881. Those settling in the area used irrigation techniques from the Mormons and with the sunny climate, began producing a vast array of crops. At the 1884 World's Fair in New Orleans, Valencia oranges from San Bernardino created quite a stir as "no one could imagine oranges grown in the western United States."[25]

By 1900, the population reached 100,000 and increased fourfold over the next five years. The main water source, the Los Angeles River was insufficient to sustain this growth. However, 250 miles away was Owens River Valley, situated 4,000 feet in elevation above Los Angeles, where a small but successful farming community developed after the settlers ruthlessly took the land from the Paiute. This source of water was ideal for Los Angeles as it allowed the water to flow, via aqueduct, by gravity to the growing city. Needless to say, many of the residents and farmers of Owens River Valley, not to mention the remaining Paiutes, opposed this diversion, as they believed the water belonged to them. However, The Metropolitan Water District of Los Angeles (MWD) began to purchase land that carried senior water rights in the area.

Through what can be described at best, very shady dealings, Los Angeles triumphed and the Los Angeles Aqueduct delivered its first water in 1913. Ultimately, as MWD purchased more and more water rights from Owens River Valley, Owens Lake and its lush valley virtually turned to dust. With Los Angeles diverting all the water 250 miles away, vegetation in this once thriving agricultural community disappeared and with it the economy in the valley.[26] As of 2014, this region qualified as the largest man-made danger for air-borne dust in the country.[27]

While all of the consequences of what many call the Owens River "water grab" are extreme, the real significance of this takeover of water by Los Angeles was the realization that areas that required more water for development could obtain it from other areas that had a surplus, with no regard to the consequences.

The Owens Valley water appropriation made many people in Los Angeles quite wealthy as well as provided subsidized water for irrigation to large-scale farmers in the San Fernando Valley (the Valley) adjacent to the aqueduct. To provide access to the water for irrigation, Los Angeles annexed the Valley, increasing its geographic size and determining a new model of urban development.

> *The Owens River created Los Angeles, letting a great city grow where common sense dictated that one should never be [...] From that moment, it was doomed to become a huge, sprawling, one-story conurbation hopelessly dependent on the automobile.[28]*

Thus, in the initial stages of controlling water in the West, the agrarian myth was destroyed with the development and enhancement of agribusiness or large-scale farming; water wars developed wherever water scarcity existed and a new type of city developed. Also, the reliance on technology led most to an understanding that water would magically appear if they needed it and the mistaken belief in its abundance. The early efforts of the USBR established massive subsidies for farmers and growing cities that developed the idea that water was free. All of this occurred in a region that was a desert.

The possibilities that these early water control management projects uncovered led to full-scale water wars that continue unabated to the present, pitting farmers against metropolitan areas: northern California, where the majority of the water exists within the state, against southern California; and state against state. Intense conflicts erupted over areas with limited resources attempting to obtain water from regions with sustainable supplies but uses not yet developed. In most cases those having surplus water did not have the political clout to stop growing cities like Los Angeles and San Francisco from acquiring water from distant locations.

After the Owens River "water grab" by Los Angeles and the sizable and increasing amount of water diverted from the Colorado River to the rapidly developing Imperial Valley, the six states through which the river actually flowed became extremely worried. When California began negotiations with the Bureau of Reclamation to build a dam to store a vast amount of water from the Colorado River on the Nevada and Arizona border near a town that barely existed, at that time, by the name of Las Vegas, red flags started flying. This led to the Colorado River Compact signed in 1922 that allocated the water in the river by dividing the six states that bordered the river as well as California into an Upper and Lower Basin.[29] The Colorado River Compact is discussed in detail in Chapter 4 – "Taming the Wild River".

Central Valley Project[30]

After the battle over the Colorado River Compact was settled, the dream of turning the Central Valley of California into a veritable agricultural mecca mushroomed. This vision did not foresee using any Colorado River water; however, given California's current extreme drought and Southern California's dependence on the river, an understanding of all of Southern California's water sources is necessary. With the goal of turning the desert into productive farmland the Central Valley Project (CVP) became reality.

TThe CVP, begun in 1935, constituted the largest project in the Bureau's history to that point, and transferred water from California's moister northern regions to the arid central and southern part of the state. Ultimately, CVP included the Shasta Dam and later the Friant Dam, that powered pumping stations to lift water uphill for 250 miles to irrigate the arid San Joaquin Valley. This water salvaged around 200,000 acres of farmland as well as added an additional 3,000,000 acres — all owned by private investors. Even though the project had a stated purpose of reducing groundwater pumping, this did not occur given the significant increase of acres placed under irrigation.

Prior to the project, the arid San Joaquin Valley, that received less than 5 inches of precipitation each year, relied on ground water for irrigation. By 1930, 1.5 million acres were under irrigation. This led to the water table dropping and land sinking, or subsidence. The extent of the subsidence varied, ranging between 1 and 28 feet over a fifty-year period.[30] Figure 7 is a very well-known photo that shows this land subsidence, which occurred in Mendota, California located in the San Joaquin Valley.

Land subsidence in the Central Valley continues to be a critical issue as ground water pumping increases during droughts. It is reported that

FIGURE 7 – Some of the most severe recorded land subsidence in history occurred in the western San Joaquin Valley near Mendota, where the land surface has subsided nearly 30 feet.

Retrieved from: http://water.usgs.gov/edu/earthgwlandsubside.html [32]

some areas in the San Joaquin Valley are currently finding land subsidence of one foot per year.[33]

Dam building during the Great Depression accelerated with the taming of the western rivers and added a focus on hydroelectric energy. The power generated produced more revenue than the irrigation projects but also supplied the vast amount of electricity needed to operate facilities that controlled the flow of water. Although irrigation remained a main objective, job creation was an added benefit during the depression. Also, this project provided the possibility for new farmland for those dislocated from the Great Plains due to the Dust Bowl.

Ultimately, the CVP consisted of twenty dams and reservoirs, 400 miles of major canals, tunnels, and conduits, and delivered seven million acre-feet of water for agricultural, urban and wildlife use. Five million acre-feet irrigated three million acres or half of the agricultural land in California. Once again, the desire to turn desert into farmland required the control of rivers in Northern California, increased the reclamation of the desert and provided needed electricity for society to continue its progress.

As the CVP neared completion, water managers in Southern California realized that future needs exceeded water they currently obtained from the Colorado River and Owens River Valley. In the winter of 1955 a devastating flood on the Sacramento River in Northern California occurred, killing sixty-four people. With this the California State Water Plan (CSWP) emerged, having as its purposes to provide more water to the San Joaquin Valley and Southern California, and establish flood control and mitigate against salt-water intrusions in San Francisco Bay.[34]

The CSWP assumed unfinished projects of the CVP and included thirty-four storage facilities and dams, twenty pumping plants, ten power plants and 701 miles of canals, pipelines and aqueducts. This information is included only to highlight the massive scope and technology involved in the CSWP, not to mention the amount of energy required to operate all these facilities. Today, the CSWP is the largest user of energy in the state. Continuing man's quest to control water, technology in the CWSP trumped Mother Nature by defying gravity and pumping water almost 2,000 feet over the Tehachapi Mountains to reach southern California. Although the total planned storage capacity of over 4 million acre-feet is not completed, due to environmental, political, economic, and regional concerns, the capability to store a total of 2.4 million acre-feet is currently a reality. Under normal conditions, almost 70% of the water currently stored goes to Southern California and the San Francisco Bay area with the remaining 30% used for irrigation in the Central Valley.

Ultimately, by controlling water, California turned desert into fertile farmland and became the leading agricultural producer in the nation as well as the most populous state in the country. It was only by taming the Colorado and most of the rivers in Northern California that this was accomplished.

> *By the late 1970s, there were 1,251 major reservoirs in California and every significant river – save one - had been dammed at least once.*[35]

Many of these dams also generated electricity for the expanding population in the state as well as provided power to the pumping stations needed to raise water over and through the mountains.

Arizona – The Central Arizona Project (CAP)[36]

Meanwhile, as California built its water infrastructure, Arizona continued to push for a storage and delivery system in the central part of the state. This of course, is the area that the Hohokam lived in for centuries. An intense conflict developed between Arizona and California as the Golden State began taking large amounts of water from the Colorado River in the early 1900s to turn the Valley of the Dead into the Imperial Valley and to support the growth of Los Angeles. As California's growth occurred long before Arizona's, the political power in California delayed any action to provide water to Phoenix and Tucson. For almost a quarter of a century a battle raged between these two states as to how to divide the Lower Basin allocation established by the Colorado River Compact. Finally, a Supreme Court decision, Arizona v. California (1963), affirmed California could take only 4.4 million acre-feet per year, and Arizona could withdraw 2.3 million acre-feet per year from the Colorado River. In addition, the court awarded Arizona the flow of the Gila and Salt Rivers as these sources were generated within the state.

Even with the 1963 Supreme Court ruling it took another five years to gain the approval of California that was desperately attempting to use as much water as possible. With the agreement that if any shortages in flow from the Colorado River occurred, Arizona would reduce the amount it took from the river but California's 4.4 million acre-feet would not change, the Central Arizona Project (CAP) gained authorization from Congress. It became the largest and most expensive water transfer project in the U.S.

Although approved by Congress in 1968, another five-year delay ensued due to the growing environmentalist movement that questioned these massive storage projects. As a result, President Carter inserted CAP on his "hit list" that included 19 federal approved water projects to be scrubbed. This essentially ended the "GO-GO Years"[37] of the USBR and COE. Fortunately, for Arizona, CAP was reinstated with the quid pro quo that the state regulate the use of groundwater. This led to the passage of the Groundwater Management Act in 1980 (GMA).

The original purpose of CAP was to provide water for agriculture in the central and southeastern part of the state, more specifically the Phoenix and Tucson basins. However, when the cost of water delivered through CAP exceeded that of pumping groundwater for irrigation, most farmers chose to continue pumping groundwater. Fortunately, for the USBR, urban areas in the central part of Arizona, Phoenix and Tucson, were starting to grow and were actively seeking water to support their development. Urban water agencies in the region sought and were awarded over 50% of the CAP water or 640,000 acre-feet and the farmers were allocated 550,000 acre-feet although junior in priority to urban users. As the Colorado River water had never flowed into this area prior to CAP, under prior appropriation the senior priority dates were granted to Phoenix and Tucson and agricultural consumption was placed in a subordinate position. But, even with the GMA, the Arizona farmers continued to use groundwater resulting in land subsidence and deep fissures in the land.

Facing intense economic pressure CAP finally reduced the price of water to farmers to "$27 per acre-foot for the first 200,000 acre-feet, $17 per acre-foot for the next 200,000 acre-feet, and $41 per acre-foot for anything beyond that, these prices increased $1 per year."[38] As CAP's cost to deliver irrigation water was around $60 per acre-foot, none of these prices made economic sense as they did not cover the cost to deliver water. This just further exemplified the major subsidies available to farmers. Thus, the water subsidies to farmers that started in 1905 when the Newlands Act was passed continued, even as the dam building phase died.

Included in this pricing, were two forms of subsidies. The first stemmed from the fact that although the highest amount charged was $41 per acre-foot, the cost to deliver the water to the farmers through CAP was $60. The second means by which the farmers were subsidized entailed the $17 price in the second tranche. No, it is not a typo. Common sense dictates that to ensure efficient use of water when one uses more water, they pay more. It is not apparent why the second tranche was $10 less than the first tier of water usage; but one cannot disagree that farmers continued to receive immense subsidies to use CAP water with little to no incentive to conserve.

However, this is not the biggest subsidy. I would be remiss in not pointing out that in this project as well as all of the other dams, storage and delivery system built by the USBR and COE during the 20th century, there was no charge for the water itself. It was free. Given the amount of water that is consumed throughout the West, that is an amazingly huge subsidy that "keeps on giving." The price of water, or lack thereof, will be discussed in detail in Chapter 9 – "What Do You Pay For Water?."

CAP water finally arrived in Phoenix in 1985 and in Tucson in 1993 through a 336-mile aqueduct system, delivering 1.5 million acre-feet/year of Colorado River from Lake Havasu that ended at the southern boundary of the San Xavier Indian Reservation, south of Tucson. Aside from the 336-mile aqueduct system, CAP consisted of fourteen pumping plants, one pump/generating plant, ten siphons under waterbeds and large washes, three tunnels and a large storage facility behind New Waddell Dam (1.1 million acre-feet capacity). To reach Tucson, required tunneling through mountains and pumping the water up almost 3000 vertical feet where CAP water then entered Tucson through a natural gravity flow.

With the construction of CAP, Arizona felt their water future was secure.

Changing View of Conservation

While the USBR continued building massive storage projects in the West that heightened both intrastate and interstate conflicts and increased expensive litigation, a change in how conservation was viewed surfaced. This added a new issue to the water wars. In the early 20th century, as President Roosevelt set aside millions of acres of nationally protected lands, the accepted view of conservation, maximized the use of water and developed it for human use. It also involved the use of technology to efficiently use water to increase production and wealth.[39] In other words, the rivers in the West were working resources and any water flowing to the ocean was considered wasted. Herbert Hoover reportedly stated:

> *True conservation of water is not the prevention of its use.*
> *Every drop of water that runs to the sea without yielding its*
> *full commercial returns to the nation is an economic waste.[40]*

This view of conservation dominated until the 1960s at which point John Muir and Aldo Leopold's vision of conservation began its journey to supremacy. The focus shifted to the preservation of nature and its resources. This revised view of conservation believed that water was required to maintain wildlife, fish and fowl instead of totally for human use. In addition, it maintained it was inappropriate to submerge beautiful canyons, petroglyphs and Native American habitats behind huge dams to store water. Instead, preserving the natural environment became paramount.

At the same time as a change in the way Americans viewed conservation happened, California was busy building its massive water empire. Colorado, Wyoming, and Utah, other states that depended on the Colorado River, grew increasingly alarmed at the exploding growth in the Golden State and the amount of water California increasingly took from the river. The Colorado River Storage Project (CRSP) resulted. This USBR project will be discussed in detail in Chapter 4 – "Taming the Wild River." But as this vast storage project was being considered, a renewed environmental movement emerged questioning the value of these massive projects given the negative impacts on the environment.

This reinvigorated movement had its seeds in the early 1920s when John Muir of the Sierra Club led a national appeal to stop the damming of the Hetch Hetchy that intended to provide water to San Francisco. Beginning in the early 1900s and lasting for almost fifty years, the Bureau of Reclamation (USBR) and the Corps of Engineers (COE) constructed major storage and diversion projects with very little opposition. This all changed with the publication of *Silent Spring* by Rachel Carson that exposed the dangers of pesticides.[41] This opened the floodgates, literally and figuratively, to the impact technology and humans inflicted on the environment.

In California, environmentalist bemoaned the destruction of the salmon and steelhead runs; the ancient Native American lands and artifacts and, of course, the natural beauty of the canyons, rock formations, and valleys formed by the rivers in the West. Also, throughout the region, people began to realize that the increased irrigated acreage resulted in declining water quality with run-off full of pesticides and fertilizers. The upshot of these splintered movements ultimately led to a nationwide organized resistance to the building of massive dams and other reclamation projects as well as the support for federal legislation that protected the environment. By the 1970s, passage of the Clean Water Act, the Endangered Species Act, Safe Water Drinking Act, the National Wild and Scenic Rivers Act, and the Water Quality Act legislated using water in a more sustainable way while placing additional restrictions on the resource and putting the brakes on massive projects. As a result, reclamation projects, such as a proposed dam in Dinosaur National Monument, never made it off the drawing board.

We Tamed Mother Nature

During the heyday of controlling the rivers and water of the West both the Bureau of Reclamation and the Corps of Engineers vied for supremacy. Their combined projects made a dramatic impact on the landscape of the West and turned millions of acres of desert into productive farmland as well as creating a massive urban sprawl.

As of 2015, the USBR indicated it is the "nation's largest wholesale water supplier" and listed its accomplishments that included:

- Operating 337 reservoirs with a total storage capacity of 245 million acre-feet
- Maintaining 475 dams and 8,116 miles of canal irrigation
- Irrigating 10 million acres of farmland that produces 60% of the nation's vegetables and 25% of its fresh fruit and nuts
- Operating 53 hydroelectricity power plants (producing 15% of the nation's power)
- Delivering 10 trillion gallons to over 31 million people each year
- Managing 289 recreation sites with 90 million visits annually

- Contributing $64.6 billion in economic output and supporting 403,241 jobs.[42]

This investment of over $7 billion and new technology led to dominion over most of the rivers in the West. Thus, one can conclude that as of the 21st century, man controlled water.

The question remains as to whether Mother Nature will reverse her trend of showing who is boss and acquiesce to the intelligence of mankind or throw another monkey wrench at those living in the Southwest and Southern California as she did in prehistory with the devastatingly persistent droughts that prevailed during the 11th and the 13th centuries. Is climate change another tool in her arsenal that will allow her to ultimately rule supreme? Or will man and his technology continue its dominion over Mother Nature?

Water is a necessity of life that required creativity and initially some manipulation and later enhanced technology to allow mankind to turn a desert into a highly productive agricultural region that supported large concentrated populations. Unfortunately, demands expanded to include filling swimming pools, watering millions of acres of lawn and providing water for fountains that shot water 100 feet into the air. Taming the water sources in the West led people to incorrectly believe water was limitless.

Many of those living in areas west of the 100th meridian are beginning to realize that Mother Nature does not stay tamed for long and that humankind needs to be controlled. Perhaps, conservation of water envisioned by men such as John Muir who started the Sierra Club and led the battle to save the Hetch Hetchy Valley and Aldo Leopold, author of *The Sand County Almanac* and proponent of a land ethic needs re-examining.[43] To date, controlling water throughout the West has been done at enormous costs, with a main goal of economic development, both urban and agricultural. Perhaps it is time for those living in the arid and semi-arid West to readjust how water is used and reused and develop a new ethic that guides our behavior.

Chapter 4

Taming the Wild River – Colorado River History

Man's relationship with water has clearly evolved over the centuries with the 20th century resulting in man's control over most of the rivers in the West. By taming the rivers, both agricultural and industrial development flourished and sprawling cities continued spreading. There were other consequences of subduing these waters as the desert turned into an agricultural and urban mecca. Reviewing the history of the Colorado River and how it was tamed provides insight into Marc Reisner's comment:

> *The Colorado's modern notoriety, however, stems not from its wild rapids and plunging canyons but from the fact that it is the most legislated, most debated, and most litigated river in the entire world. It also has more people, more industry, and a more significant economy dependent on it than any comparable river in the world.[1]*

Today most people associate the Colorado River with the Grand Canyon which is understandable as for at least the past six million years this perennial flowing river has carved through almost two billion years of geological history to form its current river bed. In some cases, this wild river is more than a mile below the rim of the canyon. As a side note, recent research indicates that in different parts of the canyon, magnificent land sculpturing may have started over seventy million years ago.[2]

The first Europeans to see the river from the top of the canyon were the Spanish in the 16th century calling it Rio Grande or Big Red. These early visitors to the Colorado River thought it was only 8 feet wide—not appreciating it was a mile down from where they stood. One thousand miles shorter than the Mississippi River and much smaller in width, the Colorado is ranked 7th in the continental United States in length. It starts as a tiny trickle at La Poudre Pass in Rocky Mountain National Park at an elevation of 10,184 feet and drains a watershed that incorporates seven states and two countries, the southwestern US and Mexico. Starting as a tiny stream, fed by snowmelt from numerous small and large tributaries, a 1,450-mile course was carved to the Gulf of California. This took at least 6 million years. Unfortunately, due to increasing consumption the Colorado River has only sporadically reached the Gulf of California over the past fifty years.

Over time, at least twenty Native American tribes used the Colorado River as their source of water; but its reach extended far beyond this. Today, the once wild-flowing river has fifteen dams on the main stem that stores this natural resource in reservoirs with around fifty more dams on its numerous tributaries. These storage facilities provide water for domestic, municipal and agricultural consumption. At this point, almost 40,000,000 people depend on the Colorado River for water and farmers and ranchers irrigate over 5.5 million acres.

Dropping from an elevation of over 10,000 feet to almost sea level this once wild river now generates hydroelectric power for most of the Southwest as well as at least 10% of the power requirements in Southern California. As a result, the conditions of the river and its annual flow are watched closely. Of course, close scrutiny has only occurred since the late 1800s as settlement in Southern California and the Southwest began. At least that is what historians would lead you to believe. But as we have already learned, it started much earlier than that.

There is evidence that over 8,000 years ago, small groups of prehistoric hunter-gatherers wandered the Colorado Plateau moving up and down canyon levels as the seasons dictated. Starting around 10,000 years ago, as ice fields retreated, the beginnings of regional variations in climate led to a gradual shift in how these ancient people adapted to their natural environment. Although it is not clear where these ancient people originated, around 450 CE various forms of sedentary agricultural civilizations emerged. Settling in different regions of the Southwest and Southern California, Native Americans, which included the Ancient Puebloans, the Hohokam, and the Chumash, manipulated the land and adapted, as necessary, to survive. Around 1000 CE, the Athabascan people (ancestors of Navajo and Apache) as well as the Yokuts and Paiute, arrived in their respective regions and lived off the land, dealing with the vagaries of Mother Nature, just as others did for centuries.

Europeans first entered the Colorado River Basin in the 16th century and although changes in both political and religious ideologies were implemented the agricultural way of life that had evolved over centuries of adaption remained the same. In fact, the Colorado River was uncharted with the headwaters unknown, at least for the Euro-Americans, until the late 19th century.

Through the mid-1800s, mainly mountain men, traversed this vast area west of the 100th meridian, trapping beavers for the lucrative hat trade in Europe. Jedediah Smith, one of the better known of these trappers, entered the Colorado River in 1826 through its tributary, the Virgin River in southwestern Utah. Smith mistakenly believed this was part of the Green River flowing out of Wyoming that the Shoshone called Seed-Kee Dee Agie, meaning Prairie Chicken River. As we now know, the Green River is actually a major tributary of the Colorado River.

Many of these mountain men continued the quest for a Northwest Passage, which preoccupied Europeans for centuries as well as a newly formed America. It happened to be one of the reasons President Jefferson commissioned the Lewis and Clark expedition. The continued quest for that passage, fostered a myth that maintained a river called, Buenaventura, ran from the Rocky Mountains to the Pacific Ocean. In 1843, John C. Fremont, the Pathfinder, finally debunked this idea with his Great Basin expedition.

In 1857, Lieutenant Joseph C. Ives, the first known Anglo-American known to navigate up the Colorado River, reached Black Canyon, where Hoover Dam stands today. Experiencing both low and high water, Ives concluded:

> *Ours has been the first, and will doubtless be the last, party of whites to visit this profitless locality. It seems intended by nature that the Colorado River, along the greater portion of its lonely and majestic way, shall be forever unvisited and undisturbed.[3]*

Boy, was he wrong!

Twelve years later, John Powell led the first known Anglo-American expedition to descend the Colorado River. It started in Green River Station, Wyoming and went to Black Canyon, where the Ives' journey ended in 1857. Twenty-six years later Powell published his journals in *Exploration of the Colorado River and its Canyons*. As Powell and his expedition entered the Grand Canyon, his journal reflected how little was known about the Colorado River.

> *We have an unknown distance yet to run; an unknown river yet to explore. What falls there are, we know not; what rocks beset the channel, we know not; what walls rise over*

the river, we know not; Ah, well! we may conjecture many things.[4]

Even with Powell's successful navigation of the river, given the wild nature of the river due to its drops in elevation and extensive deep canyons, most of the areas surrounding the river were considered uninhabitable. But, this idea would change considerably over the next hundred years.

Law of the River

So, how did such an uninhabitable region and an uncharted wild flowing river become the "most legislated, most debated and most litigated river in the entire world"? Reisner's comment about the Colorado River arose not only because so many relied on it but also due to the combination of federal and state laws, decrees and Supreme Court decisions that constitute the "Law of the River." This body of legal documents regulates, allocates and restricts water usage on the Colorado River and its tributaries. In the distant past, this overused water source that varies in quantity, depending on the season, as well as the amount of snow received in the mountains led to mass aggregations, migrations, and violence. It was the Law of the River that allowed the Southwest and Southern California to turn desert into a virtual oasis and ultimately become the fastest growing region in the U.S. in the 21st century.

Allocating Water and Prior Appropriation

What brought pioneers to the Colorado River Basin originally was not the possibility of an agricultural or ranching boom, but gold. First in central California in 1849 and then in the late 1850s small amounts were found around what is today Aurora, Arvada and Central City, Colorado; however, as of 1860 significant placer mines were in Summit County, an early tributary contributor to the Colorado River, and also in Leadville, the headwaters of the Arkansas River.

It was these early miners who created a system later adopted for allocating water throughout the West. With the Gold Rush of 1849 in California, miners panned in streams and rivers. However, many of these miners needed to divert water to mines not adjacent to a water source. As the number of miners increased and the adoption of hydraulic mining occurred, access to water became critical. Borrowing a structure used for obtaining mineral rights, the miners found their solution on how to allocate the water in the streams. This miner's system awarded whoever initially found gold in a specific part of a stream, river or mine to the rights to the minerals found in that designated area. Applied to water, if a miner needed to divert water to a mine and was first to do so, he created a priority right to the natural resource that was respected by other miners and recognized by the courts. As the West was settled and agriculture became the economic driver, this system of "first use" became the standard used to allocate water.

As the miners quickly discovered, successful hydraulic mining required funding beyond their economic capabilities; thus, some of the disgruntled returned east. However, the vast majority remained and became farmers or ranchers in this arid and semi-arid land. Understanding that irrigation was a necessity, farmers or ranchers established their homesteads near perennial flowing streams and rivers, just as ancient people had.[5]

Looking at the rivers and tributaries within the Colorado Basin in Figure 8 and given the mountainous topography where most of these streams and rivers originated, most of the land for farming and ranching was found in the valleys and flat lands along the limited watercourses.

FIGURE 8 – Colorado River Basin

Source: United States Bureau of Reclamation: Colorado River Basin Water Supply and Demand Study[6]

In Colorado, farming started on the eastern part of the state in a region that received water from the South Platte and the Cache La Poudre. It was these early farmers in Greeley and Fort Collins and the miners in both California and Colorado that originated a major element of the "Law of the River" that led to the Colorado River being the "[...] most legislated, most debated, and most litigated river in the entire world."

This, of course, was the "first use" concept or the Prior Appropriation Doctrine.

Likewise, in California, farming and ranching started in the Central and Owens valleys where the Sacramento, San Joaquin, and Owens rivers provided sufficient water for agriculture initially. As more people were lured West by success stories, new farms were established further from the riparian areas as the good acreage adjacent to the rivers were already claimed. This led to the need to divert water to these non-riparian homesteads and as a result, required a new way of allocating water.

Before settlement in the West began, Americans allocated water on a principle derived from English common law, a country where water was plentiful. The Riparian Doctrine allocated water to those living along the banks of a body of fresh water. For the first two centuries, as Europeans settled America, the riparian principle provided a structure that successfully provided water as it was more readily accessible east of the Mississippi. By its very nature, the riparian system minimized the manipulation of water that required damming or diversion. As the Industrial Revolution developed, factories established adjacent to rivers providing a source of power for these early industries. Thus began our nation's economic development. Where water was readily available, this allocation of water presented no problem; however, where this natural resource was not as accessible, development became a serious problem.

The vast expanse of land west of the Mississippi, was not located next to a water source. Early settlers found that allocating water by the riparian doctrine severely limited settlement, especially if irrigation was required. As a result, the Riparian Doctrine had a negative impact on economic development for areas not adjacent to a water source. Its predisposition against economic development did not fit the temper of the times. Very quickly, it was decided a new form of allocating water was required in the semi-arid and arid conditions that predominated the western landscape.

The system of "first use" created by the miners called prior appropriation, ultimately governed the control of water in the states west of the 100th meridian.[7] This system allocated water to the first user that diverted any quantity of water that was put to a continued beneficial use. Anyone in the West who needed water in the past or present knows very well the expression "first in time, first in right." Thus, a farmer who irrigated his land in 1895 established a "priority" for a specified amount of water at a specified location that was senior to one who started irrigating in 1899.

Another aspect of the prior appropriation system required that all water used, regardless of priority, must be put to beneficial use. This resulted in a second maxim of prior appropriation, which was "Use it or lose it." In other words, if a farmer decided to take his family and live in Africa for 5 years that required fallowing his fields during his absence, he had two options. Through a long and laborious legal process he could sell or lease his water rights to another user and transfer the priority date that the farmer had to the purchaser or lessee. The second alternative was abandonment of the right where the farmer lost any claim to the water as it was not being put to beneficial use. The water right was now available for someone else to purchase, but the farmer's more senior position or priority date was no longer valid. The new owner assumed a very junior position, receiving a priority date reflecting his "first, beneficial use."

For the western states, the prior appropriation system of water allocation proved successful given its advantages over the riparian system. Benefits of the system included a fuller utilization of the available water where it was needed and did not require proximity to a water source. It also offered more certainty regarding the availability of the water. It finally provided a more effective and efficient system to manage and administer the use of the available water.[8] The certainty the prior appropriation system provided initially supported economic development in the West by ensuring water to both mining and agricultural endeavors. This justified the expenditures of constructing irrigation systems as the region developed. As ownership of the land adjacent to a water source was not a prerequisite for using the water in a river or stream, prior appropriation provided the foundation for moving water to distant locations. This increased the amount of land available for cultivation. Once prior appropriation was adopted, the importance of water rights exploded and unlike the actual resource, water rights became a commodity that could be bought and sold, separate from the land.

When originally implemented in the late 1800s, beneficial use was an excellent means of determining how much water to allocate a specific farmer; however, given the current hydrological reality that water is limited and most sources are over allocated, beneficial use based on historical consumption does not foster conservation or the efficient use of water.

Beyond Prior Appropriation

As the West developed, the prior appropriation system worked well in the administration of water rights within each state; however, the circumstances under which it thrived consisted of individuals with similar interests, usually in the same locale or irrigation district. This local allocation changed substantially as the amount of acreage under cultivation expanded, but more significantly, as urban and industrial needs demanded more water. This shifted the understanding of water as abundant but possibly not located in the immediate vicinity. This change in the way access to water was viewed made the growth of cities in the West possible.

As hydrological technology expanded, the allocation of water was no longer just a local consideration. Prior appropriation allowed the city of Los Angeles to purchase senior water rights in Owens Valley, for water located 250 miles away. The possibility of obtaining additional sources from rivers far away permitted the West to expand into dramatically new areas. Having additional water sources from other regions allowed the population to explode and large urban areas to spread in what was formerly a desert.[9]

Remarkably, just as railroads were connecting the nation, water started dividing it. With the entry of the federal government via the Reclamation Service (changed to Bureau of Reclamation in 1923) and the construction of large projects that diverted many rivers flowing through various states, local demand was relegated to the back seat. Access to water expanded its geographical scope and grew from local to intrastate and then to interstate. This expansion only increased conflicts and litigation. The Colorado River, often called the "American Nile," surfaced as a prime example of conflicting demands of a water source related to areas outside the Colorado River Basin.[10]

Interstate issues first emerged in a 1907 Supreme Court case. In Kansas v. Colorado, Kansas (a riparian state) claimed Colorado (a prior appropriation state), through ditch diversions, depleted the Arkansas River by the time it reached Kansas. On the other hand, Colorado claimed complete control over the river that originated in its state based on state sovereignty. Colorado based its argument on the Harmon Doctrine issued by Attorney General Judson Harmon in 1895 regarding a dispute with Mexico over the Rio Grande. His opinion stipulated a country retained absolute sovereignty over an international watercourse within its boundaries.[11]

The Court's decision upheld each state's authority in controlling its respective intrastate water regulations; however, denied Colorado sovereign power in controlling an interstate river. Additionally, the ruling stipulated that although Kansas was not materially affected by the Colorado diversions on the Arkansas River, this might not hold true in the future. Thus, a new wrinkle in water rights and allocation emerged that sidestepped both the riparian and prior appropriation systems. It introduced equal appropriation. This new water ruling was based on economic equity, both now and in the future.[12] In other words, use of an interstate river relied on an understanding between states that needs could change in the future at which point the federal government could intervene if equal apportionment was violated.

Thus, one state could not totally appropriate the flow of a river or stream that ran through another state. Unfortunately, the ruling in Kansas v. Colorado did not address the real issue of how to allocate a scarce resource under a capitalist system that fostered growth and the belief that technology could provide water at anytime and anywhere. But the decision in Kansas v. Colorado established two important precedents that would directly impact the Law of the River. By ruling Colorado did not have sovereignty over an interstate river created the necessity for agreements to allocate interstate rivers. Furthermore, by instituting equal apportionment, the door was opened for intervention by the federal government. This was an anathema to the fierce independent pioneer spirit of those settling the West.

In a similar case, Wyoming v. Colorado (1911), the Court once again reinforced equal apportionment between states, even though both states followed the Prior Appropriation Doctrine. These two decisions served as a wake-up call to the western states that depended on the Colorado River and highlighted the necessity of interstate agreements to eliminate costly litigation. However, it also opened the floodgates to increased competition between the states within the Colorado River Basin. Delph Carpenter, the lead counsel for Colorado for the Wyoming v. Colorado case, felt the race to develop beneficial uses as quickly as possible would lead to increased rivalries and litigation in the future.[13] This turned out to be very prescient and reinforced comment often inaccurately attributed to Mark Twain, "Whisky is for drinking, water is for fighting'.

Another Supreme Court decision in 1908, Winters v. United States (1908), added yet another layer of water rights to the Law of the River. This involved the rights of Native Americans and established "reserved rights." The Winters decision stipulated that by creating a reservation, the land as well as the water on it, was set aside for the reservation's use. This differed significantly from prior appropriation.[14] Where prior appropriation clearly quantified the seniority and the amount of a water right based on historical, beneficial use; reserved rights stipulated that residency on land, based on a treaty with the United States, provided the right to an unspecified amount of water, anytime in the present as well as the future. Furthermore, the reserved rights were protected under federal laws and courts whereas prior appropriation followed state laws and were enforced by state courts.[15] In other words, reservations established by the federal government had senior claims on water flowing through their land even if not put to beneficial use.

Even though the federal courts had the responsibility of enforcing reserved rights, this ruling was essentially ignored for half a century while many perfected their rights under the prior appropriation system and created interstate agreements. However, once reserved rights were implemented in the latter half of the 20th century, another layer of regulations and allocations further complicated how the Colorado River was divided.

Colorado River Compact[16]

In the extreme southeastern part of California in the Sonoran and California Desert existed a region destined to be the single largest user of the Colorado River. Geologically, this desert area consisted of an 8,360 square-mile sub-sea-level basin, the Salton Sink, formed millions of years ago by the separation of various tectonic plates. For thousands of years the Colorado River sporadically changed its course forming the vast prehistoric Lake Cahuilla where ancient bands fished and camped. As the Colorado River returned to what became its normal course, flowing south to the Gulf of California, this huge lake evaporated and the land reverted to desert. By the end of the 17th century, Lake Cahuilla was completely dry. Over the centuries, during high run-off seasons, the Colorado River flooded the area again, but Mother Nature inevitably returned it to the barren land dictated by the region's precipitation and climate. Recognizing the extreme arid conditions, early Spanish explorers called this region the Land of the Dead.

In the late 1800s, a few courageous farmers started dry-farming techniques that relied on the very sporadic overflow from the Colorado River, into ditches in the Land of the Dead. In 1900, the California Development Company constructed a canal between the Colorado River and the Salton Sink, to divert water for irrigation in this region that received less than 3 inches of rainfall each year. Due to silt build-up, the diversion canal was deepened and then in 1905, because of a heavy run-off and significant rainfall, flooding destroyed the head gates and dikes that contained the diverted water. For two years, the Colorado River flowed into the Salton Sink. This is when it became the Salton Sea.[17] Figure 9 shows the extent of the ancient Lake Cahuilla, estimated to have a surface area of over 30,000 square miles. Today's Salton Sea has a surface area that changes with rainfall and run-off, of around 350 square miles.

FIGURE 9

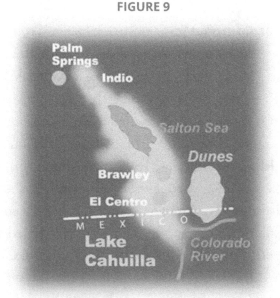

Retrieved from: http://www.blm.gov/ca/st/en/ fo/elcentro/recreation/ohvs/isdra/dunesinfo/ tio_ohv/travel_dune.print.html[18]

The sporadic flooding into the Salton Sea and its expanding agriculture motivated Southern California to propose a dam be built on the Colorado to store water to irrigate the California Desert and support Los Angeles' municipal development. The construction of Hoover Dam and its massive storage facility, Lake Mead ultimately brought over 4 million acre-feet into Southern California providing water to what became the Imperial and Coachella valleys as well as Los Angeles and San Diego. Figure 10 shows some of the major canals that currently deliver Colorado River water throughout the two valleys irrigating almost a million acres. Without this water piped from Lake Mead, this area would still be a desert.

FIGURE 10 – Major Canals From Colorado River to California

Retrieved from: https://en.wikipedia.org/wiki/
Salton_Sea#/media/File:Saltonseadrainagemap.jpg[18]

Before irrigation in the Valley of the Dead was possible and Hoover Dam constructed, the six states through which the Colorado flowed and California had to agree on how to divide the annual flow of this untamed river. This led to the most significant element of the "Law of the River," the Colorado River Compact (Compact).[20]

Due to Supreme Court decisions, recognition that no project would be forthcoming from the Reclamation Service in the absence of an interstate agreement, and the fear that California was perfecting its rights, under prior appropriation, the seven states within the Colorado River Basin negotiated the Colorado River Compact in 1922.

The Compact divided the seven basin states into Upper (Colorado, Wyoming, Utah and northern New Mexico) and Lower (California, Arizona and Utah) basins. Based on the average measured river flow near Lee Ferry, AZ between 1899-1920 of 16.9 million acre-feet as well as the Reclamation Service's estimate that the annual flow actually exceeded 17.5 million acre-feet, each basin was allocated 7.5 million acre-feet. In addition, 1 million acre-feet flowed from tributaries in Arizona allocated to the Lower Basin. Recognizing the annual fluctuations in the river's flow, the Compact also stipulated that the Upper Basin must deliver an average of 75 million acre-feet over a moving ten-year period into Lee Ferry, the dividing point of the two basins. Furthermore, a treaty between the United States and Mexico in 1944, stipulated that 1.5 million acre-feet of the Colorado would be delivered to Mexico. This increased the Upper Basin's delivery requirement to 8.23 million acre-feet each year. Thus, under the Compact, the total estimated flow of the Colorado River or 16.5 million acre-feet was completely divided between the two basins and Mexico.

It was left to each of the basins to determine how to divide their respective 7.5 million acre-feet. The Upper Colorado River Basin Compact, ratified in 1948 did not allot an absolute amount between the Upper Basin states because of "the uncertainty over how much water would remain after the Upper Basin met its obligation to the lower states."[21] Recognizing the unpredictability of the river, the Upper Basin Compact designated a percentage of the residual amount with Colorado receiving 51.75%; Utah, 23%: Wyoming, 14% and New Mexico, 11%.[22] With this, the Upper Basin states could now plan for their future development. That growth would be much slower than California until the latter part of the 20th century.

The Lower Basin continued to dispute how to divide their compact apportionment, which finally required an eleven-year and very expensive court battle. In Arizona v. California (1963), the Supreme Court allocated California 4.4 million acre-feet, Arizona 2.3 million acre-feet and Nevada 300,000 acre-feet.[23] As we will learn, California continued using more than their allocation, however, with this decision, Nevada and Arizona also obtained the ability to plan for their future.

When the Colorado River Compact was negotiated, it was assumed the Native Americans' need for water was minimal so avoided setting aside any to the Navajo Tribes, which occupied almost 25,000 arid square miles in the Colorado River Basin. This oversight changed with *Arizona v. California* in 1963 when the Supreme Court ruled the Navajo Reservation in Arizona had senior rights to over 600,000 acre-feet, or almost one-fifth of the total allocated to Arizona. Thus, with judicial decisions such as the Winters Doctrine and reserved rights, another layer of rights developed that required integration with the prior appropriation system and the interstate agreements or compacts. This, of course, added yet another layer to the Law of the River.

Issues With Compact[24]

It seemed with the ratification of the Compact, the majority of the Southwest as well as Southern California stabilized their future. However, there were several unforeseen problems. The first involved the estimated river flow used to determine the total amount allocated to the Upper and Lower Basins in 1922. The twenty-year period the USBR used to establish the annual flow of the river just happened to be among the top four wettest periods in a millennium. As a result, 16.5 million acre-feet that the Compact allocated to the two Basins and Mexico was a very aggressive number. To complicate this even further, it was determined that the device used to measure the flow at Lee Ferry during this period reported inflated numbers.

Therefore, according to the Bureau of Reclamation, the Compact assumed more water than the Colorado River, on average, actually produced. In recent studies, USBR estimated that between 1906 and 2012 the average stream-flow of the Colorado was only 15 million acre-feet.[25] Thus, based on actual average flows, the Compact allocated 1.5 million acre-feet more than the river delivered during the 20th century. Because the Upper Basin did not utilize its total allocation, the unused portion flowed into Lake Powell and the Lower Basin. Thus, the Upper Basin met the Compact's requirement but California started using substantially more than their allocation of 4.4 million acre-feet.

With the ratification of the Compact, the newly reorganized Bureau of Reclamation pursued the building of a dam and storage project in Boulder Canyon. Boulder Dam, later renamed Hoover Dam, completed in 1935 during the Depression, began storing water in Lake Mead for diversion to the Imperial Valley via the All-American Canal and for the Metropolitan Water District of Los Angeles. This massive man-made reservoir held over two times the annual flow of the entire river behind a 736-foot high dam with an initial storage capacity of more than 31 million acre-feet.

With the completion of Hoover Dam, an intense "we-they" between the Upper Basin and the Lower Basin quickly escalated for other reasons than California perfecting its rights to the water. The first stemmed from a lack of trust based on the Los Angeles Metropolitan Water District's (MWD) track record with regard to appropriating water rights in Owens Valley. The second and more disconcerting issue involved the lack of storage in the Upper Basin. This allowed surplus water during high run-off years to flow to the Lower Basin but more importantly, water allocated under the Compact but not yet consumed in the Upper Basin to run directly into Lake Mead for use by California, Arizona and Nevada. Thus, as the Depression and WWII ended, Southern California felt confident that water for their expanding population and agricultural growth was assured. The Upper Basin increasingly pushed for a storage project of their own. They wanted to stop California from taking their unused allocation and demanded a place to store or "bank" any surplus water to cover the years when snow pack was below normal.

Colorado River Storage Project [26]

It must be remembered that in the early 1930s, Southern California's population and agricultural endeavors exploded while the other six states party to the Compact did not develop until the later part of the 20th century. In addition, storage projects for the Upper Basin languished due to intrastate squabbles. This delay intensified the Upper Basin's apprehension that the Lower Basin was perfecting their rights to the river. As the Imperial Valley and Los Angeles had put water to beneficial use well before development in the Upper Basin the delay in storage projects increased the Upper Basin's apprehension. Thus, as California's growth increased, so did their demand for the Colorado River, and the state took more than the 4.4 million acre-feet awarded in 1922 and confirmed by Arizona v. California in 1963. The other states party to the Compact feared the Golden State's beneficial consumption could establish a senior right and given its increasing wealth and population, the claim might be honored. As Marc Reisner wrote, "No one was going to turn off the spigot to Los Angeles, Arizona or the Imperial Valley for the sake of a few marginal irrigation projects in the Upper Basin – especially if they hadn't been built."[27] Starting in the early 1950s, the Upper Basin began pushing for the Colorado River Storage Project (CRSP) to alleviate their concerns. But other factors extraneous to the West complicated the ability of the Upper Basin to obtain storage.

Even though CRSP was on the drawing board before the publication of Rachel Carson's *Silent Spring* and before the reinvigorated environmentalist crusade of the 1960s, David Brower of the Sierra Club organized a national campaign to eliminate one of the proposed dams in the project. His target was the Echo Park Dam in Dinosaur National Monument. Remembering the beauty of the area that he rafted as a boy, he ultimately gained the support of over seventy-eight organizations.

An additional factor that led to the success of this battle stemmed from the building of a national road system that started after WWII. This massive construction of roads allowed Americans to travel and the general public enjoy the National Parks that Teddy Roosevelt started at the beginning of the century. This appeal to protect the National Parks and Monuments resonated well and gained tremendous support. The Sierra Club produced two films that gained support from the general population. The first was "The Wilderness River Trail."[28] It portrayed the beauty of Echo Park with families floating down the Colorado River through Dinosaur National Monument. The second, "Two Yosemites," compared the unsuccessful fight in defeating the Hetch Hetchy project with the proposed Echo Park project.[29] In addition, a book with pictures, written by Wallace Stegner, entitled "This is Dinosaur"[30] was published to share the beauty of Echo Park with the public. Every member of Congress was given a copy to ensure they understood the impact the dam would have on the environment.

To be successful, Brower and his supporters realized they could not fight the entire CRSP so instead offered an alternative solution to building in Dinosaur. They proposed the height of the Glen Canyon Dam located in northern Arizona be increased to compensate for the loss of storage capacity at the Echo Park site.[31] Ultimately, their appeal was successful and the Echo Park dam was scrubbed from the project.

As a result, Glen Canyon Dam and its reservoir, Lake Powell, became the second largest man-made lake in the country with almost 2,000 miles of shoreline and a capacity of 24.3 million acre-feet. In essence, Lake Powell became the savings account for the Upper Basin as it stored the mandated annual deliveries of 8.23 million acre-feet each year required by the Compact as well as any surplus water unused by the Upper Basin. With the Echo Park Dam eliminated from CRSP and the alternative of expanding the Glen Canyon project, the Upper Basin finally gained Congressional approval for their storage project.

As the dam was under construction, Brower rafted Glen Canyon and admitted his mistake in offering the expansion of the unit further down the river in lieu of building a dam in Echo Park. As the construction of the Glen Canyon Dam was completed, the Sierra Club, under Brower's leadership, published "The Place That No One Knew" which began the fight to restore Glen Canyon to its original state. This battle still rages today.

> *Glen Canyon died in 1963 and I was partly responsible for its needless death. So were you. Neither you or I, nor anyone else, knew it well enough to insist that at all costs it should endure.*[32]

This just further highlighted that the river that became over allocated and over used still remained "unknown" a hundred years after Powell described it in his 1869 journal.

Ultimately the CRSP included four separate projects dispersed throughout the Upper Basin with a storage capacity of over 35 million acre-feet. The largest unit in the CRSP was the Glen Canyon Dam located on the border of Arizona and Utah. Its reservoir, Lake Powell had a storage capacity of 27 million acre-feet and this facility represented 75% of the hydroelectric generating capability of the entire CRSP. The power generated at the Glen Canyon Power Plant was mainly for rural areas in the Southwest; however, it also provided substantial power to municipalities during peak periods (the summer months when air-conditioning is required in the region). The other elements of CRSP included the Flaming Gorge Unit, located in Wyoming that stored Green River water, the primary tributary of the Colorado River; the Aspinall Unit, in Colorado that stored the Gunnison River water behind four smaller dams and provided some hydroelectric power; and the Navajo

Unit located in Farmington, New Mexico (Ancient Puebloan territory) to control the San Juan River.

With the construction of the Glen Canyon Dam in 1963, as well as the other units of the CRSP, the Upper Basin breathed a sigh of relief. However, this was short-lived as California continued to withdraw over 800,000 acre-feet more than their Compact allocation each year. Thus, any unused Upper Basin allocation was not being "saved" in Lake Powell, but released into Lake Mead and subsequently used by California. Over time, this began to reduce the water levels in Lake Mead and Lake Powell.

RECENT CHANGES TO THE LAW OF THE RIVER

Quantification Settlement Agreement[33]

In 2002, after a severe drought in the Upper Basin, declining water levels in Lake Mead and Lake Powell, adhering to the Compact and enforcing equal apportionment, Bruce Babbitt, Secretary of the Department of Interior instructed California to develop a plan to live within their 4.4 million acre-feet allocation from the Colorado River. If not the state would face the federal government dictating what they must do. In a desperate attempt to avoid this, the interested parties negotiated the Quantification Settlement Agreement (QSA) in 2003. Regrettably, the Imperial Irrigation District (IID) determined this agreement detrimentally affected their agricultural economy as well as jeopardized the restoration of the Salton Sea, which resulted in a ten-year litigation. Finally, in June of 2013, the California Supreme Court upheld the legality of the QSA.

With this court decision, the 4.4 million acre-feet Colorado River allocation was apportioned between the IID (3.1 million acre-feet); the Coachella Valley Water District (330,000 acre-feet); the Metropolitan Water District of Los Angeles (MWD) (water transfer of 110,000 acre-feet); San Diego County Water Authority (water transfer of 200,000 acre-feet); and additional miscellaneous water transfers (310,000 acre-feet). These water transfers represent the type where San Diego, for instance, pays the IID for water, priced at $624 per acre-foot in 2015, for water historically used by farmers in the Imperial Valley. These water transfers were sourced by fallowing fields for the first 15 years of the QSA and then out of monies earned, through irrigation efficiencies funded by the purchases of the water. Unfortunately, this was only the tip of the iceberg in California's water dilemma. The U.S. Department of Interior confirmed in 2012 that all of the Lower Basin states' demands exceeded their allocation.[34]

Colorado River Interim Guidelines for Lower Basin Shortages[35]

In 2007, due to the declining levels in Lake Mead and Lake Powell; the drought, which at that time was only in its seventh year; the Lower Basin drawing more than their stated allocation; and the recognition that climate change could only further increase the problem with the overestimation of the annual flow of the Colorado River, things started to change. As a result, the 7 states in the Compact were closer to litigation than they had been in decades. To avoid expensive court costs, the Lower Basin finally acknowledged publicly the possibility of shortages in the future. The upshot of this resulted in the development of the *Colorado River Interim Guidelines for Lower Basin Shortages and Operations for Lake Powell and Lake Mead (Guidelines)* between the Department of the Interior, the State of California and the Lower Basin states. The *Guidelines* reduced Arizona's and Nevada's allocation by specified amounts based on various water levels in Lake Mead. Based on the agreement that removed California's objections to the Central Arizona Project, California's allocation remained 4.4 million acre-feet.

The *Guidelines* also defined the minimum and maximum releases from Lake Powell to Lake Mead with a goal of refilling the reservoirs by 2026. After what we have covered so far, what is the chance of that happening?

Reflecting the continuing Pollyanna belief that water will always be there, the *Guidelines* also included a complicated process of allocating any surplus water to the Lower Basin and created Intentionally Created Surplus (ICS). An ICS resulted from projects that created water efficiency, substantial conservation, or importing water from other sources into the mainstream of the Colorado River that raised levels in the two lakes. This, in essence, formed a water bank to be used in the future.

Both the QSA and the *Guidelines* are steps in the right direction of attempting to align the Law of the River with hydrological realities. However, a political issue surfaced that reflected what most of the other parties of the Compact have feared since its ratification, which is the Golden State's political power. With California allowed to maintain its full allocation, it seems that hydrological realities only apply to those states with fewer members in Congress. In the next chapter, we consider what California is doing in the face of a 5-year drought. It will be interesting to determine if Mother Nature and her facts of life have registered yet. Before that, we need to complete our understanding of the Colorado River's history.

Intrastate Squabbles[36]

Although interstate issues dominated with California possibly perfecting its rights by beneficially using more than their Compact allocation on an annual basis and Arizona, Nevada and California not agreeing to how the 7.5 million acre-feet should be divided, intrastate conflicts also began to emerge. The interstate issues forced local water managers and consumers to focus on their own needs that relied on the prior appropriation system. This resulted in a heightened sense of urgency to develop beneficial uses of water. With the invasive drought of the 1930s, that resulted in the Dust Bowl and urban demands increasing at a faster rate than irrigation, particularly in California, intrastate rivalries exploded.

The increasing demand for water in growing urban populations, throughout the West, resulted in competition between urban and rural populations, especially in California and Colorado. This intrastate conflict manifested most clearly in Colorado over trans-basin or trans-mountain diversions (TMDs). This issue continues to plague the state today. Allowed by the Colorado River Compact, a trans-basin diversion involved the movement of water from one basin having a surplus of water to another basin where water was needed. In other words, the Owens River water grab.

In Colorado, the term trans-mountain diversion (TMDs) referred to the conveyance of water from West of the Divide (an area that had over 80% of the state's surface water) to the East side of the Divide (an area containing over 80% of the state's population).

Figure 11 shows the seven river basins and the current TMDs. The history of TMDs in Colorado started almost immediately after the Compact was ratified with another USBR project, the Colorado Big Thompson.

FIGURE 11 – Transmountain Diversions in Colorado

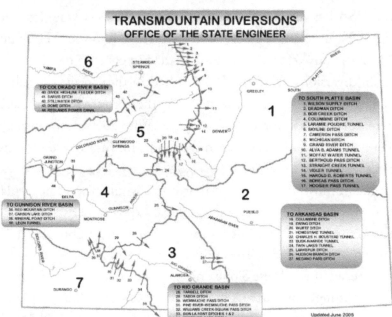

Source: Colorado Division of Water Resources [37]

Colorado Big Thompson Project (C-BT) [38]

As the Compact permitted trans-basin diversions, irrigators in the South Platte Basin located in eastern Colorado, immediately pursued this option. On the other side of the Divide, West-Slope farmers expressed strong objections to the USBR's proposal to transfer water to the Front Range via the Colorado-Big Thompson (C-BT) project. In addition, the Western Slope water districts objected to the project as they wanted sufficient water for their own development and did not want to over allocate Colorado's share of the river. They were also concerned about the requirement to deliver 8.23 million acre-feet to Lee Ferry each year. The Western Slope economy was based mainly on agriculture but looked to the future development of mineral resources and recreation in the "undeveloped and unreclaimed land,"[39] while the East-Slope needed water to support its projected population growth in Denver, Fort Collins and Colorado Springs as well as for irrigation in the eastern part of the state.

The USBR made it clear that no storage projects would occur in the Upper Basin unless the intrastate issues were resolved. Very quickly both the East and West Slopes knew they had to come to terms on trans-mountain diversions (TMDs). This resulted in the Delaney Resolution that stipulated any water diverted to the Front Range required compensatory storage for the West-Slope. With this compromise, the C-BT was approved and established the model for future water transfers, especially with Denver Water.

Although most users assumed that water would always be available for all purposes, water management officials knew otherwise. After the C-BT was approved, a renewed scramble for water rights and TMDs erupted within Colorado. The prior appropriation system resulted in conflicts between the West-Slope and Denver Water of the East-Slope that raged throughout much of the twentieth century, thus stalling most storage projects in the state. As a result, surplus water continued to flow to the Lower Basin.

This highlights the issue of intrastate conflicts in Colorado due to the fact that none of the Colorado River drains naturally into the Front Range where both irrigation and population consumption exceeds that west of the Divide.

Since the construction of the C-BT, constant litigation has enriched water rights lawyers and pitted the East Slope against the West Slope, which must meet their urban, recreational and rural needs as well as assure that the Colorado River continues meeting its obligation of delivering 8.23 million acre-feet to the Lower Basin. TMD's make this more and more problematic, especially with continued drought and the unknowns of climate change. Currently TMDs from west of the Divide to the Front Range ranges between 450,000 and 600,000 acre-feet each year.[40]

While the battle over TMDs raged in Colorado, California experienced serious conflicts that divided the northern part of the state that had sustainable water sources and Southern California that required diverted water to support urban needs in Los Angeles and San Diego as well as irrigation in the Central, Imperial and Coachella valleys. In addition, urban versus rural divisions escalated. All of this squabbling on an intrastate basis recognized the scarcity of water in areas that had grown far beyond the ability of the environment to sustain a growing population and agriculture. Instead of addressing possibilities of limiting water use in the future, the quest for new sources of water continued unabated.

OTHER ISSUES

Evaporation

Another consideration that complicates the responsibility of the Upper Basin delivering the required water each year to Lee Ferry is the loss of over 800,000 acre feet through seepage and evaporation in Lake Mead[41] with an additional 860,000 acre feet lost in Lake Powell.[42] Even though the Upper Basin continues to meet the ten-year rolling average of 75 million acre-feet, with the evaporation loss and Southern California using almost 1 million acre feet more than allocated, is it any wonder that Lake Mead and Lake Powell fell to less than 50% capacity in 2015? Even though the Compact allocated more water than it can deliver and the Upper Basin usage is increasing, the 1922 document still remains the basis for the Law of the River.

Salinity

Unfortunately, just as the Hohokam and Anasazi cultures, which only attained the second stage of water development by just manipulating the landscape, encountered insurmountable problems, the third stage, or man controlling nature, also faces troubles. Starting over a billion years ago, Mother Nature and her water cycle deposited salts and minerals into the sediment as inland seas evaporated. Around 6 million years ago, as the Colorado River carved its course, dropping over 10,000 feet on its journey to the Gulf of California, it cut through many geological layers. Before man controlled the river, during the spring snowmelt, water "cascaded furiously down from the mountains at 300,000 cubic feet per second (nearly 2.3 million gallons), tearing away mountainsides and smashing boulders."[43] This wild and flowing river eroded the rock and soil and dissolved the minerals deposited over millions of years.

Salinity, or the amount of salt and minerals dissolved in water, is a naturally occurring fact of nature and affects all water quality. Just as the Hohokam learned, irrigation increases the salinity of the soil. As irrigated water infiltrates the soil, the salts and minerals remain in the earth as the water returns to the atmosphere through evapotranspiration. On the other hand, irrigated water that infiltrates the soil and returns to the water source, picks up additional salts in the soil and the salinity of the water increases.

Thus, salinity affects water quality. Return flows from irrigated lands increases the salinity for farmers located further downstream. In turn the salinity of their soil goes up also. Increased salinity of either soil or water negatively affects crop productivity and over time eliminates the possibility of growing high-value crops.[44]

Before the West was developed and with it the expansion of irrigation, the salinity of the Colorado River at Lee Ferry was within the normal range or .5 parts per million (ppm). This changed as more acreage was irrigated and the salinity increased substantially further downstream, destroying fish habitat as well as increased soil salinity to levels that actually diminished agricultural production.[45]

In 1974 the Colorado River Basin Salinity Control Act passed to control salinity in the water delivered downstream. With enhanced drainage and new technologies, the salinity of the Colorado River became better managed.[46] However, it has been at considerable expense.

Salinity in the rivers and soils destroyed the early civilization of Sumeria and contributed to the demise of the Hohokam culture. Managing this natural occurring phenomenon, exacerbated by the millions of acres of irrigated farmland added over the past century, becomes increasingly critical. Is water assuming control over man once again?

Silt Behind the Dams

Another adverse consequence with unknown future effects includes the accumulation of silt behind dams. Reisner indicated that the Colorado River "[…] is one of the siltiest rivers in the world – the virgin Colorado could carry sediment loads close to those of the much larger Mississippi."[47] Silt is sand, clay and minerals carried by running water and deposited as sediment in a river bed or delta. Throughout history, this process has created fertile soil.

> *Most distinctive, its enormous, wild energy made the reddish-brown Colorado one of the siltiest rivers in the world…. 17 times more than the Mississippi…… Before its taming by dams, the Colorado's rampaging floods*

periodically turned the dry lowlands of Southern California and Mexico into huge swamps that left behind exceptionally fertile soil when the floodwaters evaporated.[48]

This natural process of depositing sediment was circumvented by building of Hoover Dam. Instead of building up land, this sediment now is deposited behind the dam, where it remains.

As the Colorado River carries more silt than most rivers, this is and will increasingly become an issue. Already, the storage capacity in both Lake Mead and Lake Powell has reduced 20% and 10% respectively. The fact that Lake Powell was built 30 years after Lake Mead explains the latter's lower percentage reduction. Conversely, since Lake Powell was constructed in 1963, sediment build-up in Lake Mead has reduced significantly. It is estimated that each year, 100 million tons of sediment is deposited into Lake Powell. This is the equivalent of 30,000 dump trucks depositing their loads daily.[49]

In 1986, the estimate to remove the years of accumulated silt in Lake Mead totaled $1.5 billion. Added to the cost was the more complex problem of where to put the silt once removed. Between 1967 and 1977, Los Angeles spent $29.1 million to remove 23.7 million cubic yards of silt. Unfortunately, most hydrologists believe removing silt is not the answer and construction of a new dam is required once a dam silts up.[50]

Needless to say, this issue does not just relate to the Colorado River Basin as almost a thousand massive and aging dams built over the past 85 years have silt issues as well as maintenance concerns. Thus, we see the power of water thwarting man's technological achievements and once again another example of Mother Nature exerting her control and strength. In the end who will triumph, water or man?

Groundwater

Thus far, the rights discussed have related only to surface water. However, ground water provides a substantial amount for irrigation and urban needs throughout the Colorado River Basin and California. Currently, groundwater is only regulated in Arizona and Colorado. California recently passed groundwater legislation that, unfortunately, will not be implemented for at least another 25 years, even with the constant negative press on its depletion.

In the Introduction, alluvial aquifers were described. To recap, these are usually shallow underground storage areas located near a water source that transfers the natural resource between surface streams and the aquifer. Thus, drilling wells into alluvial aquifers impacts directly on the total flow of a river or stream.

As with everything else connected with water, this natural resource stored underground is a bit more complicated, and includes various types of aquifers depending on sediment, permeability, depth and a multitude of other factors. To simplify things, the two most basic types of aquifers are confined and unconfined. A confined aquifer is normally quite deep and does not allow any surface water to infiltrate. In essence, the water is trapped between two impermeable dirt/rock layers. To refill or "recharge" a confined aquifer occurs through fractures in the rock; thus, recharge is minimal.

On the other hand, an unconfined aquifer is refilled or "recharged" as rain or snowmelt infiltrates the permeable sediment. There are various types of unconfined aquifers that were formed millions of years ago and may reach a depth of between one foot and one thousand feet. The Ogallala Aquifer is a prime example.

Although not in the Colorado River Basin, the massive Ogallala Aquifer, also called High Plains and depicted in Figure 12, provides interesting insights. Located in the eastern part of Colorado and extending north and east into Nebraska and Kansas and southeast into Texas and Oklahoma, there is a very heavy reliance on this groundwater.

FIGURE 12 – Ogallala Aquifer

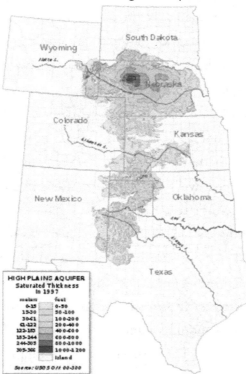

Retrieved from: https://en.wikipedia.org/wiki/Ogallala_Aquifer[51]

The Ogallala, under the surface of what was the Great American Desert, is one of the largest aquifers in the world containing 2 to 3 billion acre-feet. It contained "more water than the Mississippi had carried to the Gulf in two hundred years."[52] What is even more amazing is that this aquifer was formed over 6,000,000 years ago as the Rocky Mountains eroded and began to fill with water from long extinct lakes that carried sediment. Then, around 25,000 years ago as rivers and streams from receding glaciers infiltrated the permeable landforms, this aquifer became massive.

After WWII, technology, or more specifically the centrifugal pump, the high-lift turbine; center-pivot irrigation; and the availability of energy permitted the pumping of vast quantities of water. What seemed to be an unlimited water supply turned the Great American Desert that the buffalo roamed in search of water and food, into America's Breadbasket.[53] Once again, technology allowed man to overcome Mother Nature.

It took centuries, if not many millennia, to fill this vast water source. As rivers and glaciers no longer infiltrate the aquifer, and as current precipitation is only between 10 and 20 inches on an annual basis, the recharge rate is now less than half an inch each year. With over 325 billion gallons of water being pumped each year since 1980, the water table in some areas dropped over 150 feet.[53] By 1980, farming and mining operations withdrew ten times the replenishment or recharge rate.[54]

In water terms, the deficit between replenishment/recharge and usage is referred to as overdraft.[55] Aside from the cost of the wells and the energy required to pump the water, the ground water was free with two different principles governing it: reasonable use and right of capture. Reasonable use refers to the purpose for pumping the water, similar to beneficial use, and right of capture essentially means, that if the water was under your land, you were allowed to pump indiscriminately. The water belonged to the owner of the land. In neither situation was the quantity restricted.[56] It is estimated that this vast amount of water stored in the Ogallala for centuries will be unavailable within the next 50 years due to water levels being too deep to economically pump.[57]

Thus, unlike surface water, the unrestricted use of ground water did not address the scarcity of water, which unfortunately many predict will result in a day of reckoning or "Tragedy of the Commons."[58] This concept dates back to the early 1800s and involved individuals making rational decisions that were in their own best interest (Smith's invisible hand) yet not in the best interests of the community. As a result, a common resource is depleted. Today, the state economies that rely heavily on the Ogallala for irrigation need to find other sources of water or revert back to the grasslands that defined the Great Plains for centuries.

Unfortunately, this increases the chances for another Dust Bowl. During the droughts of 1974-1976 and 2000-2003, some blowing sand storms occurred but it was nothing like the '30s.[59] This was attributed to federal soil conservations programs that reduced soil erosion. In addition, irrigation from the Ogallala Aquifer now provides moisture via irrigation that was not available in the 1930s. This begs the question as to what will happen in future droughts when the Ogallala water is not readily available to irrigate parched land.

How does this relate to the Colorado River Basin? In the past several years huge dust storms, known as a haboob, have darkened the skies of Phoenix, similar to the storms during the Depression where visibility reduced to zero, power lost and temperatures soared to triple digits.[60] Fortunately, these were short-lived, but could they be a harbinger of things to come? Remember the water grab that permitted Los Angeles to become the sprawling city it is today and also turned the Owens River Valley into a moonscape and created a health hazard?[61] Consider what could happen if the Central Valley could no longer use groundwater and much of the irrigated acres fallowed due to lack of water?

So why should those in the Colorado River Basin worry about what is happening outside its drainage area, especially in California or the Front Range of Colorado? Those overseeing the basin water do not have to worry about other states not part of the Compact; however, the farmers in eastern Colorado are a different matter. Remember those irrigators in eastern Colorado that ultimately succeeded in obtaining the USBR's support in the Colorado-Big Thompson (C-BT) trans-mountain diversion (TMD)? As it becomes more expensive to pump water from the underground sources those same farmers will increase their demand for water currently sent into the South Platte River and Arkansas River Basins via various TMD's. This will only further increase the demand on the Colorado River, which according to many is already fully allocated as well as intensify the conflict between rural and urban sectors and the West and East Slopes of Colorado.

So, What Does All This Mean?

As the Colorado River Basin and Southern California developed over the past 200 years, federal and state laws, Supreme Court decisions, and interstate agreements created the Law of the River. Even though water rights happened in recognition that this natural resource was limited, the allocation was done mainly on the basis of demand that was not regulated and the belief of the continued availability of water. In the case of the Compact, more water was allocated than the river could deliver. The technology that developed during the twentieth century led to increased urbanization and expanding populations in areas that were never suitable for a large group of humans. Supreme Court decisions established additional restrictions, such as equal apportionment and reserved rights, which diluted the certainty of water rights under prior apportionment. On the other hand, recognizing that increasing demand required certainty of water's availability, interstate agreements developed that placed another layer on the rights established under the prior appropriation system. Finally, the environmentalist movement of the 1970s added additional demands on the river with the Endangered Species Act, Clean Water Act, etc.

In the end, all of these conflicting and complicated layers of allocating water assumed if the current sources of water were fully used, new supply could be obtained by melting snow in Alaska and piping it to California, or diverting water from the Great Lakes, Columbia River or the Mississippi River to the Southwest. In other words, if water was needed, supply was not an issue. Fortunately, costs for such projects as well as local, environmental and preservation concerns have dampened enthusiasm for such ideas. Today, increasing demand, droughts and climate change increasingly highlight the need to focus on how water is used instead of obtaining new sources.

Unfortunately, as we examine how California, Arizona, Las Vegas and Colorado continue to increase demand with minimal attempts to conserve except in a crisis, it becomes increasingly apparent that the current trajectory of water use is not sustainable.

Chapter 5

'California Dreamin'[1] – California Today

California and the Drought

During 2015, one could not pick up a newspaper without reading about the devastating five-year drought occurring in California. Bear with me for a couple of pages as I throw a bunch of numbers and percentages at you. Unfortunately, it is the most efficient means of showing the magnitude of this drought. Most of Southern California averages between 3 and 18 inches of precipitation on an annual basis; however, since 2011, the entire state experienced a substantial shortfall in rain. Meteorologist, Jan Null, reported that between 2011 and 2014, precipitation deficits in various regions of California ranged from 12.78 inches in San Diego and 79.09 inches in San Joaquin.[2] To complicate this, increasing aridity accompanied unusually high temperatures, especially in Southern California that only increased the evaporation rate.

Even with the much heralded El Niño, as of March 2016 the Drought Monitor continued showing alarming conditions. Sixty percent of the state remained in either exceptional or extreme drought and an additional 22% still suffered severe arid conditions.[3] While this was an improvement over the previous three months when exceptional, extreme and severe drought was found in over 92% of the state, the situation still remained quite disturbing.

What made the lack of rainfall even worse was a diminished snow pack. Yes, skiers and boarders constantly summon Khione, the Greek goddess of snow to disperse more of the white fluffy stuff so they can strap on one or two strips of laminated wood and defy gravity by flying down the mountain.

However, everyone living in California should be praying to all the gods for more snow as it normally provides 30% to 40% of California's annual water needs. The snowpack feeds the many reservoirs built by the state over the last century. Given the persistent drought as well as the huge demand in the state, snow pack was only 5% of normal as of April 1, 2015.[4] With less snow, there was less run-off and water levels in lakes and reservoirs declined. El Niño helped somewhat as a year later, the California Department of Water Resources reported the statewide snow pack was at 88% of the April 1 average.[5] Unfortunately, 100% of normal would not be enough to erase the effects of the past five years. While snow increased, it certainly was not an epic year. In fact, more than several consecutive epic years are needed for California to return to normal.

By early July conditions improved further with only 42.8% of the state in extreme or exceptional drought (including the Central Valley, Los Angeles and San Diego) and an additional 16% experiencing severe drought (including the Imperial, Coachella and San Joaquin valleys and the north western part of the state).[6] These conditions will only deteriorate over the next several months as the state enters its hot and dry season.

California currently has over 1,500 surface water storage facilities with a total capacity of just under 50 million acre-feet. The six largest reservoirs in the state are located in or on the perimeter of the Central Valley. Constructed under the Central Valley Project (CVP) and later the State Water Plan (CSWP), they represent one-third of the state's total storage capacity. An examination of the percent of capacity at each of these reservoirs, detailed in Chart 2 raises some interesting points.

By looking at the historical averages for the two dates at each of the six storage facilities, one is struck by the seasonality of the water collected behind each dam. In October, when I first researched the water levels, I was shocked at how little water was held in each of the reservoirs.

CHART 2 – % of Capacity of 6 Largest Reservoirs as of
October 16, 2015 and March 20, 2016 in million acre-feet (maf)

Storage Facility	Total Capacity	10/16/15 % of Capacity Hist. Av.	10/16/15 % of Capacity	3/20/16 % of Capacity Hist. Av	3/20/16 % of Capacity	7/6/16 % of Capacity Hist. Av.	7/6/16 % of Capacity
Lake Shasta	4.6	55%	33%	110%	86%	108	85
Lake Oroville	3.5	48%	29%	109%	80%	100	80
Trinity Lake	2.4	32%	21%	63%	49%	61	51
New Melones	2,4	20%	11%	38%	24%	41	26
San Luis	2.04	35%	18%	57%	50%	26	16
Don Pedro	2.03	47%	31%	78%	57%	96	76

Source: Adapted from California Department of Water Resources [7]

At first, I neglected to focus on what the percentage of capacity was usually at that time of year. Comparing the historical average for the same day minimized my initial shock. What continues to be of concern is that even with El Niño, the percentage of capacity at each reservoir as of March 20, 2016 and July 6, 2016, still lags behind the historical average. This reinforces NASA reporting it would take 11 trillion gallons (almost 34 million acre-feet) to recover from the five-year drought.[8] To put this in perspective, that is more than Lake Mead's capacity. The bottom line is "it could take several years of average to above average rainfall and snowmelt before California's water supply can return to anything close to normal."[9]

In July of 2014, Governor Jerry Brown requested a voluntary reduction in water usage. You would think that this would have put people in the state on notice that there was a problem. I was appalled to find this was not the case. A dear and very intelligent friend who lives in Newport Beach visited us the month after Governor Brown's voluntary appeal. When asked how they were handling the drought?", he responded, "What drought?" He clearly continued to live in a dream world, as did most of the population of the area as six months later, water use had actually increased in Southern California.[10]

Our friend's reaction is only one example of how most are unaware of or actually deny the hydrological realities in the West and still believe in water's abundance. *The Washington Post* reported that Steve Yuhas, a radio commentator in southern California felt as wealthier residents pay more in property taxes, they "should not be forced to live on property with brown lawns, golf on brown courses or apologize for wanting their gardens to be beautiful." He further stated that, "And, no, we're not all equal when it comes to water."[11] Yuhas made this comment soon after Governor Brown's Executive Order implemented mandatory water rationing in the spring of 2015.[12]

Thus, the 25% mandatory reduction in residential use Governor Brown instituted by Executive Order on April 1, 2015 should not have been a surprise, as voluntary conservation clearly was not in the cards. This is another example of people living in Fantasyland and our elected officials continuing to ignore reality until a crisis erupts. Given the lack of understanding of the total water problem and the severity of the drought, Governor Brown had no other choice. He had to act. I must admit, I found it highly ironic that such an action, which should have been issued years earlier, was enacted on April Fool's Day. Hopefully, this mandatory reduction in consumption will become permanent and the new normal in California.

So why does California's drought affect the Colorado River Basin? Included in the State Water Project is the California Aqueduct that not only provides water to the San Joaquin farmers but to Los Angeles, Santa Barbara and Riverside in the Coachella Valley.[13] Both L.A. and the Coachella farmers also receive Colorado River water via the

240-mile California Aqueduct and the eighty-mile All American Canal, both downstream from Lake Mead. Due to the drought that plagued California, water deliveries from Northern California reduced to 20% of contracted water supplies.[14] As a result, there was a greater reliance on other sources. This meant groundwater and the Colorado River.

The timing of this drought could not be worse. Just as water deliveries from Northern California were reduced due to the low snow pack and shrinking reservoirs, Southern California dealt with reduced deliveries from the Colorado River due to the Quantification Settlement Agreement.[15] More bluntly stated, the state was no longer allowed to draw more than their allocation under the Colorado River Compact.

Imperial Valley and the Salton Sea

With agriculture in the Imperial Valley receiving the largest single allocation of the Colorado River, it is important to understand what is occurring there. As previously indicated, the 2002 Quantification Settlement Agreement (QSA) finally restricted California, more specifically, the Imperial Valley and Los Angeles, taking more than the 4.4 million acre-feet designated in the Colorado River Compact. However, QSA encompassed more than just restricting California's consumption.

In addition to developing a plan to reduce the amount of the Colorado River diverted by the state, the QSA included the restoration of the Salton Sea. Located to the north of the Imperial Valley and south of the Coachella, this body of water formed in 1906 when the Colorado River flooded the Salton Sink. After the completion of Hoover Dam, the Imperial Valley received a constant and never-ending flow of water that allowed the region to become a veritable Garden of Eden. Sitting at an elevation of 234 feet below sea level, with no outlet and in a region where temperatures reaches over 100^0 F., evaporation increases the salt and mineral content to where the Salton Sea has a salinity level higher than the Pacific Ocean.

Over time, the Imperial Valley increased its consumption of the Colorado River for irrigation to over 3 million acre-feet each year. Of this amount, one million acre-feet returned to the Salton Sea as agricultural run-off. This became the main source of water for the Salton Sea. These return flows included salts leeching through the soil as well as pesticides, and other pollutants, thereby reducing the quality of the water even further.[16]

The QSA mandated irrigation efficiencies such as fallowing fields or drip irrigation to ensure Southern California could live within the designated Compact allocation. With the reduction of irrigated acres and the adoption of more efficient farming methods, the shrinking of the Salton Sea will only increase. Added to this is the high evaporation rate that continues to see the Salton Sea decline at an alarming rate.

So why is there such a big hullabaloo over the restoration of a body of water created by man just a century ago that for centuries Mother Nature eliminated? Some feel it is outrageous to send water from the Colorado River to "evaporate a lake that's already saltier than the ocean while Lake Mead threatens to shrink low enough to shut down Las Vegas' water intakes and the turbines at Hoover Dam."[17]

Conversely, there is the decimation of wildlife that relies on the Salton Sea. In the past, the California Department of Fish and Game introduced a wide variety of fish into the sea. With increasing salinity, only tilapia remain. As the salinity continues to rise, they too will disappear. In addition to the fish, a wide variety of waterfowl rely on the Salton Sea to include, pelicans, cormorants, ibis, geese and ducks. If the tilapia disappear, so will the fish eating birds. So there is a very real and negative impact on the wildlife that have migrated to the area over the past 100 years.[18]

It is not just wildlife that is feeling the effect of this failing body of water. A recent article in the New Yorker, entitled *The Dying Sea,* indicated the drying of the Salton Sea was causing a disturbing increase in human respiratory health issues.[19] The cause of this was the extremely fine dust remaining as water evaporated. The article told of the plight of the Valdez family, focusing on their four-year-old son, Axel, who developed environmental asthma. Due to his condition, Axel missed school ten days out of 30; was unable to play outside; and the family was forced to cover all the windows with heavy curtains to keep the dust outside.

The Imperial Valley landowners that use the majority of the water from the Colorado River for irrigation are mainly absentee; thus, the majority of the population living in the Imperial Valley consists of low paid farmworkers. As a result, many very likely have no health insurance to cover chronic conditions, such as asthma. Given the environmental conditions, the region has the highest incidents of childhood asthma-related hospital stays in the state. This health issue does not affect just children as we also are told that that Michelle Valdez, Axel's mother, developed COPD and Antonio, the husband also had a respiratory infection.

Without a doubt, the Salton Sea dramatically exemplifies the water issue in the West. If technology had not delivered water on a consistent and stable schedule starting in the early 20th century, the Imperial Valley would have remained the Valley of the Dead and the area would have continued as Mother Nature intended. The winter vegetables grown there would have been planted in areas with more precipitation and the 900,000 acres currently irrigated, would still be desert. With all of this, the Salton Sea would have remained the Salton Sink, except for periodic flooding in epic snow pack years. Few people would have chosen to live in this desolate and barren environment. If the "Grande Dame" had been allowed to keep this area the way she envisioned, the current health issues would be minimal.

On the other hand, this area now produces 70% of the nation's winter vegetables, which has certainly been a benefit by keeping prices low for many Americans. More importantly, the Imperial Valley does exist as does the Salton Sea. The tilapia, and the waterfowl now call it home. In addition, there are over 175,000 people that live, work and play in the valley. Can Mother Nature be allowed to claim this area once again?

In addition to the substantial health hazard, other human impacts include the elimination of recreation and the reduction in property values. A recent study completed by Michael Cohen of the think-tank, Pacific Institute, indicated that inaction on the Salton Sea could have a potential economic impact of between $29 and $70 billion over the next 35 years.[20] The state's plan to restore the Salton Sea totaled $9 billion but given the financially strapped condition of the state that has more severe water issues to resolve, it appears that a 2017 deadline to reinvigorate the Salton Sea is "dead in the water". Forgive the pun.

Passing the deadline with no action has even broader implications. As it was a condition included in the QSA, posturing has already begun between the Imperial Irrigation District (IID) and San Diego. The IID maintains that the water transfer of up to 200 million acre-feet to San Diego is in jeopardy if the state does not address the restoration of the Salton Sea. On the other hand, the Water Authority of San Diego maintains the water transfer, was a separate transaction. How this will play out is anyone's guess. Even though the IID owns the senior rights to the water from the Colorado River that were established early in the 20th century, will the state of California allow the IID to deny San Diego water?

San Diego and Desalination

Did you know that San Diego has over 1.3 million people, receives an average of ten inches of rain each year and has no natural source of water? Without technology and the Colorado River this city would not exist. The source of the city's water is the Colorado River (64%), the State Water Project (19%), local supplies that consist of limited rainfall, conservation and two wastewater plants (17%), reclaiming up to forty-five million gallons each day.[21]

To increase water availability to the city, San Diego pursued desalination. This coastal town's Carlsbad desalination plant went on line late 2015 at a cost of $1 billion. The plant has the capability of producing 50,000,000 gallons per day or almost 153,000 acre-feet per year.[22]

In the past, desalination was considered too expensive as a new source of water, especially when the federal government was still in the business of building dams and reservoirs. Today, it is still a very expensive alternative. The cost of the desalination plant in San Diego, was at least double that of building a new reservoir or a waste water treatment plant. Also, it was four times more expensive than various conservation methods, such as more efficient irrigation. Looking to the future, San Diego realized it could not count on the Colorado River for more water and found with the drought and the reduced state deliveries, they had to think outside the box. They decided: "You cannot conserve or recycle what you do not have."[23] What a novel idea!

As a result, they proceeded with this $1 billion project, at a cost of $2,000 per acre-foot, which is still just over a half a penny per gallon. Even at this cost, the San Diego Water Authority was willing to pay almost three times what they paid the Imperial Irrigation District for water. This reflected the growing awareness in some parts of the state that water was in fact a scarce commodity. It is estimated that this billion-dollar project will only produce less than 10% of the city's total consumption. Pursuing desalination reflected a change in the way water was viewed as it was deemed necessary for the future at any cost.[24]

California and Desalination

Environmental concerns considerably complicated the planning and construction of the Carlsbad project. Current desalination technology produces one gallon of potable water from every two gallons withdrawn from the ocean. The remaining gallon, or brine, is discarded, but with double the salt content. If discarded directly into the ocean, there is a dramatic negative impact on the marine ecosystem. To gain approval for the Carlsbad Plant, San Diego was required to build sixty-six acres of wetlands to filter the brine. An additional infusion of seawater into the brine using a 5:1 ratio was also mandated before flushing it back into the ocean.[25] These remedies dramatically increased the price of construction.[26]

The Carlsbad Plant was permitted to utilize ocean intakes from an aging power plant that reduced total capital required for the project. This will not occur for future plants constructed along the state's coast due to the decimation of the marine life as water is sucked into the plant. Instead, buried pipes further out in the ocean will be required. This will also increase costs substantially. Another downside is the plant consumes enormous amounts of energy.[27] Even with the high capital costs of the Carlsbad plant, San Diego decided it was important to pay for more certainty in their water future.

There is a growing consensus that desalination plants may be in California's future, but not immediately. Currently there are seventeen desalination plants at different points in the planning stages, all anxiously waiting to determine the success of San Diego's project. Environmentalists increasingly express grave concerns over the impact on both the environment and marine life. And of course the high costs of such technology remains a real factor. In the 21st century, desalination will become the issue that Hetch Hetchy and Echo Park were in the 20th century.

The Carlsbad Plant took twelve years of planning, a six-year approval process and over three years of construction. So, this option is clearly a long-term solution and not just a back-up plan during droughts. Santa Barbara found this out the hard way.[28] After constructing a plant for $34 million to supplement water during a drought in 1980, it was decommissioned in 1992 and partially dismantled as the rains returned. In July of 2015, the Santa Barbara City Council approved the reactivation of the "mothballed" plant at an additional cost of $55 million.[29] This is more than they paid to construct the plant initially and is another example of looking at water supply in a short-term framework and not addressing "hydrological realities."[30] In other words, water is limited, seasonal and subject to the vagaries of Mother Nature.

As an aside, Santa Barbara is also stuck in the traditional way of valuing water. Friends who live in Santa Barbara recently renovated their home which called for new landscaping. They requested a delay in planting until the drought was over to minimize water consumption. Both the HOA and the city rejected this proposal. The irony of this rejection was it occurred several months after the Governor's Executive Order to reduce residential water consumption by 25%. Clearly, land use requirements within the HOA as well as the city continue living in the past and do not consider hydrological realities of the West.

As of March 2016, Lake Cachuma, the reservoir that supplies 55% of the water to Santa Barbara was at 15% capacity.[31] In May, given the disappointing El Niño in Southern California, it was reported that the lake could fall to around 6% of capacity by the end of the year.[32] Santa Barbara remains in a dream world that clearly perpetuates Reisner's "fraud."

California and Agriculture

Are you prepared for more minutiae? Unfortunately, these details are necessary to place the urban/rural conflict over water in perspective. With agriculture consuming between 70% and 80% of water in the West and California irrigating the largest amount of acreage, an understanding of how the water is being used is important. Since 1948, the Golden State has been the country's largest agricultural producer, accounting for around 12% of the total U.S. crop and livestock revenue.[33] As of 2015, there were around nine million irrigated acres in the state that contributed around 2% of the state's revenue but produced half of the nation's fruit, vegetables, nuts and wine. Interestingly, as of 2013, four commodities, accounted for over 47% of the agricultural revenue. In rank order they were milk (16.4%); almonds (12.4%); grapes (12%); and cattle (6.5%).[34]

Groundwater depletion in California has constantly been in the news over the past year, with farmers and ranchers pumping the lion's share of this source. Added to the drought and the attention to over-pumping is the belief that water under any land owned is there for the taking. With all the finger-pointing, something had to take the blame. For a while, almonds became the monster causing the depletion of the groundwater.

Over the past decade, many farmers in the Central Valley shifted to higher profit crops, such as almonds. For instance, California is now the leading producer of almonds in the world and since 2000, increased irrigated acreage by 44% for this one crop. In 2014, almonds produced $11 billion in revenues for the state, but also used 13% of the state's water.[35] Unlike lettuce or broccoli, almonds, just like citrus and other orchard crops, require water year round. Additionally, it is not possible to fallow a field of almond or lemon trees as can be done with the annual production of vegetables. As a result, this highly nutritious nut became the "demon" as it takes 1.1 gallons of water to produce a single almond.[36]

Are almonds the real devil incarnate as they provided $11 billion in revenue in 2014 or 15% of the total agricultural revenue for the state? *The L.A. Times* provided an interactive site that calculated the amount of water needed to produce different types of food. A summary of the site is found in Chart 3. The calculation included not only the irrigation needed to sustain the livestock or grow almonds but also the water needed to grow the food for the livestock.

CHART 3 – Amount of water to produce one ounce

Category			
Fruits and Vegetables	Crop	Gallons required per ounce	Comments
	Avocados	9.05	California produced 88% in US
	Grapes	3.12	California produced 91% in US.
	Broccoli & Cauliflower	2.44	California produced 95% of the broccoli and 89% of cauliflower in US
	Tomatoes	.95	California produced 91% in US
Protein	Beef	106.28	California had 610,00 cows in 2013
	Chicken	16.61	California ranked 12th in nation for producing chicken meat
Starch	Rice	16.26	California produced 99% of glutinous rice in US

Source: Adapted from Kyle, Kim, Schleuss, Jon, and Krishnakumar, Priya. (2015). *989 Gallons of Water Went to Make this Plate. LA Times.* April 7, 2015[37]

Thus, the type of crop planted and the method of irrigation employed significantly impacts the amount of water consumed. Reviewing this makes one question why the type of crops planted are not considered in an arid or semi-arid region that experiences droughts and continues to deplete its groundwater at an alarming rate.

Although intuitively I understood that whatever a cow drank remained in its muscle and tissues or was "recycled" I never considered how much water a 1200-pound cow required nor the amount of water needed to grow the food it needed. I was shocked to find that one-ounce of beef required 106.28 gallons of water. So in effect, the almond is not the biggest villain. Does this mean we may all have to become vegetarians if we wish to live in the West?

Looking at another crop, alfalfa, which is the main food for cattle, offers additional thought-provoking issues. As of 2007, more acres were devoted to alfalfa than any other crop in California, with the majority of the production in the Central Valley (70%) and the Imperial Valley (17%). To produce this crop, irrigation is required. Furthermore, the main method of irrigation used on alfalfa in California is flood or border, which is very inefficient and requires larger quantities of water than most other methods.[38]

This low tech and inexpensive method has been around for centuries and essentially involves delivering the water through an open ditch and the water flowing over the ground to water the crop. It is estimated that over half of water lost to evaporation, runoff, infiltration and evapotranspiration is due to flood irrigation.

Blake Hansen of the Department of Land Air and Water Resources at UC Davis reports on the water use of the more abundant crops in the state. Chart 4 shows that on average, alfalfa used almost 5.5 million acre-feet each year, or 17% of the total water used for agriculture in California.

CHART 4

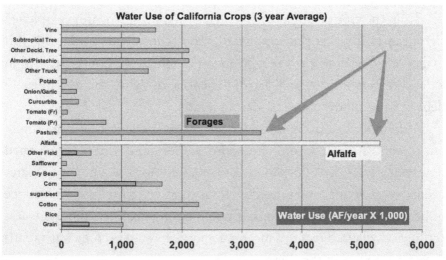

Source: Hanson, *Blaine. Irrigation of Agricultural Crops in California.* University of California, Davis[39]

Interestingly, when other forages consumed by livestock were combined with alfalfa, over 8.5 million acre-feet/year was consumed in California. This represented over 25% of water consumed by agriculture in the state. In 2013, alfalfa and other forage crops generated $1.3 billion in receipts. Compare this to the top agricultural revenue producing commodity, milk, that provided $9.4 billion or almonds with $5.9 billion in revenues.[40]

So, why does a crop that uses over 25% of the water and provides just over 2% of the agricultural revenue continue to use the largest amount of irrigated acres and a lot of water? A likely explanation is that prior to the current drought, dairy farms consumed almost 70% of the crop. Also, with milk and cattle combined, revenues amounted to 24% of the state's total agricultural receipts. Thus, alfalfa becomes a necessary crop if California wants to remain the top agricultural state in the United States.

However, the drought has presented another wrinkle in considering how water is used. Over the past five years, the number of cattle producers fell due to the arid conditions, but alfalfa production remained constant. As a result, one-third of the 2015 alfalfa crop was exported. Remember the water cycle? Given the amount of water used and retained in the alfalfa, "the state is indirectly exporting billions of gallons of water overseas due to alfalfa's water-hungry biology."[41]

And then there is the fact that everyone pays next to nothing for this valuable resource.[42] The price of water will be discussed in detail in Chapter 9, but suffice it to say that since the USBR started its mega-projects that facilitated the growth and expansion of the West, huge subsidies for water infrastructure prevailed. As a result, we all got used to paying very little for water.

So, what do farmers pay for water? Currently, an irrigator in the Imperial Valley pays between 6¢ and $2.45 for 1000 gallons. An article in *The New York Times*, "The Risks of Cheap Water," describes how such low, subsidized rates "explain why about half the 60 million acres of irrigated land in the United States use flood irrigation, just flooding the fields with water, which is about as wasteful a method as there is."[43] But most water providers and utilities are loath to raise rates that would foster conservation as it reduces their revenues. Added to this is the "use it or lose it" stipulation of prior appropriation, that provides no incentive for farmers with senior rights to become more efficient, especially when water is practically given away?

Issues regarding flood irrigation, type of crop and the amount of water it consumes, price of water, reliance on groundwater and its depletion, water rights, over allocation of surface water, and the benefit of domestic production for food supplies all must be honestly and openly addressed if there is any hope of solving the increasing supply demand gap in the West as well as the urban/rural conflict. Increasingly it is becoming apparent how interconnected and complex this natural resource becomes in the social, economic and political spheres of our everyday life.

California and Groundwater

Another major issue the drought in California finally surfaced is the overuse of groundwater, particularly in the Central Valley. Jay Famiglietti, the NASA Jet Propulsion Water Expert, and our disaster movie producer added another aspect to his pending catastrophe. He reported that between 2011 and 2014 over 12 million acre-feet of groundwater was withdrawn in the San Joaquin and Sacramento basins. This amount was more than the 40 million residents of California consumed each year.[44]

In 2002, NASA and the German Aerospace Center developed the Gravity Recovery and Climate Experiment, affectionately called GRACE. Using twin satellites scientists determined water loss over time by measuring the reduction of mass. In December of 2014, NASA analysts found the depletion of over 33 million acre-feet of groundwater in California since the project began in 2002.[45]

An image produced by GRACE, reflected in Figure 13, dramatically shows this reduction in groundwater between 2011 and 2013, which certainly has not improved over the last two years with the drought and increased reliance on groundwater.

FIGURE 13 – Groundwater Depletion 2011-2013

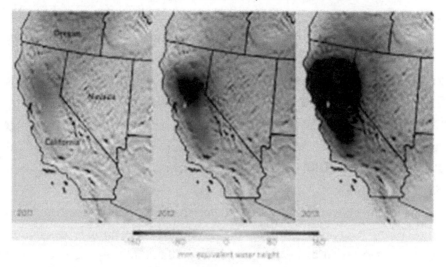

Retrieved from: http://earthobservatory.nasa.gov/blogs/earthmatters/ files/2014/11/ nclimate2425-f1.jpg[46]

According to the California Department of Water Resources, during a normal year, groundwater contributes 38% of the total water supply for the state but during a drought this reliance increases to almost 65%. And, before we blame it all on the agricultural sector, it is important to understand that around 21 million Californians also depend on groundwater for their drinking water.[47] Many in the Central Valley are finding their domestic wells going dry. Knowing that groundwater takes years to recharge, it is not difficult to understand how in some areas of the Central Valley, due to subsidence, the ground is sinking more than a foot each year. Unfortunately, for the foreseeable future it is highly unlikely this will change.

Unfortunately, GRACE is currently unable to determine the amount of water remaining underground or its quality; thus, it is unclear if and when the water level will be too low to economically pump to the surface.

In November of 2014, Lesley Stahl of 60 Minutes reported on the groundwater depletion in California. The segment, "Depleting the

Groundwater," covered the unregulated drilling in the Central Valley. When a spokesperson for Arthur and Orum Well Drilling was asked if new wells being drilled took water from neighboring farms, the response was "I would say, yeah. We are taking water from everybody. Everyone knows there is a water problem and you have to dig deeper and deeper." The reply to Stahl's question as to whether farmers had to drill or go out of business was "What choice do you have? If we don't have water to grow something it is going to be a desert."[48] How ironic! Wasn't it a desert less than 100 years ago? This is just another manifestation of Reisner's "fraud."

As the impact of climate change, extended droughts, increased population, decreased groundwater levels and continued production of water hogs, such as beef, almonds and alfalfa all converge, a perfect storm is certainly developing and is finally ringing some alarm bells. To address this, California passed legislation in late 2014 that finally addressed groundwater pumping.

It should be pointed out that even with such a heavy reliance on groundwater, California was the last western state to enact such legislation. The Sustainable Groundwater Management Act requires plans for providing a reliable water source in the face of future droughts and climate change. Emphasizing local control, the legislation omitted any overarching authority that could monitor and control groundwater withdrawals.

Even with the growing awareness of the depletion of the aquifers in the state, the traditional belief that the "water is mine" and its abundance still exists. Many of the farmers and ranchers are claiming their existing rights are being thrown out the window. They also maintain the state has insufficient storage capability to compensate for the loss of groundwater consumption on which they depend.[49] It will be interesting to see who volunteers to reduce the amount of water they currently use.

As structured, this new legislation cannot resolve the huge groundwater overdraft that developed over the past seventy-five years.

The designated deadline for achieving groundwater sustainability is twenty-five years in the future. Will Mother Nature let it go that long before the water level in the aquifers becomes too deep to economically pump or the water quality deteriorates even further? Ask anyone in the Central Valley if they drink water from the tap and most will respond in the negative, as it just does not taste good. That is, of course, if they are even able to get water out of their taps for domestic use as the drought and continued reduction in the water level has dried up many of the individual wells.

What is California's Future?

Any way you look at it, California has some very difficult decisions to make, all of which have lurked in the wings for years. Farmers, ranchers and water managers have been painfully aware for quite a while of the complicated issues the state faced. The question remains as to whether "California dreamers" understand the full scope of the problem. A two-year drought in 1976-1977 when the population was 22 million and a six-year dry period in 1986-1992 with a population of 30 million disturbed their dream world, for a while.[50] However, after the rains and snow returned, everything returned to the "same old, same old." Likewise, with the current drought, the general public's awareness finally occurred four years into the dry period with Governor Brown's mandatory restrictions. It remains to be seen whether a true appreciation of a crisis the state may encounter in the near future has penetrated the fantasy of an oasis in the desert. Or, will they close their eyes once again as precipitation returns and restrictions are removed.

Granted, California is not part of the Colorado River Basin, but as the single largest user of the Colorado River, what is happening in the entire region is connected. The Imperial Irrigation District forced to fallow fields and transfer water to San Diego, Los Angeles and the Coachella Valley while remaining within the 4.4 million acre-feet Compact allocation; the CSWP reducing water deliveries to 20% of normal during 2015;

groundwater depletion in the Central Valley increasing the clamor for new sources of water; Lake Mead water levels remaining lower than last year at this time[51]; Lake Powell water levels essentially the same as of a year ago[52]; and the Salton Sea evaporating, creating both economic and health problems are issues that can no longer be considered local in their resolution. Continuing to look at these problems as isolated situations contributes to even more difficulties. Perhaps, Famiglietti's prediction of a water crisis is not so far-fetched. Obviously, California waited too long to address these issues, so bold leadership and tough political decisions are now necessary.

Some tough decisions are being made. San Diego and Santa Barbara's desalination plants are good examples, even though the costs are exorbitant. Additionally, reuse or recycling waste water for domestic use such as facilities in Orange County are becoming a new reality. In the 1990s, activists defeated efforts both in San Diego and Los Angeles to begin what was termed "toilet to tap" programs. The "yuck" factor won the day. With the current situation and increased awareness of the hydrological realities San Diego, just approved a $3.5 billion reuse project that will produce 83 million gallons per day (around 93 million acre-feet annually) of recycled water over the next 20 years.[53] Los Angeles is also considering a massive reuse project that would ultimately generate 168,000 acre-feet each year.[54]

These programs are promising steps that reflect a change in the way water managers in southern California have traditionally obtained water to support urban development. Instead of importing new sources, the recycling of waste water will use what is imported, treat it and then reuse it.

And then, there is the way water is allocated. Water rights under prior appropriation proved successful in the past in managing water in years of shortages and provided some degree of certainty, at least to those with seniority. However, that certainty would be thrown out the window in California during an extended drought.

A study published in 2014 by the University of California-Davis found that over time the administrator of water rights in California (the State Water Resources Control Board) issued rights totaling 370 million acre-feet on an annual basis. The problem is the statewide annual average of surface water is only 50 million acre-feet.[55] Thus, rights to divert water are over seven times the amount of water available. Although many of these rights are junior and only available during surplus years, it does give a very false sense of security and continues to foster the belief of water being always available. With the promise of water in some years, these irrigators either cease operations or rely on groundwater when their rights are curtailed. It is little wonder that groundwater withdrawals have increased substantially. What are the chances any farmer or rancher forgoing income if they can use the water underneath their land? The study also claimed that demand continued to build and rights were being issued even though the water supply was not there to support any new demand.

More disturbing is a report that the state has no capacity or ability to track how much water many of the larger and more senior water rights consume. Even though State authorities reduced water deliveries to farmers and cities up to 95% in 2015, anyone with water rights that predated 1914 were exempt from any cuts. In other words, monitoring the more senior right holders, which in most cases were also the larger consumers of water was not done. Additionally, the Associated Press reported the state's information system relied on self-reporting. This led to incomplete records, numerous errors and information that was years out of date.[56] It is believed that California's inability to track its usage and its over allocation will cause increased conflict and an even larger deficits of water in the future.[57]

As farmers currently use around 80% of the water in California and account for less than 2% of the state's revenue, this sector seems the logical choice to reduce water use. But wait, these farmers provide the United States with half its fruit, vegetables, nuts and wine—all basic necessities, especially the wine! What would happen to the price of food in our country if one-quarter of the production in the Central, Coachella and Imperial Valleys was eliminated while allowing golf courses and lush lawns and gardens in Beverly Hills, Newport Beach, San Francisco and Palm Springs to flourish? If you eliminate agricultural production, how do you decide what gets slashed? Do you base it on prior appropriation where the more senior water users continue producing? If that is done, some of the more senior rights in the Central Valley belong to cattle and dairy farms and alfalfa production. Do you let the water guzzlers continue when other crops would use less water and also keep fruit and vegetable prices stable for the country? Do you focus on high-value crops regardless of water use? Or do you tell Los Angeles that they will not get their drinking water in August? How do you decide?

It gets very complicated with a myriad of conflicting interests on a personal, local, and regional level. It does not take a rocket scientist to figure out why our elected officials have not dealt with these problems on a timely basis. If the drought continues as it did a thousand years ago for almost a century, the state will no longer have a choice. Clearly, one could make a very strong argument that even if El Niño lasts for several years and refills the major reservoirs in California, that the state has only dodged a bullet with another crisis, just another drought away.

Groundwater Recharge

Of course, there is always technology to bail California out of their water woes. Unfortunately, most of these solutions are years away from reality. Desalination, construction of new storage facilities, or the expansion of existing operations is constantly being discussed. Another option that is gaining traction is groundwater recharge and storage. It is estimated that underground storage capacity in the state is between 850 million and 1.3 billion acre feet.[58] This is massive considering that total surface water storage capacity is less than 50 million acre-feet. Many claim that this option could also contribute to solving the groundwater depletion crisis the state also faces.

Recharge is an interesting solution. Studies have found it much less expensive than reservoir expansion or desalination. Advantages include, less water loss through evaporation, reduced energy requirements and the replenishment of groundwater.[59]

What is not addressed is that aside from the expensive option of desalination, the remaining alternatives rely on new or increased renewable sources of water. Groundwater storage or expansion of surface water capacity only works if you have the snow pack or rainfall that exceeds average amounts. With the current drought, the state cannot even fill its existing storage facilities. UC Davis reports that expanding storage capacity is not the solution as sufficient capacity already exists. As an example the San Joaquin watershed has around 8.7 million acre-feet of capacity but an average annual runoff of only 6 million acre-feet.[60] Once again, we are stuck in the traditional belief that water can be made available and not the hydrological reality that this natural resource is limited.

It will be very interesting to see how this all plays out over the next couple of years in the state, especially if the sea surface temperatures do warm and El Niño brings blockbuster snow falls. If the precipitation returns, will everyone go back to the status quo of watering lawns, filling swimming pools and growing alfalfa using flood irrigation? As of mid-October 2015, Los Angeles experienced torrential rains, causing massive mudslides that closed sections of I-5. Forecasters are saying more rain is on the way. So, is the drought really over? Unfortunately, as of July, 2016, Los Angeles is still looking for more rain and continues in an exceptional drought.

Will Californians continue to believe that droughts are short in duration and that Mother Nature will always provide the natural resource they use so freely in a desert environment? Or will they finally realize the need for a realistic plan for the future that addresses the hydrological reality of limited availability of water in an area that has grown well beyond its carrying capacity? Hopefully the devastating extent of the recent drought will force the state legislators to look at water in its totality, and the public to understand the status quo is just not acceptable.

The 2016 Drought Contingency Plan for the Central Valley and State Water projects issued by the California Department of Water Resources, reflected a pessimistic outlook even though the El Niño increased snowfall in the northern and central mountains and precipitation in both the Central Valley and the San Joaquin Valley improved.

> *Although current forecasts indicate the present wet hydrology will continue into spring 2016, there is a potential that dry conditions may return during WY {water year} 2016. In addition, precipitation gains observed under our present wet hydrology may not fully alleviate the effects of consecutive years of dry conditions during WY 2016.[61]*

Comments such as this deviate from the norm of resuming status quo behavior as soon as precipitation returns. The contingency plan issued on January 19, 2016 also mentioned that even though precipitation was above normal in many places in the state for the 2015/2016 water year, runoff is significantly below average due to extremely low moisture content and a reduced groundwater table.[62] The good news is the increased precipitation is providing much needed groundwater. However, given the rate it is being depleted it certainly is not increasing water levels.[62]

I certainly hope, for those living in California, as well as the rest of the Colorado River Basin, that the Sierra Nevada will have epic snowfalls that extend well beyond 2016. If not the future could become quite traumatic. If Mother Nature does decide to allow the snow gods to provide ample snow, and climatologists predictions come to pass, it will still take several years of blockbuster snowfalls to eliminate the deficits of the past 5 years in California. The same holds true for the past 15 years in the Colorado River Basin. Unfortunately, even with one good wet year, it is highly likely a return to the old ways will continue and highly unlikely that any long-term solutions will be implemented. Won't this only delay the inevitable crisis? Famiglietti's disaster movie is becoming a distinct possibility!

Chapter 6

"DROUGHT DOES NOT EQUAL A WATER SHORTAGE"[1]
– ARIZONA TODAY

ARIZONA'S ABILITY TO PLAN FOR its water future began with the Supreme Court decision, Arizona v. California (1963) that guaranteed the state of Arizona 2.8 million acre-feet under the Colorado River Compact, and approximately 1 million acre-feet from in-state rivers, delivered through the Salt River Project. In 1968, Congress approved the Central Arizona Project Act (CAP) and the residents of Tucson and Phoenix could rest easily. The water that flowed 334 miles via a canal from Lake Havasu, located below Lake Mead, solved the significant overdraft or depletion occurring in groundwater in central Arizona that the Hohokam occupied almost one thousand years before. But Arizona's future still required a great deal of creativity and attention.

Central Arizona Project & Ground Water in Arizona

CAP was originally conceived as a project to save agriculture in the central part of the state totally dependent on groundwater and causing land fissures and subsidence in many areas. However, the agricultural sector in the area found it cheaper to continue pumping than signing long-term contracts to receive water through CAP. Ultimately, it was Phoenix and Tucson that agreed to the long-term contracts with the federal government and pushed for the passage of CAP with the promise to provide water at prices equal to or less than what pumping groundwater cost. Without these agreements, the water available to the central part of the state which totaled around 1.5 million acre-feet would not be used and thus CAP not economically feasible.

Reflecting President Carter's concern about the overdraft in groundwater in the state, a quid pro quo for passage of CAP mandated Arizona enact legislation to administer groundwater resources. The Groundwater Management Act of 1980 (GMA) identified areas within the state having the most severe groundwater overdraft; where recharge was less than withdrawal.[2] Three levels of management were created, each having different requirements. The major goal of the GMA was to achieve a "safe yield" or a long-term balance of withdrawals and replenishment of the underground aquifers by 2025, within the areas having the most significant overdrafts in groundwater.

The GMA gets a bit confusing given the different levels and their respective requirements; hopefully Chart 5 simplifies the information and makes this groundbreaking legislation more understandable.

CHART 5 – Arizona Groundwater Management Act Overview

Level of Management	Characteristics of Level	Requirements of Level
Active Management Area (AMA)	* Identified 5 areas * 4 abutted CAP canals * 3 surrounding large metropolitan areas * 1 not abutting canal, but using substantial groundwater * Includes 80% of population * Accounted for 70% of overdraft	* Prohibited any new land under irrigation * Grandfathered rights to pump groundwater if under irrigation between 1975-1980 * Established system of groundwater permits and rights * Required meters and reporting of use * Required farmers abutting canal to use CAP water * New municipal growth must demonstrate a continuous supply for 100 years.

Irrigation Non-Expansion Area (INA)	* 3 areas identified * rural areas * groundwater overdraft not as severe as in AMA	* Prohibited any new land under irrigation * Required meters * Required reporting of use * No restriction on usage * New municipal growth must demonstrate a continuous supply for 100 years. No recharge required
General Level	* rural and not near CAP	* No restrictions under GMA

One element of the GMA requires some explanation. As previously mentioned, the purpose of this legislation was to reduce the reliance on groundwater in the Central part of the state. Although revolutionary at the time, the GMA did not address the pumping of groundwater in any of the areas other than that deemed at high risk of groundwater depletion, or the Active Management Areas (AMAs). Additionally, farmers and ranchers within the AMAs were compelled to use CAP water. As there had been no prior appropriation water rights regarding groundwater, land where water had been pumped for generations was now junior to urban areas.

As a reminder, to eliminate California's long-running objection to Arizona's water project and gain passage of CAP, it was agreed that in the event of any shortage in the Colorado River, the Golden State did not have to reduce its 4.4 million acre-feet allotment. This agreement is clearly reflected in the *Interim Guidelines for Shortages*, discussed in Chapter 3.[3] Thus, the Colorado River allocations to Arizona and Nevada would be curtailed first and due to a junior position on CAP water, farmers and ranchers would find their allotments reduced before the misters, swimming pools and residential irrigation systems in Tucson and Phoenix experienced any cutback in deliveries.

Given the junior position of farmers, the GMA stipulated that any land under irrigation between 1975 and 1980 were grandfathered and permitted to return to pumping groundwater if their water via CAP was curtailed.[4] So, although GMA reduced the reliance on groundwater in certain areas in Arizona, it provided the ability to return to pumping groundwater if and when the Colorado River Basin faced scarcity. Once again, political and local interests trumped hydrological realities.

Problems with CAP

Water first reached Phoenix in 1985 and Tucson in 1992, with both of these urban areas looking forward to reducing their reliance on groundwater. Unfortunately, CAP water deliveries in Tucson initially resulted in a real fiasco. Colorado River water, delivered through the canal, passed through a water treatment plant and then directly into the taps of those living and working in Tucson. Immediately, residents complained about the taste of the water and within days, many turned on the tap to see brown water flowing. Tucson Water determined that the higher salinity of the Colorado River water not only affected the taste, but also corroded the aging piping infrastructure, pieced together over the years. In addition, increased water pressure caused by shifting from a number of different wells to distributing the water to a system with only one source, increased corrosion as well as increased the number of burst pipes. This increased deterioration of the delivery infrastructure flowed right into the taps throughout Tucson.

Residents reacted to this foul-tasting, brown water by installing in-home water-treatment systems and used only bottled water for their potable uses. Very quickly, CAP eliminated the direct delivery of water and Tucson returned to their reliance on the higher quality groundwater.[5] Given GMA regulations, Tucson Water developed a recharge and recovery program that infused the water from CAP into the aquifers where it was naturally filtered and combined with the groundwater for treatment and delivery to municipal and industrial users.

Briefly, recharge or replenishment of groundwater occurs two ways.[6] The first happens naturally as precipitation, melting snow or seepage from water sources infiltrates the ground and collects in an aquifer. The second, or artificial recharge, involves redirecting and placing a surface water source into the ground or actually pumping the water into an aquifer. Through recharge, the incidence of land subsidence and fissures reduces as long as the amount of water infiltrating into the aquifer balances the amount of water withdrawn. The artificial recharge not only provides the possibility of reducing or at least minimizing groundwater overdrafts, it also allows for water banking.

Currently there are two recharge facilities for the metro area of Tucson with a total recharge capacity of 140,000 acre-feet/year, that essentially equals the area's CAP allocation of 144,172 acre-feet/year for the basin. In addition, a State of Arizona project, located to the south of the metro area has a recharge capacity of 30,000 acre-feet/year.[7]

Planning for anticipated shortages, The Arizona Municipal Water Users Association (2015) reports Phoenix and Tucson recently began a pilot project for Phoenix to store some of its unused CAP water recharged in aquifers in Tucson available to Tucson Water Authority for use during shortages. In return, during a drought, Phoenix could access a corresponding amount of Tucson's CAP allocation. Such a relationship accomplished two important goals, which involved raising the water level in in the Tucson Basin aquifers and also eliminating the need to spend millions of dollars on recharge and recovery facilities in Phoenix.[8]

Phoenix, on the other hand obtains 51% of its water from the Salt River Project that has a surface water storage capacity of over 2 million acre-feet; 37% from CAP, 7% groundwater and the remaining from surface and reclaimed water. Like Tucson, Phoenix has developed a recharge program that has a permitted capacity of over 517,000 acre-feet. These recharge facilities serve two purposes for this large metropolitan area. The first is to raise groundwater levels that have been depleted over the years. The second and more important is water banking.[9]

Water Banking

Water banking is technically defined as "an institutional mechanism designed to facilitate transfers of water on a temporary, intermittent or permanent basis through voluntary exchange."[9] In layman's terms, water banks are like savings accounts that store water via different agreements for access at a future time. Established in 1996, the Arizona Water Banking Authority (AWBA) enabled the storage in underground aquifers for those holding rights to any surplus CAP water. The amount stored created a credit for future use or for irrigators to use instead of pumping groundwater.

The AWBA reported a total of 4 million acre-feet of credits have been created, as of 2014, through its water banking program, 3.4 million acre-feet for the state and 600,000 acre-feet for Nevada.[10] According to Arizona Department of Water Resources, the total water used by the state each year is 6.96 million acre-feet[11]; thus, the water credits amount to only seven months of the annual total water consumption in Arizona. While this reflects solid water management, one has to wonder, how many years it would take for those credits to be used while at the same time not replenishing or recharging the aquifers?

Does Arizona Face Problems

The pilot project between Phoenix and Tucson as well as water banking are excellent examples of how those in water management in Arizona are planning ahead. However, the Arizona Municipal Water Users Association convinced themselves that "Drought does not equal a water shortage" as they claimed they have planned ahead for such an eventuality.[12] Although these programs and projects were totally rational, they fell into the same pitfalls of relying on both technology and agriculture bailing out urban areas in the event of a drought, planning based on droughts that only last five to seven years, addressing supply and ignoring demand.

While there is a growing recognition that the Colorado River Compact promised more water than the river could deliver over the long term, Arizona has also failed to consider the fact that climate change may reduce the flow of the Colorado River between 5 and 20%.[13]

Due to the California drought, those other than water managers have finally been alerted to the fact that the drought has actually lasted more than the normal five years and that given the current level of Lake Mead, the 2007 Colorado River *Guidelines*, shortages may actually reduce the amount of CAP water delivered to the central part of the state. However, according to Pamela Packard, the President of the Central Arizona Project Board, the cutbacks will impact the irrigators first with up to half of their water allocation slashed. Even with the reduced flow from the Colorado River, municipalities do not have to worry about receiving their water due to water they have placed in the water bank.[14]

As a result, those living in Arizona, other than the farmers, feel they can continue life as usual. Recently this was clearly apparent when friends who we worked with in the financial industry in New York 35 years ago described a home they just purchased in Carefree, located around 35 miles north of downtown Phoenix. This town has its own water system that until 1999 depended solely on the Cave Creek Aquifer, which was being depleted. As the town was in an AMA that restricted any additional wells, planned build out was not possible, so the Carefree Water Company secured a CAP allocation and currently receives over 60% of its water from CAP with the remainder from the aquifer.[15]

I was in the middle of working on this chapter, when our friends visited and was shocked as they described their new home that included a large swimming pool and a covered patio with a mister to reduce the outside temperature and make it more comfortable during hot weather. A misting system used 10 hours a day with 10 nozzles consumes between 50 and 150 gallons a day, depending on the nozzle size. In fairness, our friends, recognized the fact that they were moving to a desert and planned on replacing their lush green lawn with xeriscaping. Yet, one only has to wonder why the connection between a water shortage throughout the

Colorado River Basin with misters and swimming pools is conspicuously absent.

This disconnect between hydrological realities and Arizona's upscale residential areas is blatantly apparent when one looks at homes for sale over $1,000,000. Most if not all have good sized swimming pools. In an area where evaporation exceeds precipitation, does this make sense? Granted, green lawns account for the majority of residential water use, but in an arid environment where the average temperature exceeds 90 degrees for at least five months of the year, the evaporation rate in swimming pools is enormous. This basic knowledge of the water cycle continues to escape many living in the Southwest.

Cost of Water in Arizona

Many of those who relocated to the Southwest moved there for a lifestyle that included air-conditioning, swimming pools and golf courses. In the arid climate, one would think people would be willing to pay for the quality of life that requires a large amount of water and makes these amenities possible. However, in 2015, an average monthly water bill in Phoenix was $37.75 for around 7,000 gallons. Compare that amount to an average monthly water bill in Boston, where water is more abundant. For 5,400 gallons, Bostonians pay $84.30.[16] This comparison defies basic economics.

Even though Arizona does not adequately charge for water usage, it appears that Arizona worked out a system that determined how water should be allocated in a worst-case scenario. The farmers would either start pumping water again or go fallow until the water supply increased again. In addition, through the water-banking program in the state there is some cushion in stored water in the underground aquifers. So, aside from those irrigators that will lose the water they received either through CAP or pumping groundwater for generations, the catastrophe movie will not be filmed in Arizona

Again, if it were that simple! There are others out there who saw the potential for a disaster movie in Arizona. There is, of course, the fictional *Water Knife* that depicted Arizona at the mercy of the Las Vegas water controllers. Unfortunately there are those well researched books like *A Great Aridness: Climate Change and the Future of the American Southwest* by William deBuys that indicated Phoenix and Tucson will be able to continue their lifestyle, albeit reduced, only if climate change does not happen; extended and pervasive droughts that prevailed during pre-history do not reoccur; urban growth does not exceed the cushion resulting from agricultural water rights being junior to metropolitan areas; and the Upper Basin does not fully use its Compact allocation and continue sending surplus water to the Lower Basin. According to deBuys the belief that any of these options will not occur is "like believing in the Tooth Fairy."[17] Perhaps, California is not the only opportunity for the next Hollywood blockbuster.

Arizona and Agriculture

Agriculture, as in the other states that rely on the Colorado River, is the major consumer of water in Arizona. Although there was little consensus on how much water was actually consumed by agriculture, estimates indicated that irrigation accounted for between two-thirds and three-quarters of the 6.96 million acre-feet of water consumed in the state. The past ten years witnessed a decline in irrigated acreage, particularly in the Phoenix Basin as the urban areas replaced farmland. In addition, a reduction in irrigated acres occurred in areas not adjacent to the main stem of the water delivered by CAP from the Colorado River.[18] This is attributed to the Groundwater Management Act of 1980 that restricted pumping water from the aquifers.

Remember the grandfathered rights for irrigators under GMA? If a farmer used groundwater for irrigation between 1975 and 1980 and CAP water was curtailed, they could revert to pumping groundwater as these farmers were grandfathered. So, GMA that aimed to reduce the dependence on aquifers since the early 1980s lost some of its teeth. Furthermore, the fact that development in areas outside of the Active Management Areas pumped water for 30 years, basically unrestricted, minimized some of the savings that the farmers switching to CAP water created.

Perhaps there is another disaster movie in the wings for the rural parts of Arizona. Is there any way the agricultural sector can avoid starring in this nightmare? An examination of the agricultural economy in the state provides some potential solutions. As of 2013, the Pacific Institute indicated that 60% of the irrigated acres in Arizona were devoted to water guzzling crops. These water hogs consisted of alfalfa and forage (40%) and cotton (20%). The remaining irrigated acreage was divided between vegetables (15%) and wheat (10%).[19]

In 2015, *Holy Crop* published by ProPublica reported that both California and Arizona cotton farmers have twice the per acre yield over Texas and Georgia as the western states use "two to four times as much water per acre."[20] Most of the farmers use the inefficient flood irrigation technique to grow cotton. This is the method used in California on alfalfa crops. Even with this increased productivity per acre, the article explained that given labor, land, equipment and other expenses, cotton farmers in Arizona essentially only broke even.

Subsidies

The logical question is why continue in this stressful and back-breaking endeavor? The answer, pure and simple, is government subsidies. These subsidies, included in the Farm Bill that started during the Great Depression of the 1930s, make it economically advantageous for farmers to continue planting cotton in the desert. A good percentage of clothing uses cotton, and based on a long-standing tradition in the United States, cotton is an important crop and the cotton lobbies reflect this.

After being exposed to how much water different crops used, I was curious as to how much water was needed to make a basic piece of clothing. I was shocked. Did you know that it takes over 700 gallons of water to produce enough cotton to make a simple T-shirt? That is enough water to provide sixty-four ounces of drinking water daily for almost four people for an entire year.[21] That's a lot of water, which makes it even more difficult to understand why these cotton subsidies continue to exist.

Subsidies have been an integral part of the agricultural sector for almost 100 years. In 1961, Joseph Heller wrote about the father of Major Major, a character in *Catch 22*, that made a living not growing alfalfa.

> *His specialty was alfalfa, and he made a good thing out of not growing any. The government paid him well for every bushel of alfalfa he did not grow. The more alfalfa he did not grow, the more money the government gave him, and he spent every penny he didn't earn on new land to increase the amount of alfalfa he did not produce.[22]*

The nature of subsidies changed over the years, and as of 2014 were in the form of insurance that protected the farmer against declining demand, reduced prices or poor yields; thereby, reducing most of the risks the farmer faced for planting the crop. So, cotton farmers received subsidies for the water they used to irrigate the crops as well as subsidies to plant a crop that exposed the grower to little, if any risk. The extent of these cotton subsidies is mind-boggling with Arizona receiving over $1 billion since 1995 and California over $3 billion.[23]

Although Congress reassesses the appropriations every six years, these subsidies, albeit in a different form, continued to pass as of 2014. Even though there has to be a growing awareness of the water crisis in the West, (or am I assuming too much?), the cotton lobbyists continue to convince our elected officials to increase the subsidies. This is just another example of the overarching issue of a looming water supply and demand gap being brushed under the rug for the political expediency of supporting powerful interests.

If subsidies are to continue, why not use them to foster the intelligent use of water and award them to crops that do not use as much of the natural resource? Crop substitution is a logical option for reducing water usage. For instance, by switching from cotton to wheat on around 80,000 acres, the Pacific Institute reported that the Lower Basin could save around 101,000 acre feet of water annually. In a scenario of shifting 74,000 acres of alfalfa to wheat saw a saving of 250,000 acre-feet annually.[24]

As mentioned previously, 40% of the irrigated acres in Arizona were devoted to alfalfa and forage. With flood irrigation used to increase productivity, we know that this is truly a water guzzler. The Pacific Institute suggested that by using deficit irrigation or stressing the alfalfa crops and watering less, productivity would decline only slightly. However, annual consumption in the Colorado River Basin would decline by an estimated 970,000 acre-feet.[25] Clearly, there are options for different subsidies that could help reduce the amount of water consumed. Of course, this would require the Department of Interior talking to the Department of Agriculture as well as convincing the cotton lobbyists to become advocates of broccoli. I know, I know, this is an "unreachable star," but I can dream.

If Arizona as well as the other Colorado River Basin states and California adopted more efficient irrigation methods and changed to crops that were not as thirsty as cotton and alfalfa a substantial amount of water would be available for the growing metropolitan areas in the central part of the state. However, unless federal agricultural subsidies change, or the implementation of federal and state incentives that promote farmers eliminating flood water farming and adopting more efficient means of watering their crops occur, there is little chance of this water savings happening. And then, there is prior appropriation and its

"Use it or lose it" caveat that eliminates the possibility of any decrease in consumption of surface water.

Lately there have been numerous articles in various state journals acknowledging a shortage is very likely in 2016 in the worst case and definitely in 2017 in the best case.[26] These articles all indicate that Phoenix and Tucson have nothing to worry about given the forward planning of the state as if and when there is a shortage, and the *Guidelines* activated, the farmers will absorb any cutbacks.

This is extremely shortsighted and does not address the possibility of a drought lasting 50 years, climate change or the potential increase in the depletion of groundwater that will occur if farmers' CAP water is curtailed. This is just another example of the myth of water's abundance and any drought will reverse itself in short order.

With continued rapid growth, climate change and no revision in current laws or restrictions, the area that was once home to the Hohokam for around 1,000 years may once again reach its carrying capacity. Something or someone has to give. With time, it may have to be more than the agricultural sector.

Chapter 7

"What Happens in Vegas Does Not Stay in Vegas" – Las Vegas Today

There is evidence that prehistoric Native Americans, including ancestors of the Paiute and the Virgin Anasazi, inhabited the Las Vegas Valley as far back as 10,000 BCE. As the climate changed and the region became more arid, it is believed that during the winter months these ancient people lived near the Las Vegas Wash, an artesian spring, storing food for their subsistence. These springs and the Wash formed by Ice Age water created a mini-oasis in the Mojave Desert.[1] The Spanish named the area Las Vegas, meaning the "meadow" after the short spring-fed grasses that existed at the time. Later, serving as an irrigation community for Mormons for a short period and a railroad stop for those traveling between southern California and Phoenix, the Las Vegas Valley remained an isolated community for farmers. Upon incorporation in 1910, the population of the entire county was 3,321. With the legalization of gaming and the construction of the Hoover Dam during the Depression, the city started its expansion. Las Vegas exploded after 1970 as the county grew from 227,230 to over 2 million by 2014. With this massive residential and commercial development, the artesian springs and the Las Vegas Wash became distant memories.

Las Vegas changed from a small one-horse-town with several casinos to a gambling mecca when Bugsy Siegel and Meyer Lansky purchased the Flamingo Hotel and started the expansion of gambling in 1945. In 1966 Howard Hughes started revamping the Strip and eliminated the mob's influence. Ultimately, modern entrepreneurs like Steve Wynn, transformed the city into an international entertainment destination in the late 1980s. Today Las Vegas has some of the largest 5-star hotels in the world, many adorned with elaborate water features.[2] With this, the illusion of water's abundance became reality in in this desert town.

The Illusion in the Desert

Why 2 million people live in and 40 million tourists visit the driest large city in the United States, remains an enigma for many. Even more troubling for many "water huggers" are the massive fountains, lagoons and other flamboyant water guzzlers found on the Strip. In *The Big Thirst: The Secret Life and Turbulent Future of Water,* Charles Fishman takes the reader on a stroll down the Strip. Starting at Mandalay Bay with its two massive waterfalls and the 1.6 million-gallon Shark Reef Aquarium, to New York, New York, which shows New York Harbor in all its glory including a fireboat spewing water, twenty-four-seven. Next, one encounters the 4,000-room Aria Hotel with one of its two waterfalls 281-feet wide and 24-feet high. On the same block, one is mesmerized by the fountains at the Bellagio Hotel atop an 8.5-acre lake ejecting water up to 400-feet from the 1,214 jets and orchestrated to Handel's "Hallelujah Chorus." Of course, what visitor would miss Bellagio's Cirque du Soleil's *O* inside the 2-million-gallon tank? Next, one walks past the Mirage Hotel where an erupting volcano is located in a lagoon. Inside the Mirage is another 2.5-million-gallon aquarium for blue nose dolphins. Crossing the street one is transported to the canals of Venice and serenaded by singing gondoliers. Crossing the street again, and next to the Mirage, is Treasure Island where until 2003, battles between pirates took place in a large lagoon.[3] Today the lagoon is smaller and the nightly battles have stopped. In the next block Wynn Las Vegas has the Lake of Dreams with its 40-foot waterfall with nightly shows plus the aqua theater-in-the-round where Le Rêve is performed five nights each week. All of these water features certainly created an illusion of an oasis in the desert.

How can all this spectacular use of water take place in a city that receives less than four inches of rain each year and, I repeat, it is the driest large city in the United States? How can one walk the Strip and not feel that water is readily available, even in the desert?

None of this would have been possible without the construction of Hoover Dam, Lake Mead and of course, the Colorado Compact that allocated 4% or 300,000 acre-feet of the Colorado River to Nevada; and Las Vegas got it all!

Situated a little over 30 miles from Lake Mead, Las Vegas was in an ideal spot to develop this oasis mecca; however, as the population exploded in the 1990s and the tourists arrived in droves, Patricia Mulroy, the General Manager of the Southern Nevada Water Authority (SNWA) realized that 300,000 acre-feet was insufficient to continue supplying the water guzzling fountains that appealed to the 40,000,0000 tourists. These visitors also needed to drink water, shower and go swimming in all of the hotel pools; play on at least one of the 61 golf courses in the area, and of course admire the lush green lawns, the almost 800,000 living in the town at that time, watered on a daily basis. Often criticized for her no-nonsense, aggressive approach and her relentless quest for more water for Las Vegas, Mulroy accomplished something that most water managers in the West should emulate, which involved keeping water consumption steady with a population more than doubling. Instilling a pragmatic view of water continued as her major goal.

When Mulroy assumed the position of General Manager in 1989, she immediately attempted to eliminate the countless water features both on the Strip as well as in shopping centers, medical centers, and new residential developments. This met with immediate resistance from a range of sources, including Steve Wynn, who was just starting construction on his second hotel, Treasure Island. In an interview in

2014, upon her retirement, Mulroy described her "come to Jesus moment" occurred when Wynn said to her that the growth of Las Vegas stemmed from the fact that it sold "virtual reality."[4] In other words, Las Vegas, like Disneyland, was selling a fantasy that required water in the desert. He further stated, "Don't tell me I can't have fountains and water features. Tell me what I can do to do it."[5] Mulroy told him to use recycled water for the hotel and purified water for the lagoon and fountains. And he did! He double plumbed the 3,000-room hotel and installed a water treatment facility in the basement.

Thus, began the "Law of the Strip" that required developers to use wells on their property and access limited ground water that had the distinct possibility of going dry or use treated wastewater for any water feature. Aggressive and groundbreaking, yes and indeed it did save water. However, the Bellagio still requires between 12 and 22 million gallons (37 to 67 acre-feet) each year to compensate for leaks and evaporation. Currently, all of the water features on the Strip in Las Vegas use around 3% of the water drawn from Lake Mead. In fact, each of the 60 plus golf courses located within 30 minutes of the Strip use more water than Steve Wynn's Bellagio.

Conservation in Las Vegas

Mulroy next dealt with the many golf courses that watered acres of turf. Angel Park, a public, 36-hole, Arnold Palmer-designed course used up to 2,000,000 gallons each night to keep the fairways and greens in tip-top shape. Under Mulroy's tutelage, Angel Park reduced the amount of turf by 30% by returning the course to a desert landscape; using recycled wastewater or reclaimed water instead of Lake Mead's potable water; and installing a computer-controlled irrigation system.[6] The net effect was a reduction in water consumption by over 268 million gallons or 368 acre-feet on an annual basis and a reduction of their water bill by over $300,000.[7] This 40% reduction in water use also led to reduction in fuel costs and other materials, as 80 acres no longer needed mowing, reseeding or fertilizing. This savings in water from just one golf course was enough water for 5,000 people for an entire year. Clearly, this was a win-win solution for everyone, except the fuel and chemical companies.

Today, each of the golf courses that initially irrigated turf with water from Lake Mead are on tight water budgets with most using recycled waste water purchased from the Las Vegas city sewage treatment facility. With rebates approximating $40,000 per acre, many of the golf courses re-landscaped and reduced turf, returning many of the fairways to a desert environment.[8] Angel Park and many of the other golf courses within 30 minutes of the Las Vegas Strip were forced to look at the way they used water and adapt. This forced the golf club owners as well as golfers to look at water differently.

Industrial usage did not escape Mulroy's conservation crusade, either. For example, just imagine how much laundry 40,000,000 tourists create. One laundry facility uses four massive washing machines, each over 45 feet long. The company installed a recycling system for one of their machines at a cost of $800,000. Although a large capital expense, it paid for itself in just over a year due to a reduction in the water, heat and natural gas bills. In addition, to support this conservation of water, the Southern Nevada Water Authority (SNWA) provided a $150,000 rebate to install a second system at another of the three other plants the company owned. With the two systems operating this company saved over 300,000 gallons each day of operation or 400 acre-feet on an annual basis. Previously this water would have been drawn from Lake Mead. There are plans to install the system in the remaining two plants.[9] This is just another example of Mulroy changing the water culture in Sin City.

Finally, Mulroy turned her attention to residential use. She realized that turning off water as one brushed their teeth was less than a drop in the bucket in conserving water as the major residential consumer of water was the expanse of bluegrass lawns that flourished in the town. Thus, restrictions prohibiting turf on the front lawn in new developments and limiting grass to only 50% in the back lawn were implemented. In addition, the SNWA offered rebates for residential customers to replace lawn with either xeriscaping or artificial turf. To date, this "cash for grass" program has replaced 168 million acres of turf, saving billions of gallons of water annually.[10] In addition, strict water schedules were implemented with constant surveillance and violators fined. All of this, as well as a tiered rate system, compelled residents to evaluate their water use. Has it been successful?

Even though Las Vegas sits in the desert and has no reliable water source except Lake Mead, water rates remained among the lowest in the country as of 2015.[11] Mulroy and her successors continue to be criticized for this; however, it is part and parcel of Mulroy's philosophy on water pricing. Mulroy feels:

> *Yeah, you have a basic human right to water. Here's your bucket, you can go down to Lake Mead, and you can take all the water out of Lake Mead that you want. But you don't have the basic human right to have that water treated to an absolute guaranteed safe standard, delivered to your home in whatever quantities you want to use.*[12]

In 2012, SNWA, under Mulroy's leadership, initiated a surcharge that increased monthly residential bills by $5. This increased revenue was needed to cover outstanding debt resulting from the SNWA's massive infrastructure construction and rebate programs. As of 2015, a quarterly residential bill in Las Vegas still averaged around $55.40 and $60.94 with a pool or just over half a penny per gallon.[13] Compared to what we pay for bottled water, which is at a minimum 200% higher, water is "dirt cheap." However, as dirt costs anywhere from 4 to 8 cents per gallon, perhaps the expression should be changed to "water cheap."

In addition, residential consumption per person continues around 200 gallons per day, one of the higher usages in the country. With all of Mulroy's efforts, the swimming pools that required constant refilling due to evaporation in this hot and arid desert, the resistance for some to forego lush lawn and the continued growth in both residential development and tourism complicated the task. In fairness, the 40,000,000 tourists, even with recycled and reused water inflates the gallons per day per person. Most believe the low rates charged for water in this desert oasis need to be revised if Las Vegas wants to continue to live within their 300,000 acre-feet allocation from the Colorado River.

Forward Planning

Just after Mulroy assumed management of SNWA in 1989, Las Vegas began drawing down more than the 300,000 acre-feet allocated under the Compact. This was possible as Lake Mead and Lake Powell were both near capacity and the Upper Basin was not fully using their 7.5 million acre-feet annual allocation, so just as California was doing, Las Vegas took what was there.[14]

As General Manager, Mulroy quickly realized this could not continue so she began searching for any new source of water that included groundwater currently used for ranching in eastern and central Nevada, piping water from the Mississippi River and barging ice from Alaska.[15] These various options reinforced many water managers' opinions of Mulroy's aggressive and outlandish approach. Realizing the political and economic obstacles for each of these options, Mulroy also began constructing plant recycling facilities that took all the water used indoors, which was flushed down the toilet, used in dishwashers, washing machines, showers and drinking fountains, cleaned it up and returned it to Lake Mead. Of the water used for indoor purposes, 90% is now recycled and returned to Lake Mead.

Under the return-flow credit, Las Vegas continues using more than its allocation as long as the overage is returned. Without this return-flow credit, Las Vegas would have run out of its water allocation in 1992.[16] This situation of Las Vegas withdrawing more than their Compact allocation highlights the difference in demand and consumption.

Water use or demand is the total amount of water taken from a source. For example, if a farmer requires one acre-foot to produce a crop, the entire acre-foot is considered used. On the other hand, consumption refers to the amount of water used and not returned to the source. In other words, the farmer's consumption includes the amount of water absorbed and retained in the plant or evaporated but does not include any of the return flow or the water restored to the water source.

Even though the SNWA draws down 440,00 acre-feet from Lake Mead each year actual consumption is only 227,000 acre-feet given the water credit. Thus, through Mulroy's programs and her focus on consumption, 213,000 acre-feet returns to Lake Mead each year. So, what happens in Vegas does NOT stay in Vegas. This allows Las Vegas to continue to grow, expanding the Strip and its "virtual reality" of an oasis in the desert.

Realizing that a 90% dependence on the Colorado River was not sustainable if Las Vegas was going to continue its growth, Mulroy continued the quest for other sources within the state. Under her leadership, the SNWA pursued available ground water in central and eastern Nevada. SNWA hoped to pipe around 91 million acre-feet via a 400-mile pipeline; but, given the intense resistance from both the ranchers and the Mormon Church this project was placed on the back burner.[17] Upon her retirement in February 2015, Mulroy indicated that this concept may still be needed in the future with the rationale that Las Vegas contributes over 90% of the state of Nevada's revenue. She often said, "If Las Vegas dies, Nevada dies."[18]

Another innovative concept Mulroy utilized involved water banking in both underground storage and reservoirs, like Lake Mead. Las Vegas currently has water credits in Nevada (337,000 acre-feet), Arizona (600,000 acre-feet) and California (205,000 acre-feet). In essence, this stored water is a savings account to be used in the future. When Las Vegas needs to use some of its "banked" water, it will withdraw it from Lake Mead at which point Arizona or California gains access to the "banked water" held in their underground aquifer. With the expanding and persistent drought since the turn of the century and declining levels of Lake Mead, access to surplus water may become more difficult to find and, thus to bank.[19] However, Mulroy has 2.5 years of demand banked, which is a nice cushion.

Lake Mead

In 1998, Lake Mead was at full pool or the reservoir level at the greatest operational capacity, so there appeared to be nothing to worry about. However, this changed as the water level in Lake Mead continued to drop due to drought, reduced snow pack, evaporation and, of course, California consuming 800,000 acre-feet over their allocation for almost two decades. Fortunately, for Las Vegas, Mulroy also focused on the two intake pipes or "straws" that transported water from Lake Mead to the SNWA for distribution. As designed, the first intake pipe stopped pulling water to Las Vegas when the water level in Lake Mead reached 1,050 feet and the second intake tunnel would not deliver water to the city if the level fell lower than 1,000 feet.

Initially, all believed Las Vegas had nothing to worry about as a reservoir level below the first and second straws at Hoover Dam would jeopardize hydroelectricity production. Over 19 million people in Southern California depend on the power generated at Hoover Dam with the remaining 43% of power generated going to Arizona and Nevada. Reality began to intrude on the western illusion of water's abundance when Lake Mead's water level was 1,075 feet and falling.[20] The bathtub rings in both Lake Mead and Lake Powell graphically showed the disappearing water. Figure 14 reflects the bath tub rings in Lake Mead.

By way of explanation, hydroelectric power depends on how far water falls as well as the amount of water falling. With the water level in Lake Mead declining, the distance water drops became critical. At Hoover Dam, the minimum elevation for efficient power generation in Lake Mead is 1050 feet. At 895 feet, water cannot drain into the dam's outlets so power generation becomes impossible. When the water level drops below 895 feet, dead pool exists.

FIGURE 14 – Bathtub Ring in Lake Mead

Source: Danson, Casey Coates. (2013). *Dwindling Colorado River Forces First-Ever Cuts in Lake Powell Water Releases.* Global Possibilities date august 21, 2013. Retrieved from: http://www.globalpossibilities. org/dwindling-colorado-river-forces-first-ever-cuts-in-lake-powell-water-releases/[21]

Even though the chance of dead pool occurring was highly unlikely, SNWA began construction of a third straw in 2008 and completed in late 2015. As of June 2015, the water level was 25 feet from the first intake pipe "sucking air" and the reservoir continued shrinking. At a cost of over $800,000,000, the third intake tunnel's level will be at 860 feet and will allow Las Vegas to continue withdrawing its allocation from Lake Mead even if Hoover Dam is unable to generate electricity. Although this "third straw" is ready for operation, it still requires an additional pump at a cost of around $600,000,000. This will be the next major project for SNWA.[22]

Given her brash and often outrageous style, Patricia Mulroy has been called the "water witch," the "water czar" and, of course, many more explicit and derogatory terms. In fact, the villain in *Water Knife,* Catherine Case, who ruthlessly guaranteed that Las Vegas continued to bloom in the desert, strikes an unmistakable resemblance to the SNWA General Manager. Mulroy, also known for her outlandish suggestions for additional water sources such as piping water from the Mississippi

River to alleviate flooding or barging ice from Alaska, gained her quite a reputation during her 25 years as General Manager of the SNWA. Of course, most water managers find the showy water features, the number of golf courses and the continued expansion of massive and opulent hotels a flagrant abuse of water in a desert environment.

However, this "water witch" has accomplished a great deal to the envy of most water managers throughout the West. When the Colorado Compact was signed in 1922, Las Vegas was essentially a "whistle stop" on the way to California and except for cattle ranching in eastern and northern Nevada that relied on groundwater, the state's consumptive water needs were minimal. As a result, when the Colorado River was "divvied up," Nevada received only 4% of the Lower Basin allocation, or 300,000 acre-feet. As Las Vegas and its surrounding area expanded and the population doubled over the past twenty years and as tourism mushroomed from just over 20,000,000 to over 40,000,000 in the same period, Mulroy made the limited water available work. In fact, by adopting a forward-looking view of water in an arid environment she essentially assured a future for Las Vegas even if Lake Mead declines below the "dead pool" level. Looking out even further, if climate change reduces the flow of the Colorado, there are millions of gallons still available by shutting down golf courses, and turning off the water features.

What are the odds for Las Vegas?

Clearly, living in Las Vegas one has to be swayed with the culture of risk taking and playing the odds, and that is exactly what Mulroy and the SNWA has done. Instead of ignoring the *possibility* of the level of Lake Mead dropping below the second intake pipe; discounting the *probability* of climate change; disregarding the *chance* that the *Guidelines* could reduce the city's Compact allocation or *betting* that innovative conservation and reuse programs would cover any shortages, Las Vegas *played the odds and won*. Under Mulroy's leadership, one of the top 20 fastest growing cities in the U.S. in 2015 that welcomes 40,000,000 tourists each year has actually reduced its net water consumption. The city is positioned well for the foreseeable future.

Of course, Las Vegas does not have all the issues that the other states in the Colorado River Basin face. Agriculture is not part of the demand the city must provide. Even though Las Vegas does not have to provide water for food production, it has taken the risks needed to position the city for many of the possible scenarios the future may present.

Interestingly, prior to Mulroy's retirement in 2014, she adopted a different approach for solving the issues the West faces in the 21st century. Instead of the insular "all men for themselves" tactics reflecting the intense competition between the states and various water consumers, she realized that for the future the best odds for being successful was through cooperation.[23] In an exit interview Mulroy indicated:

> *Once we stop thinking in terms of districts, communities and states and start thinking we are citizens of a larger region, then we can start looking at how regions interconnect with each other. Does that provide any opportunities for us? Does it provide opportunities for them? Are there opportunities for mutual problem solving?*[24]

Thus far, Las Vegas appears to have played the "dog-eat-dog" game well and has positioned itself for the foreseeable future; thus, cooperation is much easier to espouse. For the most part, others in the Colorado River Basin seem to be rooted in the past of depending on technology for new sources, not evaluating how water is used, and focusing on their own local needs. Given all the possibilities of what could happen in the future in the Colorado River Basin, this spirit of cooperation that Mulroy now advocates represents an intriguing approach that could avoid future crises. This path will not be easy, as so many ingrained ideas and values that dictated decisions in the past will need to be cast aside. People do not like change. However, a change is needed.

Chapter 8

"The Trouble I'm In"[1]
— Colorado River Today

As I sit, gazing out at the Ten-Mile Range in Breckenridge, seeing a great deal of snow-pack on the mountains in a town that has very senior water rights, and after an unusually very snowy month of May, I have to wonder why everyone is so worried. I, too, take the Blue River that runs near our home for granted. Currently running at 1,030 cubic feet per second (cfs) or over 745,000 acre-feet per year, I must remind myself that this peak run-off period lasts for less than one month each year. From August through April the Upper Blue runs at less than 60 cfs, which is only 43,400 acre-feet per year. This is half of one percent of the amount the Upper Basin must send to the Lower Basin.[2] The Upper Blue flows into Lake Dillon, owned by Denver Water, with a storage capacity of around 250,000 acre-feet (81.5 billion gallons) that is diverted through the 23.3-mile, Roberts Tunnel, built in 1962, running under the Continental Divide. Although Denver Water's priority is junior to many downstream rights on the Western slope, mainly agricultural consumers, as well as the Shoshone Power Plant, one has to wonder in the event of a major water shortage, who would take priority, the farmers or the people of Denver? Supposedly, under prior appropriation, the farmers get their water first.

The more I read and researched water issues in the Colorado River Basin, I discovered that for many years I also lived in a dream world. I never gave it a second thought as to whether the quality or the quantity of water would be there anytime I turned on the tap…it just was. When I read Cynthia Barnett's *Blue Revolution: Unmaking America's Water Crisis*[3], several years ago, I realized I knew next to nothing about this basic necessity of life.[3] This led me to reading Marc Reisner's seminal work, *Cadillac Desert: The American West and Its Disappearing Water*,[4] and then other well researched and informative books by Charles Fishman,[5] Robert Glennon,[6] Norris Hundley, Jr.,[7] Steven Solomon[8] and Daniel Worster.[9] I was also intrigued how ancient civilizations survived in the arid West to glean any lessons to apply to what is occurring today.

What I discovered was a massive amount of information, recent research, rules, regulations, legislation, ad nauseam all creating a confusing, complicated and multi-layered knowledge base. Of course, Mother Nature only made matters worse by changing the rules. My husband often admonishes me not to bore our friends with some new detail I uncover. Unfortunately, to truly understand what the future holds, all of this minutiae is necessary.

With the mistaken belief that water was abundant and that technology could magically make water appear when there was a problem, the arid desert began to bloom and prosper. Any time more water was needed to increase acreage under irrigation, provide water for an expanding population or turn an area that was as dry as the Sahel into a virtual oasis with a proliferation of golf courses and water fountains, the USBR built new dams and water managers obtained new diversions from sources miles away. Needless to say, the costs to do so increased exponentially. But to the "average Joe or Josephine," the water technology was hidden and all we did was turn on the tap and it magically appeared. Cold, hot, lukewarm, it did not matter. It is little wonder that we continue taking water for granted.

Given this fallacious view of water, and as the Colorado continues as the most over allocated and litigated river, with almost 40,000,000 people depending on it and almost 6,000,000 acres of farmland requiring its water, the Colorado River Basin faces some significant issues in the future — some man-made, some natural.

Once the centrifugal pump made it possible to mine for water and the massive Bureau of Reclamation projects stored years of water and diverted it over and through mountains, there was no stopping the growth in the West. In 1900, the population in Southern California was just over 304,000 with Los Angeles totaling around 102,500. As of the 2010 census, the population in Southern California was over 24 million.

It took air-conditioning, swimming pools and gambling for the growth in the rest of the Southwest to start. As of 1900, Arizona had a population of 122,000 in the entire state and Colorado totaled 539,700 of which 134,000 were in Denver. During the same year, Nevada had a total population of 42,335 but only 25 lived in Las Vegas. By the 2010 census, Arizona grew to over 6.7 million; Colorado to over 5 million; and Las Vegas to 2 million.[10] This growth from a total of less than 1,000,000 people to around 40,000,000 in 110 years required the constant availability of water to build a virtual reality or a Fantasyland that continues to exist throughout the Southwest and Southern California today.

Even with this massive influx of people and the increased demand for water, the major increase in consumption of this natural resource was due to the expansion of agriculture in a desert environment. In the West, it is estimated that almost 90% of the pasture and cropland requires irrigation. Furthermore, more than half the irrigated land supports livestock, with alfalfa planted in more than a quarter of the irrigated land in the Colorado River Basin.[11]

It has also been determined that the Lower Basin uses three times the amount of water for irrigation compared to the Upper Basin. To a large degree, this relates to climate as the Upper Basin has a shorter growing season than the Lower Basin.[12] In addition, the mountainous areas that dominate the Upper Basin and produce the snow pack that feed the Colorado River are not conducive to agriculture. In addition, the Lower Basin has a wider diversity of crops, again attributed to their growing season as well as warmer weather.[13]

Since the 1930s, the single largest user of the Colorado River was the Imperial Valley that received at least 3.1 million acre-feet annually and produced over 70% of the country's winter vegetables, such as lettuce, carrots, broccoli and cabbage. This desert, which the Colorado River clearly allowed to "bloom", produced over $2 billion in revenue in 2013. The Imperial County Agricultural Crop and Livestock Report of 2013 revealed some very interesting data, summarized in Chart 6.

CHART 6 – Imperial Valley Crop Facts

Crop	# of Gallons Per Ounce	Total Revenue	# of Irrigated Acres	Yield Per Acre
Broccoli	2.44	$112.139,000	16,000	$7,009
Various Lettuce	0.85	$210,000,000	32,500	$6,462
Alfalfa & Alfalfa Seed	4.21	$213,728,000	141,322	$1,640

Source: Information adapted from Imperial County: Agricultural Crop & Livestock Report and Oldham County water District: Interesting Water Facts[14]

Thus, a water guzzling crop that used almost three times the amount of acreage as broccoli and lettuce combined, resulted in a per acre yield less than 25% of the vegetables and used immeasurably more water.

It remains a mystery why cattle ranching continues and along with it the vast irrigated acreage needed to produce the food that requires over 600 gallons of water for a six-ounce steak. This could only occur in an environment where virtual reality exists! Also, why farmers are permitted to dig deeper wells to access the quickly depleting groundwater throughout the basin is just not rational.

All of this underscores the basic characteristic of the West which is the rugged individualism that was necessary to survive in this arid and semi-arid region in the 19th century. This fierce independence, coupled with the 20th century belief of water's abundance and technology's ability to deliver from sources miles away, becomes an obstacle when Mother Nature flexes her muscles and attempts to return the land to what she believes to be its natural state. All of this creates an environment that perpetuates a Fantasyland and a dream world that made the desert bloom and as Reisner indicated, created a "fraud."

With 70% to 80% of water devoted to irrigation, many assume that agriculture will provide water by fallowing fields, utilizing more efficient irrigation systems or the outright sale of their water rights, which in many cases have very senior priority dates. Take a moment and consider how you would react to being enticed or pressured to sell rights that have been in the family for generations, or being told you will not receive water to irrigate half of your crops for one year as people in San Diego, Phoenix, Denver, Las Vegas or Los Angeles need water for their lawns and swimming pools? By the way, that is occurring in California currently and is also a bone of contention in Colorado and Arizona.

On the other hand, we confront the natural issues. Mother Nature has exerted her power in the Colorado River Basin since the beginning of the 21st century with a drought that covers most of the region. In fact, many claim this is the worst drought in over 1,000 years. In addition, there is climate change and its unknown impact on the region. Whether it is caused by man or naturally occurring is irrelevant; but no one can argue with the fact that average temperatures have increased over the past fifty years. Recent articles have indicated that 2015 was the warmest in recorded history since 1880.[15] And, 2016, was even warmer.

Mother Nature is finally flexing her muscles after a century of man attempting to control her. And, of course, there is the Law of the River that attempts to manage both Mother Nature as well as an expanding population and irrigate millions of acres. The natural issues that the

West faces in the future include climate change and the possibility of a persistent and devastating drought lasting more than 10 years. Wait a minute, doesn't that describe conditions thus far this century?

As of July 2016, the Drought Monitor revealed that over 77% of the Colorado River Basin was experiencing abnormally dry conditions as well as moderate to severe drought. Although an improvement over previous years, the arid climate of the Southwest and West is clearly apparent.

In 1997, climate researchers identified the presence of the Pacific Decadal Oscillation (PDO), a long-lived pattern associated with sea surface temperature fluctuations along the Pacific coastline. Paleo-climatologists claim extended and prolonged droughts in the past, similar to that experienced by the Hohokam and Ancient Puebloans during the Medieval Climate Anomaly, occurred when sea surface temperatures in the northeastern Pacific remained cooler for longer periods. This lower temperature formed high-pressure systems that blocked precipitation in California and the Southwest.[17] These cooler temperatures have been present for most of the last 14 years.

As of March of 2015, there was an indication that the temperatures in the Northeastern Pacific Ocean were increasing and hopefully, for the West, indicating an oscillation to a warmer phase, or El Niño, that is associated with more moisture.[18] As of the last quarter of 2015, Los Angeles received torrential rainfall that led to mudslides and Hurricane Patricia went from a tropical storm to a Category 5 in less than 24 hours. Many were hopeful this meant a return of snow pack to the Sierra Nevada and Rockies and more rainfall throughout the West. As 2016 progressed, Northern California received some relief; however, Southern California remained in extreme or exceptional drought.

As an aside, I have to giggle when one talks of a drought in a region where most of the area receives less than nine inches of precipitation a year anyway and in many of the more concentrated agricultural areas, less than five inches a year. According to the *Merriam-Webster Dictionary*, any area receiving less than 10 inches a year is a desert. But that did not stop many industrious Americans turning this region into an oasis. The growth of the Southwest and much of Southern California including countless square miles of lawns along with its 6 million irrigated acres blossomed only because of the Colorado River and groundwater.

During the 20th century, those living in the West experienced a relatively wet period with droughts lasting less than five years. When these droughts occurred, most westerners temporarily tightened their belts, watered their lawns less and farmers cut back on production, increasing the price of food. Yet, as soon as any of the dry periods ended those living in the region quickly turned on the hoses, sprinklers, and irrigation nozzles, taking water for granted once again.

Scott Stine, professor of environmental studies at Cal State and the paleo-climatologists that introduced the connection between the MCA and the Native Americans changing lifestyles has warned policy makers in the West that water managers continued to plan as if droughts lasted only 5 to 7 years and thus, 'We're living in a dream world'." In another interview in 1994, Stine indicated that with the current consumption of water throughout the West, that unlike prehistory, by the 15th year of a drought, "the damage is done."[19] In other words, it no longer takes a dry period lasting 50 to 100 years to upset the applecart.

Due to development of both urban and agricultural sectors, even with all of our advanced technology, extended droughts develop a carrying capacity problem throughout the West. But, if we build another dam to store water, it should provide a safety net in the event of a continued and long-lived drought. Once again, relying on technology will save the day.

Unfortunately, that is a rabbit that cannot be pulled out of the hat with regard to the Colorado River. All one has to do is look at the water levels of Lake Mead and Lake Powell to understand that the high-tech magician is not going to be able to wave his magic wand and make everything right. These two man-made lakes are the major storage facilities and "make up 85% of surface water in the basin," with a combined capacity of almost 50 million acre-feet.[20] Today these two reservoirs contain a combined total of 22.2 million acre-feet or 44% of total capacity.

Lake Mead, the largest reservoir in the U.S. built during the Depression, stores water for Southern California, Arizona, and Nevada. After construction, Lake Mead storage capacity totaled 32,471,000 acre-feet. However, due to sedimentation from the silty Colorado, today's capacity is 26,120,000 acre-feet. Over the last 14 years, the Colorado River Basin has experienced different levels of drought and the water level of Lake Mead has fallen from 1,204.22 feet to a low of 1,071.61 or around 36.1% of capacity as of July 4, 2016.[21]

Lake Powell, constructed in 1963 to store unused and surplus water from the Upper Basin, reflected the same trend as Lake Mead over the past fourteen years due to the continued drought conditions in the basin. The original capacity of the reservoir was 27 million acre-feet but, again, due to sedimentation, the reservoir storage capacity dropped to 24,322,000 acre-feet. As of July 4, 2016, Lake Powell was at 3,620.36 feet or at 57.22% capacity.[22]

Last year, the *LA Times* referred to a "May Miracle" when a great deal of unusual precipitation increased the monthly average by over 300% in some areas of the Upper Colorado River Basin.[23] The title of the article, "Water Managers Dodge Bullet With 'May Miracle' Rains," highlights the continuing misconception that droughts are short-lived and Mother Nature ultimately provides the needed precipitation to allow a return to the virtual reality of the West. Referring to it as a May Miracle also underscores the hydrological reality of the unpredictable variations in this water source on which so many people rely.

The bottom line is that with all the technology in the world, building another massive dam and a reservoir will not solve anything if the snow pack and precipitation in the Upper Basin is not there. If we can't fill Lake Mead and Lake Powell, how can we fill another massive storage project? To date, we have developed the expertise to store, divert, recycle, reuse, and desalinate water but unfortunately, no one has discovered a process to create water.

Compact Compliance

According to the Colorado River Compact, the Upper Basin must deliver a 10-year running average of 75 million acre-feet at Lee Ferry, which since 2000, has not fallen below 84 million acre-feet. The annual requirement of 8.23 million acre-feet was not met in 2002 when only 5.6 million acre-feet flowed into Lake Powell. Unfortunately, the trend is not promising. In the past 14 years the 10-year average has been under 9 million acre-feet nine times.[24] "Miracle May" plus what turned into an unusual "Jubilant June" and "Joyous July" increased the flow so what was an average to below average snow pack year allowed the Upper Basin to remain in compliance. But it certainly did not produce the surplus necessary to raise the water levels of Lake Mead and Lake Powell to any significant degree.

Even though the Upper Basin continued to be in compliance with the required deliveries to Lee Ferry, this was due to a few good years since 2000 when the drought began. It is also a result of the Upper Basin not fully using its total allocation. Thus, the Upper Basin has been able to comply with the Compact to date even when the flow of the river was reduced. But will this continue in the future with increased demand in Colorado, Wyoming and Utah as well as climate change?

Just do the math:

Average Supply and Demand on Colorado River
(in million acre-feet {maf})

Lower Basin Allocation per Compact	7.5 maf
Mexico Allocation per 1944 Treaty	1.5 maf
Combined Allocation for Lower Basin & Mexico	9.0 maf
Average Flow of Colorado per USGS	15.0 maf
Amount Available for Upper Basin	6.0 maf
Shortage to Upper Basin per Compact	1.5 maf

As the Upper Basin's population expands (Colorado forecasts a doubling of the state's population by 2050 to over 9,000,000 people[25]) and begins to use a larger share of the Compact allocation, how will the 1.5 million acre-feet gap be covered?

So as it stands today, the Upper Basin continues to underuse its Compact allocations; the Lower Basin continues to find ways to overuse their allotment; Lake Mead and Lake Powell continue to decline in acre-feet stored; the region continues as the fastest growing in the country and irrigation remains at an all-time high with an alarming rate of groundwater depletion. All of this while Mother Nature continues a 14-year unabated drought, except for some relief in the Upper Basin in the summer of 2015. Considering all these factors, the USBR projects a 3.2 million acre-feet short fall by 2060 for the Colorado River System.[26]

Does this mean the Upper Basin will have to curtail water deliveries to irrigators or the Front Range in Colorado, which currently receives 500,000 acre-feet in trans-mountain diversions (TMDs)? We must face the facts that all the cloud seeding and sacrifices to the rain and snow gods will not make this gap in supply and demand in water disappear.

Groundwater and the Colorado River Basin

Our California disaster movie producer also sees potential for a sequel in the Colorado River Basin by indicating the overuse of groundwater could be the final nail in the coffin. "Combined with declining snowpack and population growth, this will likely threaten the long-term ability of the basin to meet its water allocation commitments to the seven basin states and to Mexico."[27]

Sandra Postel, founder of the Global Water Policy Project and a leading authority on international freshwater, indicates that during droughts both farmers and urban users pump more water in an effort to meet their normal demand.[28] We already know that storage in Lake Mead and Lake Powell reduced to under 50% capacity; but what about groundwater? Researchers at the University of California-Irvine in conjunction with NASA's GRACE, those twin satellites that measure changes in mass over time, determined that between 2004 and 2013, the Colorado River Basin lost almost 53 million acre-feet of water. To put this in perspective, that amount of water is the equivalent of two full Lake Meads. What is more disturbing, 77% or 41 million acre-feet of that total was groundwater depletion, largely in the Lower Basin.[29] To put that amount in perspective, Postel indicates, "That's enough to meet the home water use of the entire US population for *eight years.*"[30]

Although, everyone has heard endlessly about the groundwater depletion in California, particularly the Central Valley, this study did not include areas outside the Colorado River Basin. I REPEAT THIS STUDY DID NOT INCLUDE THE CENTRAL VALLEY!

If you really want to get depressed, research the groundwater depletion occurring in the Ogallala Aquifer that extends from South Dakota to Texas and currently provides 81% of the water used on the Great Plains; using 15.7 million gallons each day for irrigation. "Today the Ogallala Aquifer is being depleted at an annual volume equivalent to 18 Colorado Rivers."[31] This vast aquifer enabled the United States and more specifically the Midwest to become the breadbasket of the world during the twentieth century. Prior to that, remember what it was called? The Great American Desert!

Who would have thought this area that received less than 9 inches of precipitation and had very few perennial rivers and streams contained between 2 and 3 million acre-feet below the surface that the Great Plains Native Americans and the buffalo roamed? In addition, who knew the water in the Ogallala accumulated over the past million years? Regrettably, with current usage it is predicted water in this once vast unconfined aquifer will be too low to economically pump within 50 years.[32]

What is even more alarming, our doomsday movie producer indicated that the Arabian Aquifer, a source providing water to 60 million people in Saudi Arabia, Iraq, Syria and Yemen, is the most overly stressed aquifer on earth with almost no recharge.[33] This area is volatile enough without adding an additional problem of running out of water. Although the Ogallala and the Arabian aquifers are not part of the Colorado River Basin, they highlight how water is overused throughout the world and other potential Famiglietti catastrophe movies.

Famiglietti also points out that the water laws that currently regulate and allocate water were crafted over one hundred years ago and in most cases do not deal with the symbiotic relationship between surface and groundwater. He recommends a more holistic approach to managing water that acknowledges this connection as well as the impact of climate change.[34]

Climate Change and the Colorado River Basin

And then of course, there is climate change. Whether the warming of the earth is caused by human actions or it is just a naturally occurring phase is immaterial as it relates to the Colorado River Basin. What does matter is the increased temperatures that are actually occurring and its impact on the flow of the Colorado River as well as the amount of precipitation throughout the basin. According to the Colorado Water Conservation Board (CWCB) scientific evidence has proven that the state's temperature has already risen by 2 degrees since 1977 and will continue to rise another 2 degrees by 2050 if nothing is done to reduce our carbon emissions into the atmosphere.[35] In fact, the National Research Council reports that the Colorado River Basin has seen a rise in temperature greater than any other area in the country.[36]

Another factor that cannot be disputed is that with increased temperature, the evaporation rate increases, (a basic fact of the hydrological cycle) thereby drawing water from the Colorado River and its reservoirs into the atmosphere and dropping it as rainfall in the Midwest, East Coast or over the Atlantic Ocean. This, of course, reduces the amount of water in the Basin.

What climatologists cannot get their arms around is the impact increasing temperatures will have on precipitation and thus the snowpack in the Upper Basin. Countless models of how climate change will affect precipitation in the basin range from a "5% decrease to a 6% increase by mid-century."[37] The difficulty in predicting what will happen to the quantity of precipitation reflects the wide variations in elevation and other environmental factors that exist in the Colorado River Basin.

There is consensus that regardless of the change in precipitation, snow melt and its run-off will occur earlier and of course, evaporation will increase, especially in storage facilities.[38] As run-off will occur earlier and not available when farmers require it for irrigation, increased storage in the Upper Basin will be needed. Larger reservoirs with a warmer climate will expand the amount of water lost through evaporation. So, as the Upper Basin begins to approach using its full allocation, evaporation will increase which will result in a reduced amount of water delivered to Lee Ferry.

In 2007, the National Research Council reported that:

> *Collectively, the body of research on prospective future changes in Colorado River flows points to a future in which warmer conditions across the region are likely to contribute to reductions in snowpack, an earlier peak in spring snowmelt, higher rates of evapotranspiration, reduced late spring and summer flows, and reductions in annual runoff and stream-flow.[39]*

Attempting to wade through the studies and models was definitely beyond my understanding and competence; however, the Intergovernmental Panel on Climate Change (IPCC) concluded that the Southwest would get much drier during the 21st century. There is a growing consensus that the Lower Basin will also experience a decline in precipitation. An explanation for this is an intensification of the water cycle as well as the basic climate of the region. Thus, as temperatures increase, more water vapor is held in the atmosphere, which then is transported to wetter regions.[40]

Jonathan Overpeck and Brad Udall added another wrinkle to the effects of climate change. Although they also believe the Southwest will get drier; they believe that when it does rain in the Southwest, the storms will be much more intense resulting in more floods and mud slides.[41] Hurricane Patricia and the mudslides occurring in the fall of 2015 support this. Also the flooding in the South during 2016 is yet another example of what Overpeck and Udall feel will be part of our future. Thus, between a decrease in precipitation in a region that already has minimal rainfall and the increasing evaporation rate, supply in Southern California, Arizona and Nevada will naturally decrease. In fact, a report in the Bulletin of the American Meteorologist Society concluded, "We estimate a future streamflow change that ranges approximately from –5% to –35%."[42]

So, how do we address the fact that by mid-century, the Colorado River may not be able to meet all of its demands, especially in the Lower Basin. Also hydroelectric power could be reduced by up to 40% due to reduced reservoir levels.[43]

What are we waiting for?

Researchers, climatologists, water managers, the Bureau of Reclamation and water elite have known for quite some time that change is necessary, but it is just beginning to arise to a semi-conscious level within the general public. In 2011 an article in the National Academy of Engineering indicated,

> *Future choices for water use will no doubt unfold in complex, perhaps unanticipated, ways, and future warming and droughts may reduce the availability of water resources even further. Current scientific understanding of the river's*

historical flows and regional droughts, coupled with the potential for future reductions in flows, raises fundamental questions about the sustainability of current population growth and development. Moreover, some existing paradigms and principles that have governed Colorado River water use in the past will undoubtedly have to be adjusted to fit these realities.[45]

With rising temperatures, extended drought, increased population, decreased groundwater levels, and continued production of water hogs, such as alfalfa and almonds continue unabated, a water crisis will be hard to avoid. The expanding drought as well as the decline in groundwater has finally mobilized some action. California's very tardy regulation of groundwater, the 2007 Guidelines and the long overdue mandatory restrictions in California are good examples. However, they are not enough if one is concerned about future generations.

So why has it taken so long for politicians, municipal water providers, farmers, and for that matter, anyone who lives in the West, to act? This delay in action can be attributed to three things. The first involves Stine's belief that water managers continue to plan for a five-to-seven-year time period. After 14 years of drought one would think this would change. The second and perhaps main contributor to this lack of action is the belief that water is abundant, even in the desert. Through the technology that stored and delivered water from over 400 miles away, to major subsidies farmers received starting with the formation of the Bureau of Reclamation and of course, the very low price everyone paid for water, one was automatically lulled into believing this illusion.

The third, and I feel more disturbing and daunting, is interstate and intrastate politics has delayed action. This just lures the general public further into a false sense of water availability. Again just as the causes of climate change are beyond the purview of this book, so are politics. However, one cannot deny the impact politics continue to play on water in the West. Although it ultimately may have to be the elected officials that have to assume control of the situation. Hopefully it will not be too late.

This political inaction is also due in part to the water providers as well as the system and laws that date back almost 100 years. Recently, I attended a seminar hosted by Denver Water that discussed the growing issues that the state faces with regard to the looming supply and demand gap. During a discussion on ways to curb demand in the urban areas, representatives of Denver Water were asked why irrigation efficiencies were not mandated for residential users. The gist of the response was that if a residential user contacted them about implementing drip systems, they would provide information; however, they did not feel it was their role to dictate what type of irrigation people should use or tell them to replace their lawns with xeriscaping.

Likewise, one of the participants asked why a program such as Patricia Mulroy's "Cash for Grass" was not in the works. The response was it cost too much and that money was better spent on storing surplus water underground, like Arizona was doing. It is indeed unfortunate that the largest water provider to the residents of the Front Range is not using this golden opportunity to exhibit leadership and address the expanse of green lawns seen throughout the metropolitan area in an effort to secure a sustainable water future for the state.

Instead, Denver Water continues using the traditional view of water. In other words, technology will provide water to a region that projects to have a population of 9 million by 2050, yet has no new sources of water. This is the pitfall most water managers in California, the Imperial Valley, and the Front Range of Colorado have fallen into, which is always looking for a new source of water, instead of addressing their current and future demand.

Another very Machiavellian way of looking at Denver Water's responses is that if customers reduce their amount of demand to water lawns, which by the way accounts for at least 40% of residential usage, revenues of the utility decline. What corporate manager voluntarily cuts a revenue stream that has no new incremental costs? Although Denver Water has a tiered rate system that is designed to foster conservation, residential customers in the first tranche are only charged $2.75 per thousand gallons up to 11,000 gallons per month.[46] Thus, a residential customer using 11,000 gallons of water only pays $30.25. As both Fishman, and Glennon point out, water is cheap when compared to cable, phone and Internet bills.[47] There clearly is some room to increase the rate but again would the increase offset the decline in usage and thus reduce revenues to the water providers?

On the other hand, what elected official is going to tell his constituency that all the subsidized water that has been flowing freely for decades may have to be curtailed or the groundwater that is supposed to be the safety net in dry periods won't be available for the next ten years as time to recharge the aquifer is required? If you lived in Northern California, would you vote for someone who supported cutting your water allocation so someone in Beverly Hills could water their lawns or fill their pool? Fat chance that official will be re-elected. Why do you think the recently passed groundwater legislation in California was phased in over 15 years?

In Colorado, what West Slope politicians would see another term if they supported a new trans-mountain diversion (TMD) for the Front Range? Just as in our nation's Capital, in the West, we have gridlock over water. Unfortunately, our political structure does not work when looking at an interstate river as there are too many interstate and intrastate issues that dictate water consumption and do not address the main problem, which is demand is exceeding supply throughout the Colorado River Basin.

Interstate problems get even more complicated as one encounters the political tug-of-war between states. We know that the Colorado Compact allocated more water than the river delivered over the long-term. As a result, people living in the Upper Basin consistently ask the question, why not change the amount allocated to each basin, and address the river's realities? The response is the Lower Basin has 72 votes in Congress compared to only 12 in the Upper Basin. Better the devil you know than the one you don't.

Colorado Water Plan (The Plan)

It is not just California where politics play into the manner in which water is managed. After the devastating low snow pack year of 2002, Governor John Hickenlooper directed the Colorado Water Conservation Board (CWCB) to identify current and future water demand in an attempt to discover any potential regional deficits within the state. This led to an Executive Order in 2013 authorizing the CWCB to develop the Colorado Water Plan (The Plan) to be completed by December 2015.[48] It is important to understand the Plan given its direct implications on the basin as the state supplies 70% of the water that flows in the Colorado River Basin. Thus, the Plan, which is focused mainly on state issues will affect the Law of the River and place yet another layer of issues and restrictions on an interstate water source that is already "the most legislated, most debated and most litigated river…" Are you getting tired of this quote?

The stated goals of The Plan were:

- a productive economy that supports vibrant and sustainable cities, viable and productive agriculture, and a robust skiing, recreation, and tourism industry.
- efficient and effective water infrastructure promoting smart land use.
- a strong environment that includes healthy watersheds, rivers and streams and wildlife.[49]

These goals are commendable, but they cover every consumptive use possible, yet do not identify either priorities or a direction of how to determine allocation during a shortage. It was assumed that prior appropriation would address it. Furthermore, the Executive Order stipulated that the current rate of "Buy and Dry" or selling water rights was unacceptable.[50]

Common sense indicates that it will be impossible to achieve all of these objectives if one acknowledges demand will exceed supply within the entire Colorado River Basin. This being the case, what sector will not be "sustainable", "viable", "productive" or "robust"? How will those decisions be made and by whom? Will the power elite, to which Donald Worster refers in *Rivers of Empire*, drive the decisions or will it be decided on a fair and equitable basis?[51] Will there be an even playing field? This is critical as this is a statewide as well as an interstate issue and local issues cannot be the final arbiter. If this supply/demand gap is to be effectively solved for the future, a Band-Aid approach will not suffice as Colorado will find itself in the same situation California is in today: facing a real crisis with many of its options already foreclosed.

The Plan incorporated a bottoms-up process that involved each of the seven river basins in Colorado specifying demand projections through 2050, new sources and projected population and economic growth. Although each basin expressed a spirit of cooperation, I was not surprised to see local perspectives dominated and a continuation of the intrastate rivalries and conflicts that permeated Colorado water throughout the twentieth century. Some of the more glaring issues were:

- The West-Slope indicated there could be no new TMDS while the East-Slope looked to additional TMDs as new sources
- Urban areas looked to reduce irrigated acres and rural areas expressed concern about its negative economic impact
- Urban demands included the continuation of lush lawns as a "quality of life" issue while agricultural sector faced the loss of a "way of life"

- West-Slope claimed a Colorado Compact call was highly likely while East-Slope maintained the Colorado allocation of the Colorado River was not fully utilized.

Colorado had a golden opportunity to truly deal with the future of water not only within the state but also within the entire Basin. Originally, The Plan emphasized the tradition established in the 20th century of water's abundance and looked for new sources. However, the 21st century water managers now recognize that water is not readily available and while local determination is important, when faced with limited supply, a "win-lose" scenario develops. So the golden opportunity becomes obscured and The Plan is just another instance of the politics forcing virtual reality on the issue of water shortages and politicians acting like ostriches. Unfortunately, all this does is delay the inevitable crisis that will come. This is no different than what we see occurring in the nation's capital where Congress does not effectively deal with a situation until it becomes a crisis, at which point they usually just develop a patchwork approach to the problem.

Historically, water decisions in Colorado were made using values that reinforced property rights, economic considerations, equality of access (but using a seniority system), development, and beneficial use to inform policies and procedures. These are all core values of a democratic society.

Today, the regulatory and legal aspects of water, established over 100-years ago needs some readjustments. The allocation of water through the method of prior appropriation provides a key example of an area that needs addressing. This system clearly presented a solid structure for determining priorities, which was imperative when initially allocating water. Additionally, the stipulation of "beneficial use" was critical during the development of the state. But times have changed and the Plan acknowledged this.

> *And yet, the Colorado of our forefathers is very different from the Colorado we live in today.... In 1876, farming and mining were our primary ways of life. Today, these important industries are joined by technology, tourism, recreation, transportation, financial services, and many other sectors that comprise our diverse economy.[52]*

Prior appropriation presents additional issues as it is based on private ownership. Again, this is a very important American principle, however one that leads to the "Tragedy of the Commons" when faced with limited supply. In other words, although one makes a rational decision on the use of water based on prior appropriation and individual self-interest, it may not be the best for the common good.

Abraham Lustgarten described this issue in detail in his publication *Use It or Lose It: Across the West, Exercising One's Right to Use Water* by telling the story of a rancher in Gunnison, Colorado that produces hay.[53] The rancher admitted he continued using flood irrigation all summer to ensure he used his full allocation, given his senior claim. If he did not drown his fields, under the 130-year-old practice of prior appropriation, he would have to "abandon" the amount of water not used. Abandonment of any water right would have a significant impact on the economic value of the rancher's water right as well as his property.

The rancher readily acknowledges that he wastes water, but like cotton farmers in Arizona, alfalfa farmers in the Imperial Valley and ranchers throughout the Basin, he has no other choice. They have all been advised by water lawyers to protect their rights by continuing to use their full allotment. This also applies to municipalities that have purchased senior water rights and the set amount they need to use. Thus, the "use it or lose it" which made so much sense in the past just further complicates how to solve the future shortage in supply.

Unfortunately, the Colorado Water Plan approved on November 19, 2015 still affirms the continuation of the prior appropriation doctrine and private property rights[54] as it is imbedded in the Colorado State Constitution.[55] While one realizes overturning a system that served to allocate water for almost 150 years presents substantial obstacles, conditions have changed.

Being rooted in the past is not what makes this nation great. When something has been identified as wrong, like slavery, we changed it. Granted it took a Civil War to do so, but we did it. Change is never easy.

The second draft of The Plan highlighted unacceptable conditions for Colorado to attain a sustainable water future that included:

- Eliminating farm and ranchland to supply urban development
- Creating more TMDs
- Continuing use of groundwater for municipal growth
- Maintaining lush lawns prevalent in the Eastern U.S.
- Supporting regulatory processes that were inefficient and expensive
- Increasing the possibility of federal intervention
- Maintaining water laws that did not reflect current reality.[56]

This was an attempt to establish values to guide the final plan.

Many outside sources provided input and the Getchens-Wilkinson Center for Natural Resources, Energy and Environment suggested The Plan also needed to:

- Provide for watershed health
- Implement policies that support conservation and reuse
- Protect water supply
- Develop alternatives to "buy-and-dry"
- Manage and carefully scrutinize any future TMDs
- Focus on uses not just supply
- Incorporate mitigation solutions for climate change.[58]

After two years of endless meetings, the compilation of numerous Basin reports, and the input from thousands the Colorado Water Plan was submitted to Governor Hickenlooper. It stressed collaboration and established specific measurable goals that ranged from reducing the Municipal and Industrial gap to zero, instituting land use requirements, maintaining agricultural productivity, implementing residential conservation, providing new storage, and addressing water shed and climate change issues.[59]

In addition, recognizing the controversial issue of additional TMD's, especially from the Colorado River Basin (West Slope) that remained concerned with environmental, supply deficit and compact compliance issues while the East-Slope desperate for new supply looked for more TMDs, the Plan incorporated a conceptual framework reached by consensus that could guide future negotiations. While this is a major step forward in an attempt to deal with this ongoing conflict, the Plan also indicated that it was only a guide and was not binding.[60] Thus, one step forward and one step back; however, it reveals a sense of cooperation that is a real paradigm shift from the past.

Even though the Plan emphasizes the new cooperative spirit, a further examination of the Colorado River and the South Platte/Metro Basins specific comments still exposed a divergence in values.[61] In the section dealing with potential projects to reduce the future supply gap, the Colorado River Basin stated, "The most prudent planning approach [...] is to assume that there is no more water to develop for export from the Colorado Basin."[62] On the other hand, of the 63 projects identified by South Platte/Metro five new TMDs and a reliance on agricultural transfers, both not considered acceptable by guidelines established in the second draft, were included. Once again this basin holds more than 80% of the state's population with no new in-basin supply sources available.

Conservation and reuse are two methods identified for expanding current supply. Regarding conservation, the South Platte/Metro Basin, notably Denver Water, has been diligent on reducing residential water consumption and has reduced the average daily consumption per person by 20% since 2000.[63] However, when it comes to the largest residential consumer of water, lush lawns, they are hesitant to push for land use measures or adopt programs such as Cash for Grass.[64] As outside irrigation accounts for between 40% and 50% of the total residential use this seems like an ideal way to reduce demand.

On the other hand, values established in the Plan indicated the reduction in agricultural consumption to supply increased municipal demand was unacceptable yet the Plan indicated a statewide reduction of around 700,000 irrigated acres by 2050 to cover the looming gap. The South Platte accounted for over one-third of this reduction.[65] As agricultural transfers require one to give up a "way of life" either permanently or temporarily, it seems less grass or "quality of life" is an option that should be considered. But, in the spirit of cooperation, the CWCB left land use restrictions optional.

While the CWCB established a 400,000 acre-feet reduction in Municipal and Industrial use through conservation it appears the value of local authority is of greater importance. Granted, the Plan is referred to as a "living document" that will be revised as conditions change. It is unfortunate that the largest consumption in residential demand was not more effectively handled now.

Reuse

Another method of stretching existing supplies is reuse or reclamation; a technique used successfully for the water features and golf courses in Las Vegas and increasingly in California. Although Colorado has golf courses and fountains, the projected Municipal and Industrial gap by 2050, if nothing changes, would be "between 310,000 and 560,000 acre-feet". This increase in demand was to supply potable water to a population that could double in that time period.[66]

So, what is reused or reclaimed water? In blunt terms it is treated waste water that has removed solids and other impurities and can be reused for irrigation, industrial needs and, yes, drinking. YUCK! That is the normal reaction. How can anyone even consider drinking water that has come from someone's toilet? This raises what Charles Fishman termed "the Yuck Factor."[67]

A good example of the Yuck Factor was seen on the *60 Minute* segment, "Depleting Groundwater," where Lesley Stahl visited a recycling/reuse plant in Orange County that treats 96 million gallons of sewage each day. This treated water replenishes the groundwater that is the drinking water for much of Orange County, including Disney Land. In her report she gave herself a pep talk before drinking the water and stated, "I can't believe how brave I am. Forty-five minutes ago, this was sewer water."[68]

What most people do not understand is that treating sewage for reuse is not uncommon. Everyone knows water is treated to meet water quality guidelines established by the Federal Government beginning in the 1970s. Those living in the mountains along the Continental Divide drink treated water to eliminate naturally occurring bacteria like giardia and other pollutants. When I flush my toilet, take a shower or wash the dishes, water flows into the sewer and straight to a water treatment facility that empties into Lake Dillon, the major storage facility for Denver Water.

When I informed my mother-in-law and brother-in-law that live in the Denver metro area that they were probably drinking the same water that they flushed down the toilet when visiting us, they blanched. They also claimed that they would not be able to drink tap water again. Clearly, the Yuck Factor affected their thinking.

Although the technology exists that turns waste water into potable or drinking water, due to this aversion, reuse is often downplayed and thus the ability to more completely stretch the available water supply requires substantial public education, technological improvements and vast funding resources to retrofit the current infrastructure. Steve Wynn, double plumbing Treasure Island, while very costly, was only a drop in the bucket compared to Denver attempting to obtain reused water to irrigate golf courses and the lawns that provide a "quality of life" along the Front Range.

The Plan addresses reuse with the South Platte/Metro Basin proposing 12 projects that could yield at least 58,135 acre-feet by 2050.[69] With no specific information available on the projects, I can only assume that these are "low hanging fruit" that will not require the exorbitant capital outlays to retrofit current infrastructure. Additionally, energy costs for the current reuse technology are quite high. It should be noted that reuse is an integral element in the water management systems in both Singapore and Israel. How and why this works will be described in detail in Chapter 10, "Teach Your Children Well." This option should be actively investigated with a focus on improving the technology to reduce the amount of energy required as well as developing an educational element to reduce the Yuck Factor.

Colorado's Future

The Colorado Water Plan provided a wonderful opportunity to establish values to serve as a road map for attaining a sustainable water supply for future generations. And, it went a long way in doing so; however, by emphasizing local autonomy over sustainability, real solutions face more obstacles. Hopefully, the spirit of cooperation and collaboration that permeates the verbiage in the Plan will lead all Basins to realize we are in the same boat, so to speak, and eliminate everyone protecting their "turf." Until this happens, the issues plaguing the state for over a century will continue and the chances of attaining water sustainability for Colorado remain uncertain.

While indicating a reduction in agricultural lands to supply municipal demand was not acceptable, the Plan did not suggest incentives/subsidies to replace inefficient irrigation systems nor deal with the "use it or lose it" element of prior appropriation.

Climate change is acknowledged in the Plan, which indicates "The State projects that droughts will increase in frequency and severity."[70] Unfortunately, aside from assisting in flood and drought mitigation programs, forest health and addressing regulatory barriers to combat climate change, no concrete action steps were identified.

Beyond Colorado, the Plan addresses watershed health, or how well the ecosystem is functioning, by focusing on water quality and its relationship to water quantity. If watershed health is adequately addressed, the Colorado River Basin will also be in better shape, at least as the water exits the state. But, it must be remembered, this river on which so many depend, is an interstate resource. That is why the Law of the River developed; however, each state determines how the water is used within their boundaries. As the effects of climate change become clearer, the Upper Basin starts using more of its allocation, recurring droughts of undetermined durations occur and groundwater depletions increase demand for more surface water, expensive litigation and intense conflicts will develop. So, just as the Plan in Colorado needs to step beyond local considerations, perhaps the Colorado River Basin needs a comprehensive plan of its own that looks at current and future demand more critically and finally deals with the hydrological realities that the Southwest and Southern California face in the future.

Recently, the Bureau of Reclamation formed the Colorado River Conservation Partnership that consists of the Southern Nevada Water Authority (SNWA), the Central Arizona Project (CAP), the Metropolitan Water District of Southern California (MWD) and Denver Water to address declining water levels in Lake Mead and Lake Powell. The goal of this partnership is to reduce consumption of the Colorado River in an effort to increase water levels in these massive storage facilities. Possible techniques to reduce consumption include the installing of more efficient irrigation systems, recycling municipal water, and fallowing of fields on a temporary basis. It will be very interesting to follow the progress of this cooperative endeavor as both interstate and intrastate "turf" is up for grabs.

The fact that Denver Water will be determining which programs to implement on the West-Slope is fraught with potential conflicts of interest. Furthermore, the majority of the partnerships are located in the Lower Basin. Hopefully, the USBR will help Denver Water protect the Upper Basin.

Already the battle lines are being drawn with Eric Balken, Executive Director of the Glen Canyon Institute making the case to eliminate Lake Powell to fill Lake Mead. In other words, eliminate the water bank the Upper Basin developed with the Colorado River Storage Project (CRSP). Although the chance of this occurring is very remote, Balken points out,

> But in today's 'new normal,' there is simply not enough water to maintain both Lake Powell and Lake Mead. It's time to fill Mead first.[71]

Thus, eliminating the Upper Basin water bank to ensure the Lower Basin will have access to more water becomes a real bone of contention. This of course would require the building of another major storage facility in the Upper Basin that would resurrect the Echo Park battle of the 1950s. So the interstate and intrastate conflicts that have raged for a century will only continue.

That being said, partnerships and compromises and cooperation, as seen in the Shortage Guidelines are a step in the right direction toward cooperation that Patricia Mulroy feels is necessary for a healthy Colorado River Basin. A healthy watershed is a necessity for a sustainable water supply for those that depend on the over allocated river. Hopefully, action will be taken soon which will address the entire situation that faces the Colorado River Basin.

Last Thoughts

Pete McBride, a photographer, writer and filmmaker, born and raised in Colorado, became curious as to where the irrigation water from his family ranch went. McBride rafted the Colorado River, and ultimately walked the final miles where it no longer reaches the Sea of Cortez. His passion led him to, in his words, "chase rivers" of the world, which have been published in National Geographic and The Smithsonian magazines. Although he has traveled the rivers, such as the Ganges and the Nile, his passion clearly resonates in films produced on the Colorado River. McBride produced and wrote a beautiful film entitled *I Am Red* which says it all.

I AM RED
By Peter McBride

I have run these canyons for six million years.
I have traveled from the Rocky Mountains to the desert.
Through scorching heat and freezing cold.
From the land of the dinosaurs
To the fields of wheat.

I lend my hand to seven states, 2 countries, nine National Parks
And thirty-six million people across an arid West.
I am not the strongest
or the largest
But I am the hardest working.

People love me
My playfulness
My beauty
My power
My life.

But, I don't think I can offer any more.
I am tired.
I am tired.
Tapped.
I am tired.

Of the hundreds of major rivers in the world
I am one of the few who no longer kisses the sea,
Battles to harness my soul have been won and lost.

Use me wisely and I will sustain you
Use me like you have and I will break.

My name is Red,
The Grand River Red, the American Nile, the Canyon Maker.
I am the Colorado River
And I am the most endangered river in America.[72]

Chapter 9

What Do You Pay for Water?
– Price of Water

To be perfectly honest, until I read Cynthia Barnett's *Blue Revolution: Unmaking America's Water Crisis,* I never focused on how much we paid for water each month, nor how much water we actually used. Her book made me realize that if asked what my cell phone or cable bill was, I could have responded almost to the penny what we paid each month, as well as the services used. Of course, I would have whined at the exorbitant fees, all the while knowing my grumbling would not change anything. However, if asked, "What do you pay for water?" I would have looked perplexed and said, "My husband pays that bill." After reading Barnett's book, I did look up the rate structure we pay for water and was absolutely amazed at how little water costs. Water is ridiculously cheap and highly subsidized in the United States. This only nurtures the belief that it is readily abundant.[1]

Charles Fishman devoted a whole chapter to the price of water in *The Big Thirst.* Fishman describes checking into a hotel to find two bottles of water that had tags around their necks that said,

"It's water. Of course it's free."[2]

Unfortunately, this statement epitomizes how water is viewed in the United States, regardless of where one lives.

Throughout the West, water is essentially free and users pay basically for the delivery infrastructure.[3] The highest rate Las Vegas Water District charges residential customers is $4.59 per 1,000 gallons.[4] Compare this to $4.58 per GALLON of bottled Crystal Geyser Alpine Spring Water that more than likely is just filtered tap water. In other words, a gallon of bottled water can cost around 1,000 times more than a gallon of water in Las Vegas. Likewise, the IID in the Imperial Valley currently consumes 3.1 million acre-feet from the Colorado River to irrigate the desert. The price of water for farmers in the IID is only $20 per acre-foot, or almost 326,000 gallons of water. This means they pay 6¢ for 1,000 gallons.[5] To put this in perspective, the cost of water in Las Vegas is over seventy-six times what the IID farmer pays, even though both use Colorado River water. More staggering is a gallon of bottled water costs 76,000 times more than the water used for irrigation in the Imperial Valley.

Mentioning bottled water opens another can of worms. Some of the largest companies in this $9 billion industry are doing business in drought-stricken California. According to CNN Money, there are 110 water bottling companies in the state that include Nestle, Coca-Cola, Aquafina, Crystal Geyser, Pepsi and Dasani. All of these companies consume around 3.1 billion gallons each year.[6] Even though this is less than one percent of the total water consumed annually by residents, farmers, ranchers and other industrial users it raises an interesting question. How much are these companies paying for the water that is taken from California's groundwater and municipal sources while charging thirsty Californians many multiples for the same water? The irony of this situation is that many of the same bottled water consumers probably fight tooth-and-nail any increase in water rates.

Returning to water rates, Denver Water's residential rate structure is shown in Chart 7. As a reminder, Denver Water is the provider of water in the Denver metropolitan area and one of the major recipients of the 500,000 acre-feet of TMD's from west of the Continental Divide.

CHART 7 – Denver Water 2015 Monthly Residential Rate Structure

Tiers	# of gallons	Rate/1000 gallons	Rate/ gallon
Block 1	0 - 11,000 gallons	$ 2.75	$0.0027
Block 2	12,000 – 30,000 gallons	$ 5.50	$0.0055
Block 3	31,000 – 40,000 gallons	$ 8.25	$0.00825
Block 4	over 40,000 gallons	$11.00	$0.011

Source: Denver Water. (2015). *Inside City 2015 Rates.* **Retrieved from:** http://www. denverwater.org/BillingRates/RatesCharges/2015-rates/inside-city/[7]

This is a typical tiered rate structure where pricing increases with usage and is an attempt to force residential consumers to think about their consumption. However, with such low rates, does the consumer give it a second thought? A family of 4 that uses 11,000 gallons a month or 92 gallons per person pays $30.25 each billing cycle. Amazingly, a family of 4 that uses 30,000 gallons a month only pays an additional $105.00 each month to consume over 200 gallons per day per person. Quite frankly, it is highly unlikely that any residential consumer using that much water each month is going to be concerned with an additional $100 incremental charge. Thus, the tiered structure, although well intended, does not generate sufficient discomfort to motivate many users to focus on the amount of water they use.

In 2016, Denver Water revised their rate structure. The rationale for the change was based on "the more you use the more you pay." However, when one compares the 2015 to the 2016 rate structure summarized in Chart 8, those that are using more water are actually paying less than they did under the previous pricing policy and those in Block 1 and using over 5,000 gallons are paying more.

CHART 8 – Denver Water 2015 and 2016
Monthly Residential Rate Structure

Tiers	2015 # of gallons	2015 Rate/1000 gallons	2016 # of gallons	2016 Rate/ 1000 gallons
Block 1	0 - 11,000	$ 2.75	0-5000	$2.60
Block 2	12,000 – 30,000	$ 5.50	5,000-15,000	$4.68
Block 3	31,000 – 40,000	$ 8.25	Over 15,000	$6.24
Block 4	over 40,000	$11.00		

Source: Denver Water. (2015 and 2016). *Inside City Rates.*[7]

Thus, residential customers using the most water to fill swimming pools and irrigate large expanses of lawn saw a discounted rate over 2015, while most customers experienced an increase as Block 1 was reduced by 7,000 gallons. This new rate structure seems to fly in the face of the espoused philosophy of paying more if one uses more.

The public reaction to this new rate structure was immediately quite negative. On August 14, 2016 the Denver Post ran the headlines, "Steamed: Denver Water customers are boiling mad after seeing big jumps in their bills caused by a rate hike based on "the more you use, the more you pay." This public reaction is just another indication of the belief that water is free and not limited. Clearly, Denver Water has some educating to do.

Santa Fe, New Mexico also addressed this issue and implemented a steep tiered rate structure in 2008 which does support paying for use as well as addressing the type and timing of use. This arid New Mexico city recognized the realities of the climate and that filling swimming pools and watering lawns peaked in the summer months. To reflect this the water utility raised the amount available at the lower rate by 3,000 gallons. However, the steep rate differential based on usage regardless of time of year led to a dramatic realization by customers where they actually paid attention to their water use.

CHART 9 – Santa Fe Residential Rate Structure

| September – April | $6.06/1000 gallons – for first 7,000 gallons
$21.72/1000 gallons – thereafter |
| May – August | $6.06/1000 gallons – for first 10,000 gallons
$21.72/1000 gallons – thereafter |

Source: City of Santa Fe: Water Division. **Retrieved from:** www. Santafenm.gov/ water division[8]

A *New York Times* article that compared the water fees in Fresno, California and Santa Fe commented that since this steeper rate structure was established in Santa Fe, water consumption has decreased even as its population has grown. "When water costs more as its consumption increases, people respond exactly as an economics textbook would dictate: They use less."[9]

Unfortunately, when San Juan Capistrano in Southern California attempted to implement a steeper tiered rate structure, the Orange County Appeals Court ruled it unconstitutional. Even though the highest rate assessed was $9.15 or less than half of that charged in Santa Fe, it violated California's Proposition 218 that prohibits government charging more than the cost of the service.[10] This ruling came after the April Fool's Day Executive Order to reduce residential water consumption by 25%. This, once again, highlights the disconnect between legislation and hydrological realities. Thus, even though studies indicate that water consumption declines at least 15% with tiered pricing, the entrenched concept that water should be free prevails.

In many cities, monitoring demand and pricing water based on usage is an anathema. Fresno, California is a clear example of this. The city maintains an archaic flat-rate water system that charges all users the same rate regardless of the amount of water used. As of 2013 Fresno approved an increase in water rates from around $24 to $48 over a four-year period as their water rates were "the cheapest of any major metropolitan water system within the state, and they still will be after this initial increase."[11]

However, this increase was repealed in 2014 due to a public outcry.[12] Again, just like Denver, the residents of Fresno maintained water should be free.

This ingrained belief in the right to a limitless supply of inexpensive water dated well before these rate increases were being discussed. In 1992, voters amended the Fresno City Charter to ban the use of water meters, even though this provided the city the tool to monitor water consumption. In 2004, the California legislature enacted "a bill requiring the installation of meters—by the year 2025. Talk about political courage."[13] Although the politicians acknowledged meters were a necessity, they too continued to believe that water supply was not an issue for the state and perpetuated Reisner's "fraud." This is just another example of elected officials kicking the can down the road.

With the drought in California, Fresno finally initiated a program to install meters on residential homes that was completed in 2013. Fresno was not the only town that procrastinated in installing meters. *The Sacramento Bee* reported on February 23, 2015 that the capital city had the largest amount of unmetered homes in the state but planned to accelerate a program of installing meters to be completed by 2020, five years ahead of schedule. The rationale for not installing meters earlier was that the Sacramento and American rivers both flowed through the town and provided sufficient water supply, so conservation was not needed.[14] When the intake pipes from both the American and Sacramento were close to "sucking air" early in 2014, it alerted the city managers to basic hydrological realities. As of August 2016, Sacramento had installed 70% of the residential meters.

Water meters have definitely proven successful in reducing consumption as cities without them have a higher daily per person consumption than those that have installed them. Back to Fresno, a city that resisted water meters, per capita usage was around 329 gallons per day. However Clovis, a town less than 10 minutes away from Fresno, installed meters and had a daily usage of approximately 200 gallons per day.[15] Once meters were installed, the City of Fresno Water District reported the average daily water usage dropped by over 22%.[16] Likewise, the Sacramento Bee reported the per capita daily consumption in the capital city was 165 gallons. However, these per capita usage rates are still high when compared to the statewide average of 124 gallons, Arizona's rate of 140 gallons, and Colorado's rate of 121 gallons.[17]

Even though the city of Fresno now has the ability to measure the amount of water used, until February of 2015 an average monthly water bill totaled $24.00 for around 7500 gallons or less than one-third of a penny per gallon. As mentioned previously, the City Council attempted to raise the water rates in 2013 but backed down when the electorate vigorously protested. Ultimately, hydrological realities forced the City Council to finally take action. In 2015, after many years of waffling, the City Council finally approved increasing water rates to around $48 per household over the next five years to construct and finance a recharge and treatment project. The vast majority of Fresno's water comes from groundwater, which has caused water levels to drop over 100 feet in the last 80 years. By using water discharged from the Friant Dam during surplus or wet years, treating and storing it in storage basins for dry periods the city hopes to reduce its reliance on groundwater from 88% to 36%. The increased rates will pay for this $429.1 million project.[18]

This is a clear example of how we pay for just the delivery of water. This echoes Patricia Mulroy's philosophy that everyone is entitled to water; but, they need to except the responsibility in covering the cost of the infrastructure that cleans and distributes the water, in essence the delivery system.

So, Fresno's recharge project makes imminent sense, but there are two glaring problems with it. The first is this $429 million program depends on surplus or wet years and snow melt from the Sierra Nevada. With the current drought and lack of snow pack, the chances of surplus are slim to nil of filling any storage basins. Hopefully, this drought will end soon; however, if it persists as the dry periods in the Medieval

Climate Anomaly, the recharge basins will remain empty. The second assumes that even if there are surplus water years in California's future, there is no guarantee that the surplus water is available to Fresno and not already committed to the San Joaquin Valley or Los Angeles. This is a prime example of increasing demand throughout the state, all relying on the same source. Just as the Colorado River is over allocated, the same is occurring on the state rivers throughout California.

Water as a Commodity

As Charles Fishman points out in *The Big Thirst*, there is a bias in the United States not to view water as a commodity or allocated on the basis of the ability to pay.[19] In other words, it should be free. Many others who are concerned about shortages in the future are beginning to believe that water should be treated as a commodity. Ted Turner and at one point, T. Boone Pickens, agreed as both held a vast amount of water reflecting their view that water would become a commodity.[20] However, the view that water is a natural resource and more significantly a public resource is too firmly entrenched. All other commodities have substitutes but no living thing on this planet can exist without this "blue gold."[21]

Fishman and Glennon believe it is important to view water more as a commodity, similar to oil, and allow price or the market determine how water is consumed.[22] Both Glennon and Fishman recognize that water is a necessity, thus the "first drink" issue of providing basic needs at the lowest cost must be resolved; however, both believe water should have a higher economic value.[23] Reisner also felt the price of water should be market-driven. He indicated, "If free-market mechanisms [...] were actually allowed to work, the West's water 'shortage' would be exposed for what it is: the sort of shortage you expect when inexhaustible demand chases an almost free good."[24]

Fishman also thinks that Americans' strong resistance to increasing water rates stems from believing this natural resource is readily available. If water users understood that supply was actually limited and there was a cost to water, which in most cases is subsidized, this opposition could possibly reduce. As an example, Fishman pointed out "We certainly got into the habit of free TV and now 90% of the U.S. homes pay for TV, either cable TV or satellite TV." [25] Interestingly, not only do we pay for TV we pay more for it than we do for water. Glennon reinforced this by stating, "Most Americans pay less for water than they do for cable television or cell phone service. Water is ridiculously cheap in the United States." [26]

How did the cable/satellite companies accomplish this? They increased the perceived value of their product. This must be done with water, which requires a shift in how water is valued. Adam Smith's diamond-water paradox in *An Inquiry into the Nature and Causes of the Wealth of Nations* published in 1776 still holds true today.

> *The word VALUE, it is to be observed, has two different meanings, and sometimes expresses the utility of some particular object, and sometimes the power of purchasing other goods which the possession of that object conveys. The one may be called 'value in use'; the other, 'value in exchange'. The things which have the greatest value in use have frequently little or no value in exchange; and on the contrary, those which have the greatest value in exchange have frequently little or no value in use. Nothing is more useful than water: but it will purchase scarce any thing; scarce any thing can be had in exchange for it. A diamond, on the contrary, has scarce any value in use; but a very great quantity of other goods may frequently be had in exchange for it.* [27]

Economists, like Smith argue that without assigning a value or a realistic price to water, there is no incentive to conserve. Tiered pricing addresses this issue by charging more for higher usage; however, when one looks at the facts it is apparent that for some the threshold of pain or the rate for higher usage is not affecting their water use.

As another example, the average per capita daily use for Arizona is 140 gallons; however, in Scottsdale, an-upscale area north of Phoenix, the average daily consumption per person is 249 gallons. Thus, one can only assume that the tiered rate structure has not had an impact on filling their swimming pools or supplying the misters. Chart 10 summarizes this growing city's rate structure which certainly supports that those living and working in Scottsdale place no value on water. So, a household using only 5,000 gallons would pay $22.25. Another water consumer who used 10,000 gallons would only pay an additional $14.25 for double the amount of water. It is little wonder that water consumption is not reducing in Scottsdale.

CHART 10 – Scottsdale Arizona Water Rates

Tier	Usage	Price per 1000 gallons
Tier 1	0-5000 gallons	$1.65
Tier 2	5,000-12,000 gallons	$2.85

Source: City of Scottsdale, AZ. (2015). *City of Scottsdale Water and Sewer Rate Report:* **Retrieved from:** Assets/Public+ Website/ water/ Rates+$!26+Fees/FY15Water WastewaterRateRpt.pdf[28]

Given water is essential for the survival of all life forms, this basic necessity must be provided to everyone at the lowest possible cost and most agree that the basic survival needs should be subsidized, what has not been addressed is what should be charged for lawns, swimming pools, misters and of the course the biggest and most subsidized, agriculture. With agriculture consuming 70% to 80% of the water in the West, this low price of water for farmers and ranchers needs much closer scrutiny.

Economic Determination of Water Demand

One way of evaluating demand is based on economic returns. As an example, Glennon compared the growth and harvesting of alfalfa with that of Intel producing a Core 2 Duo microchip. To produce one ton of alfalfa requires 135,000 gallons of water that sells for approximately $110. On the other hand, to make one microchip uses 10 gallons of water and sells for $400. Glennon concludes, "Each acre-foot used to grow alfalfa generates at most $264. That same acre-foot used to manufacture Core 2 Duo chips generates $13 million."[29] Thus, looking purely at water usage and the revenue produced, any economic advisor would counsel switching to building microchips; however, is economic return the value that should be used?

Glennon did not include the technological and energy costs of producing microchips in his report; so it is a bit skewed. The analysis also does not include government subsidies that alfalfa received over the years. Glennon continues to describe how Intel initially consumed over 5 million gallons a day in their Chandler, Arizona plant. The company spent unspecified millions on converting to ultra-pure water needed for the production of microchips as well as another unspecified millions to clean the discharged water. By cleaning the water, the company returns 3 billion gallons each year to the aquifer for reuse. Thus, strategies employed by Intel "save almost 4 million gallons per day, an 80% reduction in water use."[30]

This cost benefit analysis highlights the highly controversial political issue of transferring agricultural production to industrial uses. Thus, the tradeoff of taxpayers subsidizing agricultural products to maintain lower costs of putting dinner on the table versus reduced taxes and increased food costs presents a real dilemma. As climate change and future extended droughts may be in our future, shouldn't how water is allocated be part of a public dialogue? This issue was deliberated in the Colorado Water Plan with the goal of minimizing the reduction in irrigated acres; however, aside from developing different types of agricultural water transfers other than "buy and dry" no real solution was presented.

Another important aspect to be considered is the corporation's willingness to spend millions to develop the technology to change the water properties to enable the production of a product that is economically viable for them. Showing corporate responsibility, Intel also determined ways of returning the water for reuse. Compare this to the government providing subsidies for agricultural or other uses that were not economically feasible otherwise. Clearly, Intel desires to use the water for their economic benefit but realizes efficiency of its use is critical. Applying the expertise that Intel and others have developed is a different way of viewing technology as a means of stretching the water supply. It also places a different slant on using economic considerations in determining water allocation.

Charles Fishman reinforced the issue of economic return trade-offs for different uses in *The Big Thirst*. He compared the Imperial Valley's water usage to that of Las Vegas. A farmer in the Imperial Valley paid six cents for 1,000 gallons of water while, in Las Vegas, an average homeowner paid $2.71 for the same amount, even though both use the same source, the Colorado River.[31] In addition, the Imperial Valley generated a revenue of $1.5 billion each year while gambling revenue alone generated $8.8 billion in Las Vegas. Fishman did not conclude that more water should be going to Las Vegas and less to the Imperial Valley, but suggested that any time a resource was limited, choices must be made and those choices affect the future.[32]

This is key as it reflects that decisions made in the past influenced the current and future status of our water supply; who will use it and how it will be used.[32] Unfortunately, at the present time, decisions are still made based on past history when water demand did not exceed supply, and when the value of private ownership and manipulation and control of waterways by technology dominated. This surplus of water will not exist in our future; thus, leadership and revised policies are required that determines what criteria should inform these decisions. Otherwise, the ineffective policy of "kicking the can down the road" will continue and result in a water crisis in the future with no immediate remedies in sight.

Maintenance Issues

Fishman raised another very important issue that involved the maintenance costs of our current system, which not only needs replacement and, in most instances, is not capable of delivering future demand. Although the cost of maintaining the current U.S. water system totals $29 billion each year, most water utilities budget minimal amounts to maintain their systems or plan for the future. Maintenance includes the servicing and upkeep of potable water treatment plants, pump stations, pipes in the ground and wastewater treatment plants. Even with the monies spent on maintenance, it is believed that over 7 billion gallons each day is lost due to leaking water pipes.[33]

In the summer of 2014, two aging water pipes burst in Los Angeles and flooded the UCLA campus losing up to 20 million gallons of water into the sewers, destroying 300 cars and creating a 25-by-30-foot sinkhole that was 7 feet deep. These 90-year old pipes were in terrible condition with one badly corroded and the other already having five leaks prior to the rupture. Pictures of the 30-foot geyser and wasted water appeared in the *L.A. Times* at the same time Governor Brown called for a voluntary cut back of residential water usage by 20%.[34] The juxtaposition of these two items highlighted the aging infrastructure that needed replacement as water users were being asked to cut back on usage; thus, reducing revenues and the water utilities ability to afford to replace old pipes.

The California State Water Resources Control Board reports that 870,000 acre-feet of water used in urban areas is lost to leaky pipes on an annual basis. This represents 10% of the annual urban water supply in the state.[35] Much of the infrastructure is at least 100 years old; thus, at the end of its lifespan. Unfortunately, the amount lost to leaking pipes will only increase. With the financial condition of the state and all of the other social and environmental issues California currently faces, this is not a problem that will just go away. With the current low prices charged for water, how does California, or for that matter any state or municipality plan to cover future maintenance costs.

A water infrastructure that has passed its useful life is prevalent throughout the country. The 2013 Report Card for America's Infrastructure compiled by the American Society of Civil Engineers and summarized in Chart 11, gave the following very disappointing grades to America's water systems.

CHART 11 – Water Infrastructure GPA - 2013

Category	Grade	Rationale
Dams	D	Average age of the 84,000 dams in the country is 52 years and there are 4000 deficient dams
Drinking Water	D	Most of the drinking water infrastructure has passed its useful life. There are an estimated 240,000 water main breaks each year. To replace would cost $1 trillion
Waste and Storm Water	D	Pipes are insufficient to address sanitary sewer overflows necessary for expanding populations. More waste water treatment plants are needed. Over the next twenty years, almost $300 billion will be needed in capital investment and repairs.

Source: Americans Society of Civil Engineers. 2013 Report Card for America's Infrastructure[36]

Although the issue of an aging infrastructure is a country wide issue, the drought in the Colorado River Basin and California makes it even harder to address replacement issues as water managers are much more preoccupied with where they will get new sources of water to cover their growing demand. As a result, the Band-Aid approach of fixing only broken pipes will lead to more significant loss of water in the future.

Continuation of the current decision making process highlights yet another obstacle when it comes to pricing of water throughout most of the country. How will we pay for the estimated $1 trillion anticipated for repair costs over the next 25 years? Many Water Boards are elected and the public still feels water should be free. Which elected officials will support increasing water rates if they want to be re-elected? Thus, our political system remains another obstacle to deal with needed current and future maintenance costs. As Cynthia Barnett points out,

> *The problems are also laying bare the flawed way we pay for water — one that practically guarantees pipes will burst, farmers will use as much as they can and automatic sprinklers will whir over desiccated aquifers.*[37]

This presents a good news/bad news scenario. The bad news is there is not one easy fix as this occurs everywhere in the country in thousands of different pipes or treatment plants. The good news is it needs fixing which presents an opportunity to retrofit our water system to accommodate new technology that reuses water and increases water efficiency. Why continue throwing good money away to fix obsolete systems?

Cost of Groundwater

And then there is the cost of ground water. Farmers and municipalities only have to pay to dig the wells and the energy required to pump water, which becomes more expensive as water levels plummet. In other words, they too only pay for the delivery system. Thus, just as in surface water, the water itself is free. One cannot be surprised about the depletion of ground water occurring in the Central Valley or in the Lower Colorado River Basin. What will happen when the water levels in the Central Valley drop to where it is uneconomical to pump? Will the almond growers and alfalfa fields disappear, or will changes in the way water is used be implemented to minimize the effects of groundwater depletion?

What is the VALUE of water?

Water is essential for everyone, but as Adam Smith pointed out two hundred and forty years ago, it has no value. Given the large subsidies that irrigators continue to receive and the bargain-basement price everyone pays for water it is only human nature that this natural resource is taken for granted. As a result, most Americans do not give a second thought to a leaking toilet, floodwater irrigation or the type of crops being planted. We expect that when we turn on the tap, clean water will magically flow even though we have no idea what had to be done to the water to make it safe to drink, the cost of the delivery and sewer systems and their maintenance nor how much is being consumed. The fact that most of us cannot answer the question "How much do you pay for water?" clearly illustrates this.

Circle of Blue, an organization formed in 2000 by scientists and journalists that focuses on water, reports each year on water rates throughout the country. It is not surprising to see that some of the lowest rates are found in the West, notably Fresno, Denver, Las Vegas and Phoenix. In addition, Circle of Blue reports the cities that reflected the highest increase in rates from year to year and the reasons for these increases. The top three metropolitan areas that reflected the highest increase since 2014 were a 31% increase on its highest users in Austin to maintain revenues, a 15% increase in Chicago for maintenance and replacement of aging infrastructure and San Francisco boosted rates by 15% to guarantee water will be available within 24 hours after an earthquake.[38] Needless to say, this just reinforces that the natural resource is free and all we pay for is the delivery of water. It also highlights some of the fastest growing parts of the country receive water from the Colorado River also have some of the lowest rates.

There is growing support that viewing water as a commodity addresses the looming supply demand gap that the Colorado River Basin as well as the majority of the Western United States face. It is acknowledged that water is an essential for life, so the "first drink" must be protected, especially for the economically disadvantaged. The health of the watershed is another key element to be considered. Above that, if the West is going to learn to live within the water supply that Mother Nature provides and water is going to receive "VALUE," viewing it more like a commodity, such as oil, is one solution. But, before developing a market for water or any other major change in the way water is priced, we must start actually realizing that water does have VALUE and stop taking it for granted; accept that it is limited; and agree that that the hydrological realities of the Colorado River Basin demand cooperation. This is the only way we secure a sustainable water supply for our children's children.

> *Going forward, water infrastructure, supply and quality challenges intensified by the droughts, floods, temperature extremes and other influences of a changing climate will require new approaches to not only price, but also ethics: using less and polluting less, recycling more, and sharing costs among all users.*[39]

Of course, changing the way water is priced will also require a new way water is allocated and thus a revision or perhaps even abandoning the prior appropriation system that provides water rights. A new way of assessing demand or beneficial use, that may entail stricter land use regulations and a complete overhaul of the pricing structure of water is needed. Unfortunately, if this is to be done our elected officials must make some hard decisions and act on them, instead of waiting for consumers to experience an epiphany and change their behaviors. If not, we all will continue kicking the can down the road. As of today, there appears to be no one picking up the banner. One can only hope such a leader will emerge soon as Famiglietti's disaster movie is looking more like reality. Maybe not today or tomorrow, but definitely at some point in the future.

If the past is any indication, it will take a real crisis such as Denver, San Diego or Los Angeles not able to supply all of their customers with drinking water, Glen Canyon or Hoover Dam silting up or failing, Mother Nature continuing a drought for a century, ground water depletion reaching levels that eliminate the possibility of digging new and deeper wells or climate change reducing significantly the amount of precipitation that the Upper Colorado River Basin and the Sierra Nevada receives annually. Are we willing to continue betting that none of the above will happen? I am not sure the odds would be in our favor.

Chapter 10

"Teach Your Children Well" – Lessons Learned From Other Countries

Being a "Pollyanna," I tend to look at a glass half-full and do hope that at some point California and the Colorado River Basin will have a sustainable water future. Other countries have faced this issue and developed successful models that work for them. Israel, Singapore, Chile and Australia determined sitting back and waiting for a crisis to occur was foolhardy. They each realized that water was limited and shortages were, in fact, hydrological realities. All developed very different strategies in managing their limited water resources, which warrant further examination. Perhaps we can learn something from each of them.

Israel[1]

Unlike most countries, Israel was proactive and began addressing water scarcity even before it became a country in 1948. Covering just over 8,000 square miles, 60% of Israel is desert with the remainder semi-arid. In the mid-twentieth century, the population of the country was around 800,000.[2] By 2014 this rapidly expanding nation-state reported a population of 8.3 million people.[3] An ethic valuing water guided the planning and development of this water-scarce land and enabled this small country to move from uncertainty to a relatively sustainable future. By valuing water from the early stages of development, this liquid gold was not taken for granted and fostered an environment of conservation and innovation. By 2012, Israel saw the implementation of an integrated water management system for the entire country and was well on its way to a sustainable future.

In *Let There Be Water: Israel's Solution to a Water-Starved World,* Seth Siegel describes how this was accomplished. To begin, a water-respecting culture was necessary. By most realizing that water was not an abundant resource and needed preservation, a partnership between those that provided water and those that consumed it developed. With this, the government declared water belonged to all the people of Israel fostering decisions that would benefit the common good. Compare this to the western United States where water rights, once granted, are beneficially used at the discretion of the water right holder, regardless of the common good. Similarly, groundwater in the United States, in most instances, is available to anyone who lives on the land above the water, without much regulation.

Siegel outlined two major steps that permitted the country to ensure independence from drought and climate change. Realizing how decisions regarding water bogged down with political haggling, several government leaders put the nation's interest first and made some revolutionary and undemocratic changes in this democratic country. All water management decisions were concentrated in one government authority. This very controversial step resulted in taking politics out of the decision making process. As Siegel indicated, "Israel regards water as too important to be left to the whims of politicians."[4] This is consistent with water belonging to the nation and not to the holders of individual water rights.

Even though judicious use of water was a core value from the early days of statehood, just as in the United States, those living in Israel felt water should be free. The next important achievement was reversing this myth by raising water prices over 40% on everyone, regardless of use. As a side note, the government did provide support for the economically disadvantaged to provide for basic human needs. This dramatic increase in the price of water reinforced the idea that this natural resource was not to be wasted while providing funds to pay for the desalination and waste treatment plants necessary to provide water for the country's future.

Prior to this increase, water rates did not even cover the cost of the delivery systems. Oded Fixler, the current Senior Director General of Israel Water and Sewage Authority espouses a water pricing philosophy that mirrors Patricia Mulroy's.[5] Reflecting the commitment to de-politicize water management, the first Deputy General of the water authority, Professor Uri Shani told elected officials,

> *If you want to subsidize farmers or disabled people or give water to the country's neighbors, no problem. Discount it or give away all you like. But whatever you take or allocate, the government has to reimburse the water utility for the water used.... Everyone would be on the same rules. Everyone pays.*[6]

This one step of increasing rates across the board motivated the entire population to focus on how they used water, including the politicians.

The purpose of raising rates was to pay for past delivery infrastructure but, more importantly, for ongoing maintenance and construction of future desalination and recycling plants. The creation of a massive water infrastructure that connected the country allowed Israel to become self-reliant with regards to water.

Many believe what made this possible was assessing the real value of water as it "permitted market forces to work."[7] Eliminating subsidies and charging everyone what water actually cost to deliver, maintain and ensure an infrastructure for the future compelled irrigators, the largest consumer of water, to consider the "REAL" cost of producing their crops. It also saw a 25% to 30% reduction in domestic use in a country that already believed in strict conservation. This in turn fostered innovation that only further enhanced a culture that valued water.

Instead of looking for new sources, the Water Authority concentrated on using water more efficiently. A prime example of this was the development of drip irrigation by one of the early water leaders in the country. Today, 75% of farmers in Israel use this efficient form of irrigation that results in at least a 40% water savings. Studies have also revealed that "drip irrigation will produce a larger harvest and usually a higher-quality one [...] Harvests of double or more are now standard."[8]

Other innovations also increased water efficiency. This included breeding plants that required less water, such as short-stalked wheat and compact tomatoes plants having fewer leaves. In both cases, water was not wasted on the leaves or stalks. Also, Israeli seed breeders developed plants that thrived on water with higher salinity, or brackish water.

An emphasis on maximizing available resources by recycling wastewater became a central component for planning and contributed to Israel's water self-reliance. Unlike precipitation, sewage is "consistent, reliable and predictable."[9] Currently, around 85% of sewage is treated and reused with the majority of this reclaimed water being consumed by irrigation. Compare this to California recycling only 8% of its sewage and only 1% in the United States. Without recycling wastewater, Israel's agricultural economy would have faltered. Instead it currently produces 95% of the country's food requirements and also provides export revenues.

Desalination has also been a central element of the water management system in Israel. There are five desalination plants near the Mediterranean producing almost 475,000 acre-feet of water each year. The Water Authority plans to increase its desalination output to 612,000 acre-feet by 2020.[10] Another benefit of Israel's centralized water management structure, was the streamlining of approvals and implementation of plans. The country constructed all five plants during the time it took to gain regulatory approvals and construct the Carlsbad plant in San Diego. By the way, an Israeli firm engineered and constructed the Carlsbad plant.

Reclaimed water, desalination and a culture that values water enabled this arid country to become self-sufficient, but more importantly, have a sustainable water future. Today, the water infrastructure supports the eight million people living in Israel plus another four million by exporting over 46,000 acre-feet to the West Bank, and almost 8,000 acre-feet to Gaza. In addition, around 45,000 acre-feet is transferred to the Kingdom of Jordan.

Although it was very difficult to track total consumption with total demand from various conflicting sources and confirm that Israel has a sustainable water future, there is no question that the country is addressing the issue. The five desalination facilities produce 587 million cubic meters (475,000 acre-feet) on an annual basis, added to the annual mean average of freshwater from rainfall and other sources of 1,202 million cubic feet (975,00 acre-feet) potable drinking water should not be an issue for the rest of the century. Also with 86% of sewage treated and delivered to farmers for irrigation and the desalination of the brackish groundwater further supplementing irrigation, agriculture, currently using 55% of Israel's water should be able to handle most droughts and climate change.

Interestingly, Israel determined there is a downside to conservation. Using less water means there is less waste water available for treatment. Flow restrictors on all faucets, dual-flush toilets, short showers, reduced lawns and drip irrigation for shrubs and plants are all part of the water-efficient culture existing in Israel. All of this reduces the amount of water flowing into the waste treatment facilities. This reduction in sewage occurred even though the population increased. However, Siegel exposed a silver-lining in this situation that once again reinforces the importance of conservation.

With Israel's raw sewage being the least diluted, most dense, sewage found anywhere in the developed world, Israel's wastewater facilities operate at high rates of efficiency, not needing to treat excess water as is the case with the ordinarily highly diluted sewage usually found in other countries' sewage and most especially in the U.S.[11]

Another factor that must be considered is the smaller geographic size and population of this nation-state, which makes an interconnected system easier to implement, construct, manage and administer. Israel's 8019 square miles is just over one-third the geographic area of the Central Valley in California and is home to one-fifth of the thirty-nine million living in the state.

Regrettably, none of these conditions that allowed Israel to succeed exist to any great extent in the Colorado River Basin or California. Many people living in the western United States still believe that water is abundant except during droughts that will be short in duration. A culture that respects and understands the hydrological realities of the Southwest and California is not an ingrained value. During dry periods, everyone tightens their belts with city dwellers pointing fingers at almond growers or ranchers for using too much water and almond growers and farmers resenting the lush green lawns in Beverly Hills, Scottsdale and Denver. Very few of them acknowledge that under the Law of the River, prior appropriation and other regulatory statutes have over appropriated the available water and as population expands or during droughts, there is not enough to go around. 'Something's Gotta Give.'

Is such a system possible in the Colorado River Basin and California? Israel was founded in 1948 as a Jewish State that makes identification and support of the common good much more acceptable than the conditions existing in the western U.S. where a fierce independent spirit prevails. Taking the politics out of water enabled the country to address the issue of scarcity on a timely basis before a full blown crisis erupted. As Israel's

Water Authority was not shackled with ever-changing political whims, a viable water plan for the future resulted. This centralized decision-making process regarding water yielded a comprehensive and integrated plan.

Compare this to the Band-Aid approach prevalent in the Colorado River Bain and California that developed over the past one hundred and fifty years. Unfortunately, with all the complicated layers and often conflicting federal and state laws, judicial decisions and the rest of the Law of the River, removing politics may be an insurmountable hurdle in the West.

Also, the basic underpinnings of our nation rewards fierce individualism and protects private property, leading to the Tragedy of the Commons. Thus, any focus on the common good becomes very difficult. Our factions, varied political interests and numerous governmental agencies make it much more difficult to depoliticize water decisions.

The geographic size and population distinctions only further complicate the ability to take the politics out of water.

> *In a vast and heavily populated state like California, Israel's integrated and top-down approach to water management could be impossible to adopt.*[12]

The de-politicization of water and an integrated plan for the entire basin appears highly unlikely in the near future. This is quite unfortunate as ultimately this may have to happen. Hopefully a real crisis will not occur before reality sets in; but, we should not throw up our hands and claim defeat quite yet.

There are definitely things we can learn from this small nation-state. The first lesson is to plan ahead. Unfortunately, in the case of the Colorado River Basin and California that message is a bit late. However, it only makes it more important that future planning be done posthaste. Another key message is the importance of a water ethic that values water. Given our nation's heritage this will be difficult to attain, but is necessary. A third concept that stems from a new valuation of water is an emphasis on maximizing current sources and fostering innovation that focuses on water efficiencies. Another notion to take away from Israel's experience is the accurate and realistic pricing of water. This rate structure should not only include the cost of delivering the water today, but also include the ability to pay for any future infrastructure needs as well as ongoing maintenance. A final thought that demonstrated success was separating water used for urban purposes (desalination and fresh water) and that used for agricultural (recycled and brackish water). It not only encouraged innovation, it minimized the urban/rural conflict that continues to escalate in the Southwest and West.

Singapore[13]

When you think of Singapore, what comes to mind? I think of a very clean bustling economic city where no one thinks of littering and a very humid climate. Insufficient water never enters my mind. However, this 750 square mile country with a population of five million imports half of its water from Malaysia under an agreement that only lasts until 2061.

Planning ahead, the Singaporean government built two desalination plants with a plan to build more in the future that will provide up to 25% of their water needs. In addition, a reuse program was established called NEWater that as of 2015 produced 30% of the country's water requirements. Plans to triple this output over the next forty years are currently on the drawing board. Although the water quality produced by NEWater far exceeds all standards for human consumption, the water produced is currently used for industries requiring even higher purity. The Yuck Factor strikes again! However, during dry periods NEWater is added to the reservoirs, blended with raw water, retreated and then delivered as tap water. Singaporeans are slowly being converted to the benefits of reuse. As this aversion is eliminated, the main issue the water authority faces in the future is a technological problem involving the high-energy requirements of desalination and treating wastewater.

In addition to desalination and reuse the Singapore Water Authority, PUB, also constructed a separate system to collect rainwater and run-off through a comprehensive network of drains, canals, collection ponds and reservoirs. Singapore is one of the few countries in the world that harvests urban water on a large-scale to add to its water supply.

Like Israel, this tiny country leads the way in looking to the future and planning ahead. The utilization of reuse and recapture to such a large extent clearly shows an understanding that the future does not rely on looking for new sources of water. Given the country's forward planning, Singaporeans have the time to get over the yuck factor before they have no choice.

Compare this to how reuse is handled in the Front Range in Colorado. As mentioned previously, Summit County provides a good portion of water consumed by Denver. The Blue River empties into Lake Dillon at an elevation of around 9,600 feet and then is drawn through the Continental Divide via Roberts Tunnel. A good portion of the water that feeds Lake Dillon comes from the sewers of Breckenridge, which is treated prior to entering the reservoir. I would hazard a guess that a good portion of the people turning on the tap in Denver have no idea how many and what bodily functions the water they consume has experienced. This is just another example of taking water for granted.

Chile[14]

Just as in the Colorado River Basin, Chile sees wide fluctuations in precipitation on a seasonal and annual basis. This South American country is over twice as large as California and also lays claim to the driest region on earth in the Atacama Desert.

After the Allende government was overthrown by the military in 1973, a group of Chilean economists, trained at the University of Chicago and referred to as the "Chicago Boys," began a transformation of Chile's economic system. By implementing free market policies and procedures, such as privatization and widespread deregulation the country began to thrive. In 1981, using theories espoused by the Chicago Boys, a new water code, called the Chile model was adopted. Based on a free market system, the goal of this model was to encourage investment in agricultural infrastructure, promote more efficient use of water and transfer the "saved" water to higher economic uses.

> *Based on a free market and deregulation, the new code [...] strengthened private property rights, increased private autonomy in water use, and favoured free markets in water rights to a degree that was unprecedented both in Chile and in other countries. The new Water Code separated water rights from land ownership, for the first time in Chilean history, and declared them to be freely tradable: they can be bought, sold, mortgaged, inherited, and transferred like any other real estate.*[15]

Once the government granted a water right it became private property and was protected under the Chilean Constitution. These rights were also fully marketable like any commodity. Through government incentives and private trading of water rights, more productive and efficient use of water was envisioned. Operating for over thirty years, the Chilean water system is a shining star in the free-market method for water law and management.

In keeping with deregulation advocated by the Chicago Boys, Chilean authorities minimized governmental regulation and oversight as much as possible. The Dirección General de Aguas (DGA), the agency that issued water rights retained very little regulatory authority. It had no power to settle conflicts or monitor usage. As a result, once a right was granted, the water could be used for any purpose. Unlike the western United States, beneficial use did not matter.[16] Thus, the owner of a water right could change how water was used or sell the rights to an individual for a totally different use, without gaining approval or notifying any governmental agency. Similarly, if the owner of a right chose not to use or sell the water allocated, there was no penalty or consequence, such as "use it or lose it." Unfortunately, this led to increased speculation and hoarding.[17]

Additionally, due to the lack of any governing authority market price information was not readily available, leading to an informal and segmented market where it was extremely challenging to match buyers and sellers. The laissez-faire approach to an open market for water also resulted in vague or incomplete definitions of protected property rights. This thin market that lacked transparency is not dissimilar to what exists in the limited water markets in the United States.[18] With no centralized market, the number of transactions were lower than expected and trading remained local, resulting in wide price variations.[19]

While the Chilean adoption of a free-market for water produced positive economic benefits it also had its failures. Clearly, this water management system encouraged private investment in both agricultural and non-agricultural water use given the guarantee of private property. It also reallocated water in certain areas during scarcity that fostered efficiencies. Most importantly, this model of operation permitted Chile to compete quite well in the international markets for high-quality and high value agricultural products.

However, some negative aspects such as hoarding, speculation and social inequity surfaced, highlighting the need for governmental or regulatory oversight. By letting the individual water rights holders determine how, when and where water was used, the goal of increased efficiency in water use did not occur. Furthermore, peasants and poor farmers saw little, if any, of the economic benefits.[20] Currently, the value of economic efficiency overshadows social equity and environmental sustainability. Also, unintended consequences surfaced, which occur with the implementation of any new policy. The need for ongoing assessment and flexibility to deal with negative impacts was a glaring issue that required resolution. Thus, hoarding, speculation, social inequality and lack of conflict resolution were identified as problems. It required, political will and leadership to address these concerns.

After operating for twenty-seven years, the country implemented water reform to address some of the issues that lack of regulation exposed. Initially, the needed changes were vehemently resisted due to vested property rights; however, an urgent need to increase hydropower due to an electricity shortage in the country finally overcame the opposition to reform in 2008. Changes in the water code included developing an administrative record on water rights, improving management of groundwater, granting the DGA authority for future grants of water rights, instituting modest environmental oversight and establishing fees for non-use to minimize hoarding and speculation. While significant for the country, the reforms were modest and according to Carl Bauer, a research fellow at Resources for the Future and Professor at University of Arizona focusing on comparative water law, policy and economics in Latin America, the changes in the code still do not address the structural deficiencies of the Chilean model.[21]

Bauer summarized the water management model in Chile:

> In short, the Chilean experience shows that the legal and institutional arrangements that are associated with a narrow and free-market approach to water economics are not compatible with the arrangements required for integrated and sustainable water resources management over time.[22]

Even with the drawbacks, Chile's Water Code has worked and is lauded by the World Bank as an example for other water starved regions. The success of the model is seen with the increase in exports of processed fruits and vegetables totaling $32,000,000 in 1981 when the water code was enacted to $491,000,000 in 2001.[23] However, it is what did not work and why that we need to learn from Chile's experiences. The unintended consequences, such as hoarding and speculation, due to the well-intended deregulation and emphasis on personal property provide invaluable insights especially when implementing a new system. Fortunately, with the implementation of appropriate regulation and the necessary oversight, these problems are solvable.

When evaluating the Chilean model, the lack of regulation highlights a key issue that also confronts the Colorado River Basin and California, which is the absence of an integrated water management system. Assuming water resources remain static in this arid and semi-arid region, the expansion of urban populations and increases in agricultural and industrial production naturally result in water shortages. When extended droughts and the impact of climate change are considered, future water problems only increase and magnify. Local and regional water management governance cannot and will not effectively solve the conflicts and issues that the future holds. Thus, Chile's experience emphasizes the necessity of an overall, integrated system that includes all interested parties in addition to the hydrological realities. The water managers throughout the western United States that depend on the same water sources, like the Colorado River, should heed this lesson well.

Australia[24]

The country "down-under" developed a new method for allocating water that is connected to a water trading system. This approach appears to deal quite effectively with extended drought conditions that are prevalent in Australia. I must apologize up front for the long-winded description; however, as I learned the hard way, not understanding the entire workings of the system is analogous to having the ingredients to making crème brûlée but not knowing how many eggs or how much cream to use.

Australia, like the Colorado River Basin, has both annual and seasonal variability in precipitation. It is also the driest inhabited continent on earth. To enable development, the country followed the same pattern established by the USBR in the western U.S., building large dams and storage facilities during the twentieth century. In addition, the federal government provided massive subsidies for agriculture, just as the United States continues to do. Beginning in the early 1970s, it was recognized the status quo was not sustainable. After a string of extended droughts, major water reform started in the Murray-Darling Basin.

As a bit of background, this basin is located in southeast Australia and includes most of New South Wales. It covers almost 410,000 square miles, two-thirds larger than the Colorado River Basin. The water in the basin services over two million people plus an additional one million residents in Adelaide, not located in the Basin. This region has been home to the Aboriginal people of the country for over 50,000 years with thirty-four of the nations still living on their traditional lands. Agricultural is the second largest employer in the region and contributes 40% of the country's gross agricultural production and one-third of the country's food supply.[25]

This catchment basin of both the Murray and Darling rivers consists of 23 major river valleys and like the Colorado River reflects wide fluctuations in its flow. The average annual flow is around 26.6 million acre-feet (compared to 15 million acre-feet for the Colorado River) and has ranged from a high of 94.8 million acre-feet in 1956 to a low of 5.5 million acre-feet in 2006.[26] These massive swings in river flow in such an arid environment fueled by ongoing droughts stimulated the Murray-Darling Basin to adopt a revolutionary approach to allocating water. At the same time the basin shifted to a market-based trading system in the 1980s.

Just as in the United States, Australia initially began issuing licenses to allocate water when there was excess capacity. The methods adopted eventually led to over allocation of most of each country's rivers, a theme echoed throughout this book. Regrettably, surplus is not part of the hydrological reality in either the Southwest or Keith Urban or Russell

Crowe's homeland. Professor Mike Young, who holds a Research Chair in Water and Environmental Policy at the University of Adelaide maintains that with the development that occurred over the past century, demand is close to exceeding supply. He further indicates the licensure program of issuing water rights in Australia similar to the seniority system of prior appropriation used in the United States, was determined no longer an optimal way of allocating water.

> *Almost all water entitlement regimes that one can find around the world evolved during periods of relative water abundance and where rapid changes in technology were not common.*
>
> *When viewed from this perspective, in many cases, it will be more efficient to replace the existing abstraction management regime with one that is designed specifically to enable the cost effective management of the many challenges that increasing water scarcity brings to a region.[27]*

To address this, Australia eliminated their century-old allocation system and implemented water sharing.

The basic structure of Australia's water sharing system in relatively simply. It divides water into three tiers. Imagine an inverse of Maslow's Hierarchy of Needs with the most basic layer being water for the environment. This tier keeps the water source healthy. The second tier, the "maintenance layer," is for critical human requirements that includes drinking water, sanitary needs and essential city needs for hospitals, schools, etc. Once the amount allocated in the basic and maintenance layers is determined, the "sharing layer," which is around 80% of the total water available and consists mainly of agricultural and industrial demand is divided into marketable instruments. Figure 15 outlines Australia's water sharing.

FIGURE 15 – Australia's Water Sharing Concept

Sharing Layer
For irrigation, industrial and non-essential domestic needs

Maintenance Layer
For critical human needs

Basic Layer
For environment

Water sharing is based on four main premises. The first involves ascertaining the current hydrological realities, in other words, how much water exists in the system at a specific point in time. In Australia, this is determined every two weeks. This dramatically differs from requiring the Upper Colorado River to deliver 8.23 million acre-feet each year or allowing the Imperial Valley farmers to withdraw 3.3 million acre-feet to irrigate their fields based on an estimation of the stream flow during a very wet period almost a century ago. It also captures, seasonal and annual variations. By starting with the current supply of water over allocation is minimized.

Young and the late Jim McColl, Research Fellow for the Commonwealth Scientific and Industrial Research Organization (CSIRO), strongly advocated water sharing for decades and maintained that starting with the current hydrological realities was critical. It was necessary to start with the amount of water currently available to achieve a "robust system" that was flexible and had "an ability to recover gracefully from the whole range of exceptional inputs and situations in a given environment."[28]

The second foundational tenet defines and determines what the absolute essential water needs of the entire Basin total. The first fundamental requirement is a healthy watershed. It is recognized that any sustainable water management system mandates a strong and vigorous river. The second essential condition is the identification of critical human needs. This includes potable drinking water, sanitary requirements, hydroelectric power needs and essential city needs for hospitals, schools, etc. According to Young, the watershed health and critical human needs require around 20% of the average annual available water.

To determine how much water to set aside for the first two tiers requires consensus, which makes this the most difficult part of the decision making process due to politics, history and regional or individual desires. However, once established, emotions and politics are removed and economics becomes the driving value for the majority of the water that is in the third tier. Using economics as a driving value creates incentives for everyone to become more efficient and carefully evaluate how they use water. In other words, the Intel Chip versus alfalfa or broccoli versus rice or alfalfa issues are forced.

A third principle that guides this innovative allocation system involves an open and transparent market for water in the sharing tier. The rationale for this mirrors Chile adopting a system for trading water or promoting the transfer of water during shortages to higher economic uses and allowing the system to become more efficient.

The final premise is the basic economic concept of "cap and trade." In other words, determining the total amount available to be included in the sharing tier, and thus available for trading. This amount is capped or limited to the current hydrological realities less the amount earmarked for the Basic and Maintenance tiers. By capping the amount to be traded in an open market based on the water existing at that time, over allocation is minimized and the price of water reflects the actual conditions existing at that time.

Water sharing in Australia mandates the inclusion of all interested stakeholders in determining the amount allocated to the environment, human needs and the sharing tiers. Once a water sharing plan is developed, it lasts for 10 to 15 years allowing for some degree of certainty of the minimum amount of water one expects to receive. An element such as this is necessary to justify capital expenditures to transition to more efficient sytstems.[29]

Just like the stock market, the structure of the sharing tier evolved over time and required precise definitions and regulations for each of the numerous newly configured marketable securities. To simplify what is now a relatively sophisticated market, there are two basic tradable instruments. The first is entitlements that the National Water Commission defines as:

> *A water access entitlement is a perpetual or ongoing entitlement to exclusive access to a share of water from a specified consumptive pool.*[30]

Thus, an entitlement becomes a permanent access to an amount of water from an identified body of water; however, the total amount accessible to the entitlement holder is only available when the cap is set at 100%. For example, the owner of an entitlement for five acre-feet receives only four acre-feet if the cap is set at 80%.

Entitlements are further divided into two tranches; high and general reliability.[31] A high reliability entitlement is more expensive but provides more certainty whereas a general reliability entitlement costs less but does not guarantee water delivery during droughts. Think of the general reliability entitlement having a lower cap. In other words, the price one pays for an entitlement determines the level of insurance one desires for obtaining water in the event of a shortage. Entitlement trading is tied to longer term and more permanent water requirements. For example, the wine industry or citrus farmers water requirements remain relatively fixed each year and do not vary. These sectors prefer high-reliability entitlements as losing a tree or a vineyard is more of an economic disaster than a farmer who plants a seasonal crop such as wheat or rice.

With time, those overseeing the water management of the Basin saw usage actually increase by 8%, having a major negative impact on wetlands as well as other environmental conditions.[32] As the purpose of water-sharing was to become more efficient and not increase water usage, further water reform was enacted in 2009, where entitlements were "unbundled" and new forms of tradable shares were introduced. The most notable was water allocations, which the National Water Commission defines as:

> *A water allocation is a specific volume of water allocated to water access entitlements in a given season and/or given accounting period.[33]*

These market shares are temporary and helped water users respond to seasonal conditions as well as drought. During scarcity, those with flexible water demands are able to sell to those with inflexible needs. By doing this, it is now possible for the individual users of water to manage scarcity on an immediate basis while at the same time taking the government out of the equation.

I must admit it took me a lot of time, effort and the patient guidance of Professor Young to sort through this complex structure. Even my attempt to simplify this probably needs some real-life examples. For instance, 100% of the rice grown in Australia is produced in the Murray-Darling Basin.[34] This crop is a low-income producing, or a low-value crop that is quite water intensive. In past droughts, rice producers found they could switch to another crop requiring less water, reduce the land under production, or delay plantings. In essence, water demand for rice farmers is flexible, or in economic terms, elastic.

With the water trading system in place, rice irrigators in Australia now have an additional option. They can sell their entitlements or allocations to irrigators whose demand is more inelastic or inflexible. In most cases, farmers producing low–value crops, such as rice, found more positive economic benefits from selling their entitlements or allocations than actually planting and producing their crops.[35] In fact, during extended droughts, many rice farmers find that water trades are their only source of income.[36]

On the other hand, dairy farmers find the temporary allocation market quite beneficial in managing their businesses. In this agricultural sector, a major expense is providing food for the herds. In the past, dairy farmers had two options, irrigate lands for grazing or purchase fodder such as hay or alfalfa. With water sharing/trading, the price of water allocations increases during droughts. This is just basic economics. Under this scenario, dairy farmers sell their temporary access to water using the proceeds to purchase fodder. They find this is more lucrative and increases their bottom line. Alternatively, these farmers purchase allocation shares when water is more readily available and prices decline as they find purchasing fodder is more expensive.[37]

Finally, those crops that were less flexible in their water requirements, such as grapes, almonds, fruits and citrus products, found water trading quite beneficial. Farmers of these high-value crops were willing to pay higher prices for high-reliability entitlements to guarantee they had water. The water allocations were also quite valuable to these farmers during extended droughts as they were able to buy water on a temporary basis to supplement their entitlements when the cap dropped below 100%.[38] Thus, the rice farmers could sell their allocations at a profit to those producing higher-value crops that demanded a more constant amount and could afford the higher price of water. The National Water Commission of Australia concluded that:

> *Without water trading, it is likely that many long-lived horticultural assets would have been lost, at great cost to individuals and communities.*[39]

Even though quite intrigued by the system, I felt the downside was the smaller farmer or businessman could not afford the "high security" water and during a shortage would find their general liability entitlements severely curtailed. The disadvantages small farmers faced initially, resulted in further reform that "unbundled" the entitlements and the development of allocation shares. When I asked Mike Young about whether those without deep pockets were still placed at a disadvantage, he indicated:

> *In a well-designed system this is not the case. In fact, those that are poorer often gain immensely via increased opportunity and wealth. For many, it meant escape from a poverty gap.*[40]

Although this bears further examination, Young's logic is supported by basic economics.

> *To generate higher net incomes during the drought, individual rice irrigators typically sold their limited water allocations and further reduced or ceased annual production. Returns from water sales were often far greater than those that could be received from producing rice, and they were much less risky.*[41]

More than likely, a small farmer runs a break-even operation and holds either a general liability entitlement or a water allocation. In an extended drought, the value of any type of tradable water instrument should increase in price where the farmer makes more money by selling the general entitlement or the allocation than if he planted his seasonal crop.

Under this new water regime, the Australians learned it is important to include evaporation when determining the amount of water available. This is glaringly absent in the Colorado River Compact. Returning to the water cycle learned in elementary school, as precipitation declines, the inflow of water into the supply is logically reduced. At the same time, increased temperature normally associated with either drought or climate change increases evaporation rates where even less water is available. In fact, Young and McColl found that in the Murray-Darling Basin a 10% reduction of precipitation resulted in a 30% decline in streamflow.[42]

Another element the Australian government tackled was subsidies. It was recognized that to drastically change a well-ensconced water management system, carrots were needed to assist in the transition. In addition to eliminating the vast subsidies for water itself, it minimized the complicating factors of subsidies for certain crops. The government also supported the new system by instituting a $5.8 billion program to:

> *Improve the efficiency and productivity of rural water use and management, to deliver substantial and lasting water returns to the environment and to help secure a long-term sustainable future for irrigated agriculture.*[43]

Thus, instead of providing subsidies to grow cotton or alfalfa the government supported the shift to more efficient irrigation systems and practices.

The United States really needs to carefully examine the consequences of subsidies. While the massive subsidies provided for water distribution and storage enabled the development of the West it also established vested interests that now resist any change to the allocation of water or its cost. The historic as well as current policies and practices regarding subsidies contributed to American's belief that water is free and placed obstacles for more efficient use of water. By minimizing and restructuring both direct or indirect subsidies a more thorough understanding of the true hydrological realities that exist in the West may eradicate our mistaken belief in water's abundance.

Australia appears to have developed a water strategy that addresses their ever present droughts and potentially any future impacts of climate change. In 2009, at the height of a decade long drought, farmers received only one-third of their normal allocations, rice crops failed, and wild fires killed 210 people. Yet with the water sharing and trading system in place agricultural production remained at 70% of the norm.[44]

This approach had several crucial benefits that are well worth noting. To begin, demand is managed prior to any shortage or crisis. Planning ahead is a key lesson to be learned from each of the countries discussed. The Colorado Water Plan that addresses an individual state's future water gap and the Guidelines that reduces appropriations to Nevada and Arizona if water levels at Lake Mead fall below a specified level are certainly steps in the right direction. However, both are only piecemeal approaches that do not deal with all of the challenges that confront the entire Colorado River Basin and California.

Another positive feature of this water management system is it does not play favorites or place one water user over another. No one shareholder or group of shareholders receive any preferential or priority treatment; cuts are across the board and equally assessed based on the type of entitlement or allocation. The cap determines the percentage to be received by each entitlement or allocation. Thus, everyone shares in the pain of drought or reduced water availability. More efficient use of water results. Also, those having an inelastic demand have the option to pay increased prices for available allocation shares.

Compare this to the allocation of water under prior appropriation that over the past several years found many California farmers with junior priority dates receiving little or no water while those holding more senior water rights continuing to flood their fields. Remember as a child crying how "unfair" it was that Johnny got two pieces of cake while you had only one? My husband always told our children that "a fair is a picnic in the park where they serve lemonade" so there was no such thing as "unfair." I have to cry "unfair" on behalf of the junior water rights holders. Why should someone hold a senior position just because a great grandfather braved the elements in the late 1800s or someone with surplus funds purchased someone else's great grandfather's water right? It is unfair!

Another beauty of the Australian water management system is the transparency and ease of transfer of water entitlements and allocations. With the nationwide market system, buyers and sellers easily find their needs met in less than a week. As a result, farmers make informed business decisions that reflects a realistic price of water based on current conditions and individual needs. The system to transfer water rights in the United States is much more expensive and very time-consuming. If an urban water authority wishes to purchase the water right of a farmer located in the same area, it takes months or years to obtain the regulatory permits with water lawyers making a pretty penny. This definitely increases the cost to the buyer and reduces the profit to the seller.

Australia also avoids many problems that Chile experienced due to lack of regulation by precisely defining the water rights to be traded, developing an open and transparent market and providing subsidies that foster efficiency and support instead of hindering the new water management system.

A very important aspect of Australia's water management system is the new structure compelled a revision of how water was valued, recognizing demand must be more prudently assessed to foster a more efficient use of the natural resource. By providing basic necessities at a low cost and instituting a structure that forced each user to determine what they were willing to pay for water, based on economic feasibility, water conservation was forced at all levels. Instead of a priority system developed over a hundred years ago, the current water availability and a sound business determination of what one was willing to pay for the natural resource forced efficiency into a system experiencing shortages.

Another key lesson to be learned from the water sharing/trading system mirrors Israel's taking politics and special interests out of the decision making process. The Australia water management system leaves the decision to grow cotton, rice or almonds in the hands of the individual farmers. With a more realistic price of water, they are able to make their own business decisions or decide whether to plant at all. Ultimately, the current hydrological realities determine the price and the system removes the government or some water authority deciding who receives water in a shortage. The market decides. Such a structure requires a drastic revision in the water ethic, water laws and the acceptance that water is not always available for all purposes.

Another point that is worth consideration is the separation of different competing demands. Curiously, both Israel and Australia water management systems separated agriculture and urban demand, to some degree. The logic behind this makes a great deal of sense with agriculture the largest user of water.

Both countries developed different models in separating demands. In Israel's case, agriculture and urban use was separated by the type of water used, thus removing ongoing conflict between the competing demands. In Australia's situation the maintenance tier included urban demand while the sharing tier was comprised of agricultural, industrial uses and non-essential domestic uses. Assuming that strict water restrictions are in place for urban use that ensures water is not wasted on watering lawns, etc., this structure removes the urban/rural conflict—one that always surfaces in the United States during any drought or in discussions regarding water's future. The ability to remove any conflicts aids in depoliticizing water.

The final and perhaps most significant message that the Australian water sharing/trading system reveals is the importance of an integrated and interconnected system that encompasses all direct or indirect aspects of water management. Water sharing originally began within various regions of the Murray-Darling Basin that saw disparate systems developing. Each had different regulations and types of water rights. Reduced efficiencies in trading resulted between different localities within the Basin. In 1992, the Murray-Darling Basin Agreement established an integrated system for the entire Basin. By 2004, an integrated water system was adopted for the entire country.[45]

Can the systems in Chile, Israel, Singapore and Australia Work Here?

Wouldn't it be nice if we could clone some of these systems or water codes and magically eliminate the water issues that the western United States faces today? Unfortunately, the waving of a magic wand or saying "Bibbidi-Bobbidi-Boo" ten times will not turn our pumpkin into a carriage. However, each of these systems provide lessons that anyone living or working in the Colorado River Basin or California should seriously ponder.

Israel's reliance on desalination and reuse is technology already being used throughout the West, albeit on a much reduced basis. The Carlsbad Plant in San Diego, a desalination plant in Yuma, Arizona that treats water sent to Mexico, and the retrofitting of the Santa Barbara plant are prime examples of the first technology. Unfortunately, environmental concerns and high capital costs dissuade many water authorities from choosing this alternative. This resistance to desalinate based on capital costs stems from the traditional approach of looking to technology to provide water from new sources, which is definitely less expensive.

Recycling, reuse or reclamation of waste water is definitely an option to be considered. California currently recycles 8% of its wastewater. This will increasingly be a factor in the Golden State. Las Vegas uses this technology quite effectively to obtain return flow credits permitting the city to withdraw more than its Compact allocation. In the metropolitan areas within the Colorado River Basin, this technology is gaining increased attention. However, due to the yuck factor, it is mainly gray water that is finding more acceptance. Unfortunately, the double plumbing of existing structures make this cost prohibitive.

Israel dealt with the yuck factor by directing recycled wastewater to irrigation. In the Colorado River Basin, except for Denver and Las Vegas, most larger metropolitan areas that produce more sewage are located downstream from agricultural regions. California, on the other hand, has distinct possibilities in applying this concept. Sewage from the San Francisco Bay area could be treated and sent through the Central Valley and California State Water projects to the Central Valley infrastructure. This would increase water availability in an area that is depleting groundwater at an alarming rate and experienced drastic cutbacks in water during the recent drought.

Another note on the implementation of the water management model developed in Israel that emphasized desalination and reuse relates to geographic size. As Yoram Koren, professor of chemical and biomolecular engineering at UCLA pointed out size does determine the reality of refitting the infrastructure in California.

> *Israel has about 8 million citizens and is roughly 8,000 square miles in size, dwarfed by California's nearly 39 million residents and 163,600 square miles. Israel's ability to pipe water throughout nearly the entirety of its populated territory can't be duplicated in California.*[46]

While this statement holds water if one is looking at an interconnected and integrated system, reuse and desalination certainly should be considered on a regional or local basis when managing available water.

Chile's and Australia's open-market system is a concept that needs no explanation in the United States. Whether buying shares in the stock market, a pair of shoes at Nordstrom's or a condo in Los Angeles or Denver, buyer and seller must agree on a price for ownership to transfer hands. As Chile has discovered, more governmental oversight and regulation is necessary. On the other hand, Australia's water trading has developed into a fairly sophisticated market which could easily be adopted in the United States.

The obstacles to implementing such a system in the West is the manner in which water is allocated. The administrative quagmire of prior appropriation, the "use it or lose it" aspect of water rights, the uncertain value of junior priority dates, the vested interests of senior priorities and special interest groups pose overwhelming obstacles.

Perhaps the most difficult impediment is how large water right holders with senior priority dates should be compensated in water sharing as they lose not only their seniority but also potentially suffer economic losses in their property values and livelihood. This issue is currently being addressed in a potential water sharing pilot project in Nevada's Humboldt Basin and the Diamond Valley developed by Young for the Duke University's Nicholas Institute for Environmental Policy Solutions.[47] It will be very interesting to see how this will be addressed. Given the fallout of the devastating five-year drought in California, Professor Young also visited various agricultural communities in the state in May of 2016 to discuss the implementation of water sharing and trading pilot programs.

Furthermore, the idea of adopting a water sharing plan for the entire Colorado River Basin and consequently upsetting the long held traditions, laws and power base that has regulated and allocated water throughout the West for over a century appears completely unattainable. The most obvious problem is getting the various states to start looking at the entire watershed, instead of just their own respective needs. This highlights, once again, how politics, special and vested interests complicate changes to water management in the West. Historically, collaboration has not been a predominate element in making water decisions; however, since her retirement Patricia Mulroy, the "water witch," espouses this. The Colorado Water Plan also attempts to adopt this approach within the state; however, local and regional priorities still prevail. Mike Young admits an integrated plan is optimal; however, adds that initially Australia began the water sharing and trading in different regions of the Murray-Darling Basin that expanded to encompass the entire basin and then finally the entire country.[48]

Another impediment to a complete water-trading system similar to that in Australia is the sharing level, based on economic values, could favor those having surplus monetary resources and place smaller farmers at a distinct disadvantage. Chile has experienced this income inequality due to the lack of government oversight. This indeed presents an ethical dilemma that pits the value of equality, participation, empowerment and inclusiveness against stewardship and the common good to achieve economic efficiency. I am sure a resolution to this could be achieved that could possibly include transferring crop subsidies for smaller farmers that are not growing water intensive crops or irrigation efficiency support to reduce the amount of water needed. Additionally, an intermediate sharing level for qualifying smaller farmers or businesses could be established. Mike Young indicated that as water trading has increased, the smaller farmers have found they actually made more money during shortages.[49] This was also confirmed by the National Water Commission in a report in 2010.[50]

And then there is the problem that other areas outside the control of water management make it difficult, if not impossible to change from the status quo. This includes areas such as the cotton or alfalfa subsidies; the politicians and lobbyists that ensure this aid continues to be appropriated; the political imbalance in Congress among the states that depend on the Colorado River; and all the local, regional, and intrastate conflicts. Chances of de-politicizing water in the western United States seem highly unlikely. This is indeed unfortunate as both Israel and Australia's experiences stress the importance of this. Even with this very daunting obstacle, I am hopeful we will intelligently and equitably join forces and develop a system that will ensure a sustainable water future for generations.

What does this all mean to the future of the Colorado River Basin and California? Yes, there are substantial impediments if any of these models were to be implemented, but crying "uncle" is counterproductive. The conditions prehistoric people and early settlers encountered were no less daunting and look what they accomplished. It is not part of the American psyche to throw up our hands and admit defeat without pursuing all options. Let's just hope that the American ingenuity that has brought us this far will not allow vested interests, politics, special interest groups and a mistaken view of water's abundance delay considering any options.

Chapter 11

"Something's Gotta Give"
– A New Water Ethic

WHEW! THAT IS A LOT of information to absorb, but if one is to intelligently plan for the future, understanding the past, knowing how we arrived at the present, comprehending the overlapping and conflicting Law of the River, appreciating Mother Nature's influences and grasping some water basics are all necessary. Each of the states that are party to the Colorado River Compact are facing the hydrological realities of the future. Although not discussed, Wyoming is currently focused on using its full Compact allocation. Utah, the driest state in the nation, is struggling with understanding its future demand and continues pursuing a decade long $2 billion project to pump 86,000 acre-feet from Lake Mead to St. George.[2] New Mexico currently receiving 11.25% of the Upper Basin allocation is facing its own hydrological realities. It is also running out of water.[3] The four remaining Colorado River Compact states that consume the majority of the Colorado River have major challenges in their future with respect to water. Thus, it is hard to dispute that those living, working and playing in the West have some extremely difficult decisions to make. Of course, the first question that must be addressed is what is the likelihood that Famiglietti's disaster movie will actually be part of the evening news? If there is even a slight chance that it could be a possibility, action is required now. We cannot continue to be ostriches with our heads in the sand.

California has finally been forced to face reality with the severe drought that continues to wreak havoc throughout the southern part of the state. Governor Brown's Executive Order that reduces residential water use and limits new commercial or residential development to just 25% turf in landscaped areas, addresses important issues.[4] It goes without saying this is something that should have been implemented years ago. More importantly, what about the state's future? Clearly, a comprehensive evaluation of current water demand utilizing hydrological realities, including groundwater is critical. In fact, with the exception of groundwater legislation that will not see any results for 20 years, all other legislation, Executive Orders, etc. deal with the current drought only. Although many of the larger metropolitan areas are addressing problems by the construction of desalination and recycling facilities, many are not. As a state, California continues to be mired in the past. What will happen if El Niño lasts for several years and the water levels of the storage facilities rise substantially? Will the Executive Order be rescinded? Will the green lawns and rose gardens once again consume millions of gallons of water?

Colorado is in a more enviable position and is currently planning through 2050, which is very commendable. But as the Plan mainly focuses on finding new supply to meet the deficits projected to occur in 35 years, what happens in 2055? Fortunately, the state has still not utilized its full allocation under the Compact, at least with most of the annual historical flows. Remember, 51.75% of the Upper Basin allocation was apportioned to the state depended on the total annual flow of the river, which has been as low as 5 million acre-feet and as high as 22 million acre-feet. With projections that the Centennial State will double its current population by 2050 to nine million people, how would the state cope if the total flow of the river was only 5 million acre-feet for several years?

Then, there is Arizona that claims they are in a strong position given their planning, even though the farmers may not receive CAP water if the drought continues. But the farmers do not have to worry if they were irrigating their land between 1975 and 1980; they could just start pumping groundwater again, increasing subsidence and fissures. This would, of course, just increase the rate in which groundwater is being depleted in the basin.

And of course, Las Vegas has its "third straw". Granted the pump that will makes this $800 billion project operational has not been installed yet, but, not to worry as Lake Mead only needs to fall another 75 feet before the pump will be required. Given the rate the water level has declined, Las Vegas has another five or six years. There is also climate change that will result in an uptick in demand due to increasing evaporation rates and maybe increase the gap further if precipitation declines. And, of course, the real elephant in the room is the fact that the Compact allocated more water than the Colorado delivered during the twentieth century and is expected to produce in the future. All of this, at the very least, will lead to more litigation or could start another "War Between the States," all occurring in the West.

As Fishman indicates in *The Big Thirst*, the conditions that exist today are all based on judgments.[5] And decisions were made when everyone thought water was eternally flowing and available and at substantial subsidized rates. As of 2015, things have changed and the California drought finally surfaced the limited availability of water in the West for most of the public. But, water managers have wrestled with these issues since the beginning of the twentieth century.

Fortunately, the water supply shortages that face the future of those living in the West is finally chipping away at the illusion of water's abundance; however, old habits die hard. Within a week of Governor Brown issuing mandatory restrictions in April of 2015, the *LA Times* reported that a resident in Beverly Hill was doing his best to conserve by turning off the water when he brushes his teeth and washes dishes.

However, "there's also his fountain and Jacuzzi and the lemon and orange trees to consider."[6] Even as California is in the worst drought in centuries, Reisner's fraud or the oasis in the desert continues.

Going forward it is clear that "something's gotta give". Short of all-embracing litigation that could take years and every state, farmer and city dweller hoarding, stealing, pumping and consuming anything they can lay their hands on, political leadership, gumption and sacrifice by everyone will be required. Knowing that this is in our future, perhaps it would be prudent for all the interested parties to come together and determine what should inform these decisions with the goal of developing a water plan for the entire Colorado River Basin.

In *This is Dinosaur* written to educate the public on the potential effects of the dam at Echo Park in Dinosaur National Monument, Wallace Stegner wrote:

> *We are the most dangerous species of life on the planet, and every other species, even the earth itself, has cause to fear our power to exterminate. But we are also the only species, which when it chooses to do so, will go to great effort to save what it might destroy. Which, I wonder, will we ultimately choose to be?*[7]

Back in the 1950s, questions like this changed the approach of conservation that throughout the early 20th century maintained that water running wild and free to the ocean was a waste. Water was there for man to develop and use to its fullest extent. After it was decided to eliminate the dam planned for Echo Park, the view of nature changed to one of preserving what we had and sustaining it for future generations. Thus, John Muir's view of nature emerged.

Another pioneer in how the earth's resources should be used was Aldo Leopold who promulgated a "land ethic", outlined in *The Sand*

County Almanac published after his death in 1948. Leopold described his ethic best.

> *It is the principle that a thing is right when it tends to preserve the integrity, stability, and beauty of the biotic community. It is wrong if it tends otherwise.*[8]

For Leopold, man was just a member of an interdependent environment that also included soils, water, plants and animals. In this biotic community, man was not in control, but an equal partner with other members, where all were respected. This did not mean that alterations or manipulation of the earth's resources could not occur, but decisions took into consideration everyone's right to exist, be it a plant, animal, human or bird. Leopold criticized man's lack of respect for nature when he stated:

> *Do we not already sing our love for and obligation to the land of the free and home of the brave. But just what and whom do we love? Certainly not the soil, which we are sending helter-skelter downriver. Certainly not the waters, which we assume have no function except to turn turbines, float barges, and carry off sewage.*[9]

Essentially, Leopold questioned the economic values used as the driving force in determining decisions made regarding the land and its resources. Instead, he felt the biotic community was more "valued" than economics.

The Endangered Species Act, Clean Water Act and other legislation of the 1970s inserted the impact to the environment before any infrastructure projects for water or any other type of development proceeded. This, in essence, incorporated Leopold's Land Ethic or in philosophical terms an ecologically based land ethic.

Regrettably, the West faces a future where demand will exceed supply and where there will be winners and losers in what could be a water grab that could escalate into the likes of Catherine Case and her hired guns in *Water Knife*. Unfortunately, this pattern sounds similar to what the Ancient Puebloans and Hohokam faced when their supply did not meet their needs.

Before such a crisis occurs it would behoove us to determine which values and ideals should inform decisions that guarantees a sustainable water future. To wait until a crisis, such as California currently faces would be irresponsible. It would be much more prudent to have a system based on ethics that guides these difficult decisions instead of special interest groups that have the economic where-with-all to dictate who will "lose". Without such a structure, who decides whether humans, farmers, fish, animals or plants will suffer?

For the past century, and for the most part even today, it is safe to say that most decisions regarding water were made with economics and development being the underlying value. This approach meant, using and adapting Leopold's words, "It is the principle that a thing is right when it tends to preserve the integrity, stability, and possibilities of growth of the economic community. It is wrong if it tends otherwise."

This water ethic in essence uses self-interest, individual rights and economic development as its foundational values. There is nothing wrong with these values as they helped form this country; and they worked fine when there was a surplus or excess capacity. The question one must now answer is when supply is less than demand, what is the best driving value or values?

This highlights that in our complex society that a system based on one element, such as the environment or the economy, will not suffice in the future.

What Values Do We Use?

Although numerous philosophical theories exist, such as John Stuart Mills' Utilitarianism, Immanuel Kant's Libertarian or Rights-based concepts or John Rawls' Egalitarian system, it is the underlying values that inform the decisions in each of these models that are critical. This goes beyond growing almonds or watering a lawn, but should be used in determining whether almonds or lawns are ethically correct. UNESCO has identified the following as possible principles that could or should be incorporated into any water ethic:

- **Human dignity:** Must respect all life, as without water there is no life;
- **Participation:** Must include all individuals in water planning, especially the disadvantaged;
- **Solidarity:** Must acknowledge both upstream and downstream interdependence within a watershed necessitating an integrated water management approach;
- **Human equality:** Must provide everyone with the basic necessities of life and on an equitable basis;
- **Common Good:** Must respect human potential and dignity as water is a basic right;
- **Stewardship:** Must protect this natural resource by promoting a sustainable and life-enabling ecosystem for future generations;
- **Transparency and universal access to information:** Must avoid control by any one or collection of groups;
- **Inclusiveness:** Must insure minority rights are addressed;
- **Empowerment:** Must allow all stakeholders to influence decisions, not just the more powerful or larger groups.[10]

This is a very admirable list of values that few could argue are ethical. However, the ideals that have been the driving beliefs forming the water ethic of the 20th century of economic development, self-interest and private property are conspicuously missing. Are we willing to give these important principles up? After all, wasn't the American Revolution fought defending these rights?

I do not pretend to know what this water ethic should look like; however, applying various values to some existing systems is an interesting exercise. As water demand increases and supplies continue to become stressed, how water is allocated will become increasingly contentious. Looking at the West's prior appropriation and Australia's water sharing provides interesting insights.

Applying Water Ethics to Prior Appropriation

Prior appropriation establishes a priority system of allocation including two premises, "beneficial use" and "use it or lose it". As water is allocated on a first come first serve basis, it certainly can't be considered fair, inclusive, participative or empowering except for those with senior priority dates. Likewise, as a farmer with a senior priority date continues to flood fields while those with junior water rights see their water allocations curtailed, the common good and stewardship are not supported.

The values inherent in prior appropriation are self-interest and private property. When initially developed, this allocation system also reinforced economic development. Today, many argue the "use it or lose it" aspect of prior appropriation does not support economic efficiencies and development during droughts.

Applying Water Ethics to Water Sharing

Although I am personally quite intrigued with the water sharing/trading system in Australia, I don't pretend to believe it is the panacea to all of our issues. It is thought-provoking to apply different values to this method of allocation. It is also interesting to see how different principles can be used on different aspects of a system that has clearly defined processes and procedures serving different purposes.

The allocation method under water sharing is based on the three tiers, basic, maintenance and sharing. For example, for the first tier, protection of the watershed and environment could reflect UNESCO's water values of stewardship, solidarity and common good. The second tier, the maintenance layer, could be guided by values such as human dignity, participation, human equality, common good and inclusiveness.

The final or the sharing tier, the largest amount of water, relies on economics as it's driving value as well as transparency. At first, I reacted negatively to economic returns being a driving value; however, as I played with other values, I realized the efficiency of the system. For example, using equality as the driving value for the sharing layer meant the largest amount of water, which Young estimated should be around 80% of the total would be divided amongst all the users, regardless of their need. Those users that did not need all the water could sell their surplus to a water consumer that required more of the resource and at the going market rate. This provided incentives for high security water users to evaluate how much water they needed for an acceptable return as well as what product they should be producing. Unfortunately, it does not foster the low security users becoming more efficient. A prime example of this is the rice farmer who continues to flood his fields as trees in a citrus orchard began dying due to lack of water.

However, with economic returns the driving value where water prices doubled, that same rice farmer may decide to sell the allocation to the citrus farmer, fallowing the fields until the drought is over. Or he may use the proceeds to install drip irrigation. As a result, more water would be available during droughts for others to share. This clearly is much more efficient for water usage as well as economic considerations.

What Should A New Water Ethic Look Like?

Developing a new water ethic for a sustainable water future will take better minds than mine. However, the following are some of the issues that must be addressed before any new ethic is possible.

- How do we best allocate water based on current and future hydrological realities?
- How do we include all interested parties?

- Should any plan remain state or locally driven or is an integrated approach needed?
- How are basic human needs met at a reasonable price?
- How do we protect past rights but ensure an efficient and sustainable future?
- How do we design a system that values water, that does not forget the common good and supports a sustainable future?
- How do we minimize the impact on "losers" in the various water conflicts?
- How do we best protect the health of the watershed?
- How do we counteract the unknown impact of climate change?
- How do we protect the common good if personal property rights continue as a driving value?

Chapter 12

"Whiskey is for drinking and water is for fighting." – The Future

OBVIOUSLY, IT IS HARD TO envision a future anywhere in the Colorado River Basin or California where water availability, water rights and water usage will not cause conflict. The statement attributed to Mark Twain in the late 1800s, resonates once again. Reports of a water truck being filled from a public water hydrant at least 12 times over the past several years and delivered to Tom Selleck's 61-acre ranch, comments like "we're not all equal when it comes to water", mounting litigation over increasing water rates, mandatory rationing and reducing amounts of water delivered to senior water right holders—just scratch the surface of what is in our future.[1]

The indications for escalating conflicts is seen clearly in a letter to the editor in an Imperial Valley publication.

> *What does a water collapse and panic look like? You don't want to know! But you must anticipate and get prepared immediately. The cause is a Western Institution failure to plan for long term drought. In a panic - there is no information...no answers...no leadership.*

It becomes a mob and a crowd, every man for himself.
Remember, you have what they want. What is the answer?
Having anticipated such events for 30 years, I would suggest
serious consideration for an Imperial Valley solution to their
problem on our terms and conditions.[2]

The battle lines are being drawn! But, with every man for himself, how can any long-term solutions ever be realized?

Looking back at the past and evaluating where we stand today hopefully provides some insights as to how water will inform the remainder of the 21st century. Without question, this natural resource played a major role in defining our past. The question that remains is how will it determine our future?

In prehistoric times, the Ancient Puebloans and Hohokam adapted to water scarcity. The Ancient Puebloans packed up and moved either en masse or in small groups to areas where the carrying capacity of the land allowed them to survive for a while. When the climate changed they moved again. Unfortunately, given today's sedentary lifestyle, this form of adaptation is not in the cards for those living in our arid and semi-arid land. Because of the massive irrigation structures the Hohokam built, they also found mobility was not an option; instead they centralized and expanded their canals until they too surpassed the carrying capacity of the land. At that point, they also dispersed into smaller groups throughout the Southwest and into Mexico. In the end, Mother Nature reigned supreme.

The relationship between man and water in recorded history is a tale of man's evolving attempt to control water throughout the West. This taming of rivers started in earnest in the beginning of the 20th century with the formation of the USBR and the construction of massive dams, their resulting storage capacities and hydroelectric power generation. All of this allowed the desert to bloom. Ultimately, the expansion of agriculture and sprawling metropolitan areas occurred in a land deemed uninhabitable in the early part of the 19th century.

Today, the Colorado River supplies almost 40,000,000 people with water, provides irrigation that produces 15% of the nation's food supply and faces a carrying capacity issue that is rapidly reaching a crisis situation. As part of the ProPublica series, *Killing the Colorado,* the authors summarize the "structural and systemic" problems facing the region that include explosive urban growth and development, inefficient irrigation methods, federal subsidies that promote continued planting of water thirsty crops and outdated and inefficient water laws.[3] Of course, one cannot forget that the Law of the River promises more water than the Colorado River can be expected to deliver.

Technology that stored and transported water from distant locations made settlement in the arid West a possibility, but may not be able to protect those living west of the 100th meridian in the future. Given the time frame it takes to construct a storage facility or a desalination plant, there is little hope technological solutions can solve any gap in demand and supply in the near future. California found that out during the most recent drought. More importantly, the traditional solution of finding new sources is highly unlikely in the future unless American taxpayers are willing to pay at least nine billion dollars to construct and then another billion annually to maintain a project that diverts water from Alaska, the Great Lakes or the Mississippi River.

These ideas originally surfaced when Patricia Mulroy was on her quest to find more supply for Las Vegas. Fortunately, most realized that they were not realistic solutions. I must admit, I was amazed to see the USBR included the option of piping water from the Mississippi or Missouri rivers along with its astronomical costs in a 2012 report that reported by 2050 there will be a 3.2 million acre-feet Colorado River deficit.[4] When Congress has difficulty approving expenditures for long-overdue highway construction and maintenance, what do you think the chances are of this type of massive project getting past committee discussions?

Thus, if mobility and technology are not solutions how are we to adapt? And adapt, we must, as Mother Nature will inevitably step in. A recent study by NASA, and Columbia and Cornell Universities indicated that the future in the West will be much drier and warmer, increasing population and water demand and the depletion of groundwater resources. This will introduce mounting challenges for all those living in the West.

> Combined with the likelihood of a much drier future and increased demand, the loss of groundwater and higher temperatures will likely exacerbate the impacts of future droughts, presenting a major adaptation challenge for managing ecological and anthropogenic water needs in the region.[5]

If we do not want to suffer the violence similar to the Ancient Puebloans or allow the power elite to decide how water will be allocated once a crisis erupts, an integrated plan for the entire Colorado River network, that by necessity includes California, is essential. The first steps in accomplishing this requires changing the way water is viewed and then how water decisions are made. To ensure there will be a sustainable water future the status quo is no longer a possibility and there is not a lot of time left, especially if the drought the Colorado River Basin suffered since the beginning of the 21st century persists as it did during the Medieval Climate Anomaly. Even if 2016 brings increased precipitation throughout the West, what happens the next time such a drought occurs with population growing to over 50,000,000 and much of the ground water at unsustainable levels? Also, one cannot ignore the uncertain impacts of climate change and its effects on this precious resource.

With all of this, Famiglietti's disaster movie is not out of the realm of possibilities. In an Op Ed in the *LA Times*, he indicated that California faced a dire future.

> *"Whiskey is for drinking and water is for fighting."*
> *(Mark Twain) – The Future*
>
> *Right now the state has only about one year of water supply left in its reservoirs, and our strategic backup supply, groundwater, is rapidly disappearing. California has no contingency plan for a persistent drought like this one (let alone a 20-plus-year mega-drought), except, apparently, staying in emergency mode and praying for rain.*[6]

Thankfully, due to the drought, a lot of discussion, increased attention (Colorado Water Plan), and some tardy and "turtle-paced" action (California's groundwater and meter legislation) occurred. We reacted but actual strategic initiatives and planning remains conspicuously absent. None of these measures adequately addressed a sustainable water outlook for future generations.

Increasingly one hears that water is too cheap, except from most water utilities that charge for and distribute the water. As the Prior Appropriation Doctrine permits transferring a water right without selling the land, as long as the purchaser demonstrates beneficial use, the selling of water rights at market rates continue to gain popularity with urban water suppliers. An example of this is found in the Quantification Settlement Agreement (QSA) with the transfer of up to 200,000 acre-feet to San Diego at an initial price of $258 in 2007 and a current price of $624. San Diego determined that paying two-tenths of a penny per gallon is worth the certainty. Thus, the municipality guaranteed 200,000 acre-feet at a set price and the farmer is happy as the best he can do is earn $960 an acre by producing alfalfa. With labor, taxes and the minimal cost of $20 an acre foot for water, he may just breakeven.

Currently, selling water rights is an expensive, laborious and a time-consuming process under prior appropriation and other state administered legislation. Furthermore, determining the economic value of rights with priority dates after the 1920s when the Colorado River Compact was ratified remains difficult given droughts and the uncertainties of rising temperatures and reducing precipitation. Add this to the seven states vying for this prolific but limited water source, an obligation to deliver 1.5 million acre-feet to Mexico plus the vast array of intrastate issues (rural versus urban, TMDS, etc.), the future bodes well for water lawyers and the power elite. But, I am not sure if the losers of these legal battles will go "gentle into that good night."[7]

Jay Lund, a professor of civil and environmental engineering at UC Davis, indicated that under prior appropriation,

> *Farmers with senior water rights would make a huge profit, selling water at sky-high prices to cities.*[8]

This scenario takes the current dispute between agriculture and urban consumption of food production versus irrigation of lawns and golf courses to a more intense conflict. As awareness of hydrological realities grows, the lush lawns and golf courses will be transformed and the expanding urban populations will need more water for basic necessities. This establishes a "no-win" situation that pits the metropolitan areas against the farmers and ranchers who are reaping huge profits from water they have never paid for and in fact in most cases its delivery was heavily subsidized. Ultimately, the government will be required to intervene to address this issue. It seems only logical that these issues be addressed before the battle escalates and a crisis actually occurs.

Being a realist, I also know that another extended drought, like those dominating the Medieval Climate Anomaly or the impact of increasing temperatures, may be necessary to get us off square one. Continuing along the same course, where each state continues to act as if the Colorado River will always meet all the needs and ignore both present and future hydrological realities will only lead to a crisis. The question remains as to when it will happen. When it does occur, both urban and agricultural demand would have increased even further with technological solutions years away from implementation. More importantly, there will be no system, other than prior appropriation, to allocate water. Unfortunately, that allocation would not be on an equitable or an efficient basis.

What a shame we do not take the opportunity, before that crisis erupts to do the right thing. What a pity that we continue to kick the can down the road where our great grandchildren may have to decide, like the Ancient Puebloans, that they need to move to an area where they can get adequate drinking water.

The Bottom Line

Any way you look at it, something has to change. The Colorado Water Plan painted a bleak picture if nothing is done to address the looming water gap in the state's future that included futile hopes for additional TMDs, continued depletion of groundwater supplies and uninterrupted transfer of water from agriculture to urban uses. The Plan summarized the consequences of remaining with the status quo by indicating, "This is the de facto future we are handing down to our children and grandchildren if we do nothing."[9]

Famiglietti is not the only one painting a bleak picture with regards to water in the Colorado River Basin and California. In an article, Paul Rogers indicated,

> *In urban areas, most cities would eventually see water rationing at 50% of current levels. Golf courses would shut down. Cities would pass laws banning watering or installing lawns, which use half of most homes' water. Across the state, rivers and streams would dry up, wiping out salmon runs. Cities would race to build new water supply projects, similar to the $50 million wastewater recycling plant that the Santa Clara Valley Water District is now constructing in Alviso.*[10]

It is hard to envision that anyone cannot see the handwriting on the wall. Water as we know it, use it and value it will have to change if the Southwest is to continue its phenomenal growth; if climate change increases temperatures and reduces precipitation in the West but, more importantly, if our children's children want to have safe, reliable drinking water.

Ultimately, life as we know it will change for everyone. Howard Watts of the Great Basin Water Network, an organization of environmentalists, Native Americans and ranchers that focuses on the health of the Colorado River indicated,

> *We do have to eat, so we're not opposed to using water for agriculture. But everybody is going to have to make shared sacrifices, even making shifts in what's being grown by the Southwest's farmers.*[11]

As with all change, many obstacles, such as intrastate and interstate conflicts that have become so entrenched over the past 150 years; the water power elite resisting changes to the status quo; and of course the political and economic repercussions resulting from any changes will make it very difficult and cause a great deal of angst. Perhaps the most daunting challenge will be the acceptance that the development of a comprehensive and consolidated water plan for the entire Colorado River Basin is required to completely solve this highly complex, confusing, conflicting, and multi-faceted issue. Although it is not part of the culture of the West to willingly accept anything beyond local control, if far-reaching collaboration does not start soon, a future crisis may require federal intervention. And, we know that Westerners hate that idea.

It also goes without saying that any change to an existing system will experience problems and there will be unintended consequences. For instance, although the water-sharing program initiated in Australia attempted to include all stakeholders in the process, the "economic aspirations and livelihood opportunities" of the indigenous people of the country were not quantified. In many regions of the country, the reserved rights were not included.[12] In other words, any future agricultural and environmental needs were unknown as the water sharing/trading system was implemented. This is reminiscent of what occurred to the Native Americans when the Colorado River Compact was negotiated. It took Arizona v. California to begin to rectify this. Fortunately, the Australian government recognized the problem and started purchasing entitlements to maintain appropriate environmental requirements that have subsequently been identified for the indigenous people.

One cannot say with any degree of certainty that Australia's water sharing program could be the panacea. It will be interesting to see how the pilot program in Nevada turns out. I am intrigued with this option and think that it may offer a systematic approach that can address many of the problems the Southwest and California face in the not too distant future.

The Colorado Water Plan mentions water-trading a handful of times in the document; however, each time it is raised, impediments such as "loss of income, lost market share and the lack of expertise in farming new crops"[13] surface. This highlights how the current water rights system presents obstacles in the more efficient use of water. Even with this, adherence to the prior appropriation system is ultimately affirmed.

"Colorado's Water Plan recognizes the need to increase agility within Colorado's system of water law, while respecting individual property rights."[14]

One thing that is clear: prior appropriation needs a major readjustment, at the very least, to foster efficient use of the available water. It could be argued, which many do, that this system should be replaced with one that reinforces conservation and efficiency. It goes without saying that any change to prior appropriation will encounter intense resistance. Robert Glennon, author, as well as Regent's Professor and Morris K. Udall Professor of Law and Public Policy at the University of Arizona mentioned to me that he begins each course with the "water lawyers' prayer."

"Oh Lord, may the change in water law occur to someone else's client."[15]

Glennon also feels the allocation system and the Law of the River need some massaging to adapt the one-hundred-year old allocation method to current realities. I asked how he saw this happening and he made it clear one had to work with what we currently have. In other words, work within the system.

Mike Young, on the other hand, feels prior appropriation presents too many obstacles and complicates establishing water sharing. Although the partnership with Duke University is attempting to identify and resolve these issues/conflicts, Young prefers to eliminate a process he feels is obsolete and inefficient.

Another political hornet's nest involves subsidies for both crops and water itself. Clearly agricultural support from the federal government needs to complement the hydrological realities of the region and not succumb to Washington lobbyists. Unfortunately, some subsidies are so entrenched that these changes will cause seismic reactions. Just because this process will be difficult and conflict-laden, does not mean we should give up. These issues, if not addressed now will have to be resolved at some later date when our backs are up against the wall.

Other arid and semi-arid countries have designed systems that will result in a sustainable future. Israel's emphasis on expanding existing resources through desalination and recycling waste water are examples of steps local governments should consider.

Hopefully we can learn from others. Looking at how Chile, Israel, Singapore and Australia have restructured their water management systems to deal with their pressing hydrological realities provide the following key lessons:

"Whiskey is for drinking and water is for fighting."
(Mark Twain) – The Future

1. Develop an ethic that values water, recognizes its current and future limitations, and incorporates views of all stake holders on an equitable basis
2. Plan ahead
3. Implement an integrated and interconnected plan to achieve optimal efficiencies
4. Attempt to de-politicize water management where possible
5. Ensure any new system is well defined with necessary oversights and regulations included
6. Re-evaluate and restructure subsidies, grants, etc. that do not foster efficiencies and conservation
7. Price water realistically, including costs of future infrastructure.
8. Develop systems that expand existing sources of water

The implementation of any or all of these requires the adoption of a new water ethic. This revised way to value water requires consensus by all stakeholders that starts with the premise that water is not abundant and looking for new sources is not a solution. Then, with a shared vision, a plan that addresses the hydrological realities of the Colorado River Basin and California could become a possibility and a sustainable future a reality.

In the end, as Fishman pointed out, each decision or non-decision has consequences. But more importantly, we do have decisions to make as there is a distinct possibility that a water crisis may be in our future. As President John F. Kennedy indicated in a speech in 1959, "When written in Chinese, the word 'crisis' is composed of two characters. One represents danger and the other represents opportunity."[16] We can continue to "kick the can down the road" until Famiglietti's disaster movie becomes reality or we can choose to demand our political leaders start making the tough decisions that are quite frankly past due. This will call for leaders who do not have re-election as an ultimate goal. Given our political structure this will not be easy and will cause significant angst and turmoil.

In the current political climate, such a person, or group of people, may be impossible to find; however, one can only hope leadership emerges. There is always hope. As Tony Blair indicated,

> *I think the journey for a politician goes from wanting to please all the people all the time, to a political leader that realizes in the end his responsibility is to decide. And when he decides, he divides.*[17]

Hopefully, a leader will emerge that will gain control of all of the water issues that face the Colorado River Basin as well as the entire West.

Without revising the way water is currently viewed and valued, a crisis is inevitable. To ensure the Colorado River continues to provide sustenance to the environment and the 40 million people that depend on it, a new water ethic is not just an environmentalist ideal. It is necessary for a sustainable water future.

> *A willingness to make water use sensitive to the limits of natural and human communities, with an ethical concern rooted in the principles of conservation, fairness, and ecology, is central to determining the long-term success of communities in the American West.*[18]

Hopefully, I am not being Don Quixote and "tilting at windmills." I sincerely believe that there are solutions for the water supply/demand gap. Given the distinct potential for an actual water shortage either in the very near future or at least within the next 50 years; the hydrological reality that technology cannot always provide all the water we want; Mother Nature's track record of gaining the upper hand; and human nature's tendency to fight for what they believe is "theirs," some radical changes are needed now. We no longer have the luxury of avoiding the real issues. By we, I mean our elected officials, each company, each water district or water provider and every person living in the West. A dialogue that includes everyone from the MWD of Los Angeles to Denver Water to the immigrant workers in the Imperial Valley to residential homeowners who feel that a lush lawn is essential to their quality of life to farmers that continue to use flood irrigation to all water right holders regardless of priority date is essential in determining what our values and goals should be for the future. We must create a water ethic that informs all decisions. I do not want some faceless power elite making decisions about my future or my children's children's future. Do you?

Do we want special interest groups dictating how water is used? By special interest groups I mean water utilities, farmers, ranchers, Las Vegas casinos, each state in the Colorado River Basin, each locality within the basin, landscapers, golf courses, and of course each homeowner that insists that a green lawn is necessary. Sitting back and doing nothing as we feel the problem is too big, is not the answer. In other words, do we want a continuation of the status quo? If we do not change, then Stegner's question in *This is Dinosaur* is answered with confirmation that we are a species that wishes to destroy.

Hopefully, that will not be the answer and we will as an interested polity, but more importantly, as a concerned inhabitant of our beautiful arid and semi-arid environment, deemed uninhabitable in the 19th century, start realizing that we can mess with Mother Nature to a point and then she re-establishes her power. Until someone develops a way to invent more water we must call for leadership that overcomes all of the insular ways we deal with and manage water today. What has worked in the past will not work in the future and we are definitely running out of time.

Hopefully California's drought will not continue and they will receive an epic snow pack this coming winter with the return of the white powder that provided water to the Central Valley, Northern California,

San Francisco and Los Angeles in the past. Hopefully this will continue for years to come. Hopefully, the groundwater legislation will not delay its implementation for 20 years and start immediately. Hopefully, climate change will not reduce the amount of precipitation and the Colorado River flow reduced. Hopefully, snowpack in the Upper Basin will be "epic" to augment the amount lost to higher evaporation rates due to increased temperatures. Hopefully, due to shortages, agricultural fields will not be fallowed that will result in another Dust Bowl. Hopefully, Miracle May, Jubilant June and Joyous July will continue to refill Lake Mead and Lake Powell. Hopefully, groundwater depletions will not continue throughout the Colorado River Basin and the Central Valley. Hopefully, a disaster movie of California running out of water or Bacigalupi's *Water Knife* will not become reality.

Hopefully, we will develop a water ethic that will bring everyone in the West together and lead to the development of an integrated plan that will realistically deal with our hydrological realities and create water sustainability for future generations ... HOPEFULLY!

Notes

Chapter 1 Notes – "For What It's Worth"
Introduction

1. Stephen Sills. (1967). *For What It's Worth.*

2. Jay Famiglietti, *How Much Water Does California Have Left?* L.A. Times Op Ed, July 8, 2014.

3. Matt Stevens and Chris Megerian. *Southern California Lags Behind in Water Conservation.* L.A. Times, April 7, 2015

4. Robert Glennon. (2002). *Water Follies: Groundwater Pumping and the Fate of America's Fresh Water.* Island Press: Washington, D.C.

5. Ibid., Pg. 47

6. USGS. *The Water Cycle.* http://water.usgs.gov/edu/watercycle.html.

7. Ayn Rand. (1957). *Atlas Shrugged.* Random House: New York, NY

8. Paulo Bacigalupi. (2015). *The Water Knife.* Alfred A. Knopf. Alfred A Knopf. NYC, NY.

9. USGS. *Water Basics.* http://water.usgs.gov/edu/mwater.html.

10. United States Geological Survey. (2015). *The World's Water: Distribution of Earths Water.* Retrieved from: usgs.gov/edu/earthwherewater.html

11. Marc Reisner. (1993). *Cadillac Desert: The American West and Its Disappearing Water. Revised and updated edition.* Penguin Books: NYC, NY.((pg. 332)

12. California Department of Food and Agriculture. (2015). *California Agricultural Production Statistics.* Retrieved from: https://www.cdfa.ca.gov/statistics/

13. Mikhail Gorbachev wrote the Foreword of Water: The Drop of Life written by Peter Swanson.

14. Doug Kenny and Jeff Lukas. (2013). *Challenges of the Colorado River Basin presentation.* Retrieved from: http://www.slideshare.net/LearnMoreAboutClimate/climate-change-and-water-in-the-west-the-colorado-river-basin. Permission granted via Creative Commons. License obtained at: https://creativecommons.org/licenses/by-nc-sa/4.0/

15. Clark Graham. *World Prehistory: New Perspectives. Third edition.* (1977). Cambridge University Press: Cambridge, Great Britain.

16. Institute for the Environment. *Assessment of Climate Change in the Southwest United States.* (2013). Island Press: Washington DC.

17. Background on the Columbia River people came from numerous sources that included:

Cain Allen. (2007). '*Boils, swell and whorl pool': The Historical Landscape of the Dalles-Celilo Reach of the Columbia River.* Oregon Historical Quarterly. Vol. 108(4).

K. Barber & A.H. Fisher. (2007, Winter). *From Coyote to the Corps of Engineers: Recalling the History of The Dalles-Celilo Reach. Oregon Historical Quarterly, 108*(4), 520.

Virginia L. Butler. *Relic Hunting, Archaeology, and Loss of Native American Heritage at The Dalles.* (2007). Oregon Historical Quarterly. Winter 2007. (624).

P.C. Gold. *The Long Narrows: The Forgotten Geography and Cultural Wonder.* (2007). Oregon Historical Quarterly. 108(4).

William Lang. (2007). *The Meaning of Falling Water: Celilo Falls and The Dalles in Historical Literature.* Oregon Historical Quarterly. Winter 2007. (566)

Nerburn, Kent. (2006). *Chief Joseph & the Flight of the Nez Perce:*

The Untold Story of an American Tragedy. Reprint Edition. HarperOne: San Francisco, CA

18. Elwyn B. Robinson. (1974). *An Interpretation of the History of the Great Plains,* North Dakota History. 41(2), pp. 5-19

19. Lauren W. Ritterbush. (2002) *Drawn by the Bison: Late Prehistoric Native Migration into the Central Plains.* Great Plains Quarterly. Fall 22, pp.259-270

20. Elliot West. (2012). *The Essential West: Collected Essays by Elliot West.* University of Oklahoma Press: Norman, OK

21. Adam Hodge. (2012). *In Want of Nourishment to Keep Them Alive: Climate Fluctuations, Bison Scarcity, and the Smallpox Epidemic of 1780-82 on the Northern Great Plains.* Environmental History, Vol. 17 (April) pp.365-403. DOI 10.1093/envhist/emr153.

22. Marc Reisner. *Cadillac Desert,* pg. 3.

23. Jared Diamond. *Collapse: How Societies Choose to Fail or Succeed.* (2005). NYC, NY: Viking Press. Pg. 137

24. Ibid. pg. 156

25. Frederick Jackson Turner. *Contribution of the West to American Democracy.* Atlantic Monthly, January 1903, pg. 90.

26. USGS. (2014). *Colorado River Basin Area Study.* Retrieved from: http://water.usgs.gov/watercensus/colorado.html

27. Cynthia Barnett. (2011). *Blue Revolution: Unmaking America's water Crisis.* Boston, MA: Beacon Press.

Chapter 2 Notes –Who Would Want to Live There? Prehistory

1. Information regarding climate and mega droughts during prehistoric times included:

Larry Benson & Michael S. Berry. (2009). *Climate Change and Cultural Response in Prehistoric American Southwest.*U.S. Geological Survey – Published Research. Paper 725

Edward Cook; Richard Seagßer; Richard Hiem, Jr.; Russell S. Vose; Celine Herweijer; & Connie Woodhouse.(2009). *Megadroughts in North America: Placing IPCC Projections of Hydroclimatic change in a Long-term Palaeoclimate Context.* Journal of Quaternary Science 25(1) pp 48-61. DOI: 10.1002/jqs.1303

Edward R. Cook; Connie A.Woodhouse; C. Mark,Eakin: David M. Meko & David W. Stahle. (2004).*Long-term Aridity Changes in the Western United States.* Science 306(5). Pp 1015- 1018

Robert C. Euler;George J. Gumerman; Thor N. V. Karlstrom; Jeffrey S. Dean; & Richard H. Hevly. (1979). The Colorado Plateaus: Cultural Dynamics and Paleoenvironment. Science 205:1089–1101

Terry L Jones.; Gary M. Brown; L. Mark Raab; Janet L. McVickar; W. Geoffrey Spaulding; Douglas J. Kennett; Andres York; & Phillip L. Walker. (1999). *Environmental Imperative Reconsidered: Demographic Crises During the Medieval Climatic Anomaly.* Current Anthropology Vol. .40, No. 2

Terry L. Jones; & Al Schwitalla. (2007). *Archaeological Perspectives on the Effects of Medieval Drought in Prehistoric California.* Quarternary International 188. Pp. 41-58.

Stephen H. Lekson.(2008). *A History of the Ancient Southwest.* School for Advanced Research: Santa Fe, NM.

Glen M. MacDonald.*(2007). Severe and Sustained drought in Southern California and the West: Present Conditions and Insights from the Past on Causes and Impacts.* Quaternary International.173-174. pp. 87-100

Glen M. MacDonald; Constantine V. Krementetski;, & Hugo G. Hidalgo.(2008). *Southern California and the Perfect Drought: Simultaneous prolonged Drought in Southern California and the Sacramento and Colorado River Systems.* Quaternary International 199. pp. 11-23.

David M. Meko; Connie A. Woodhouse; Christopher A. Baisan; Troy Knight; Jeffrey J. Lukas; Malcolm K. Hughes; & Matthew W. Salzer (2007) *Medieval drought in the upper Colorado River Basin. AGU Publications.* DOI: 10.1029/2007GL029988

L. Mark Raab; & Daniel O. Larson. (1997). *Medieval Climatic Anomaly and Punctuated Cultural Evolution in Coastal Southern California.* American Antiquity. 62 (2). pp. 319-336.

Salzer, Matthew W. Salzer and Kurt F Kipfmueller. 2005. *Reconstructed Temperature and Precipitation of Southern Colorado*

Plateau. Climatic Change 70:465-487. DOI: 10.1007/s10584-005-5922-3

Scott Stine. 1994. Extreme and Persistent Drought in California and Patagonia During Medieval Time. Nature 369, pp. 546–549.

Woodhouse, Connie A. Woodhouse; David M.Meko; Glen M. MacDonald; Dave W. Stahle & Edward R. Cook. (2010).*A 1200-Year Perspective of 21ˢᵗ Century Drought in Southwestern North America.* Proceedings of the National Academy of Sciences. 107(50). Pg. 21283-21288. DOI:10.1073/pnas.091197107

2. Franck Lavigne; Jean-Philippe Degeai; Jean-Christophe Komorowski; Sebastien Guillet; Vincent Robert; Pierre Lahitte; Clive Oppenheimer; Markus Stoffel; Celine M. Vidal; Surono; Indyo Praromo; Patrick Wassmer; Irka Hajdas; Danang Sri Hadmoko; andEdouard de Belizal. (2013) *Source of the Great A.D. 1257 Mystery Eruption Unveiled, Samalas Volcano, Rinjani Volcanic Complex, Indonesia.* PNAS 110(42) pp. 16742-16747 doi/10.1073/pnas.1307520110

3. The information on the Ancestral Puebloans came from numerous sources, most helpful were:

    Richard V.N. Ahlstrom; Carla Van West; & Dean, Jeffrey S. Dean.(1995). *Environmental and Chronological Factors in Mesa Verde-Northern Rio Grande Migration.* Journal of Anthropological Archaeology. 14. Pp. 125-142

    Benson, Larry & Berry, Michael S. (2009). *Climate Change and Cultural Response in Prehistoric American Southwest.* U.S. Geological Survey – Published Research. Paper 725

    L.V. Benson; D.K. Ramsey; D.W. Stahle; & K.L. Petersen. (2013). *Some Thoughts on the Factors that Controlled Prehistoric*

Maize Production in the Southwest with Application to Southwestern Colorado. Journal of Archeological Science 40, pp. 2869-2880.

L.V. Benson; E.R. Griffin; J.R. Stein; R.A. Friedman; & S.W. Andrae. (2014). *Mummy Lake: An Unroofed Ceremonial Structure Within a Large Ritual Landscape.* Journal of Archaeological Science44. pp. 164-179.

Catherine Cameron. (1995). *Migration and Movement of Southwestern Peoples.* Journal of Anthropological Archaeology. 14. pp. 104-124

Craig Childs. (206). *House of Rain: Tracking a Vanished Civilization Across the American Southwest.* Little Brown and Co: New York, New York

Melissa J. Churchill;James M. Potter; & Richard H. Wilshusen. (2015). "Prehistoric Reservoirs and Water Basins in the Mesa Verde Region: Intensification of Water Collection Strategies during the Great Pueblo period." *American Antiquity* 62.4 (1997): 664+. *Academic OneFile.* Web. 25 Apr. 2015.

Cordell, Linda S.Cordell and Fred Plog.(1979).*Escaping the Confines of Normative Thought: A Reevaluation of Puebloan Prehistory.* American Antiquity. 44(3). Pp 405-429

William deBuys, (2011). *A Great Aridness: Climate Change and the Future of the American Southwest.* Oxford University Press: Oxford, U.K.

R. Euler; et.al. (1979). *The Colorado Plateaus: Cultural Dynamics and Paleoenvironment.* Science. 205(4411. Pp. 1089-1101

Joseph A. Ezzo;& T. Douglas Price. (2002), *Migration, Regional Reorganization, and Spatial Group Composition at Grasshopper Pueblo, Arizona.* Journal of Archaeological Science: 29, pg. 499-520

Kristin A. Kuckelman. (2010). *The Depopulation of Sand Canyon Pueblo, A Large Ancestral Pueblo Village in Southwestern Colorado.* American Antiquity75(3). Pg 497-525

Stephen H. Lekson; Thomas C. Windes; Jorh R. Stein; & W. James Judge. (1988). *The Chaco Canyon Community.* Scientific American. July. pp. 100-109

Stephen H. Lekson. (1995).*Introduction.* Journal Of Anthropological Archaeology. 14. Pp 99-103

Stephen H. Lekson; & Catherine Cameron. (1995). *The Abandonment of Chaco Canyon, the Mesa Verde Migration and the Reorganization of the Pueblo World.* Journal of Anthropological Archaeology 14, pp 184-202.

Stephen H. Lekson. (2008). *A History of the Ancient Southwest.* School for Advanced Research: Santa Fe, NM

William D. Lipe. (1995). *The Depopulation of the Northern San Juan: Conditions in the Turbulent 1200s.* Journal Of Anthropological Archaeology. 14 pp143-169.

Paul E. Minnis.(1995).*Social Adaptation to Food Stress: A Prehistoric Southwestern Example.* University of Chicago Press: Chicago. IL

Stephen E. Plog. (2008). *Ancient Peoples of the American Southwest. Second Edition.* Thames & Hudson. NYC:NY

Stephen E. Plog and Carrie Heitman. (2010). *Hierarchy and Social Inequality in the American Southwest, A.D. 800-1200.* Proceedings of the National Academy of Sciences. Vol. 107(46). Pp. 19619-19626.

W.H.Wills and Wetherbee Bryan Dorshow. (2012). *Agriculture and Community in Chaco Canyon: Revisiting Pueblo Alto.* Journal of Anthropological Archaeology. 31. Pp 138-155.

4.   Stephen H Lekson. (2008). Pg. 21

"A note on terminology: I use *Anasazi* as archaeological jargon,

5.   Wikipedia.(2016). *Pueblo Bonita.*

Retrieved from:https://en.wikipedia.org/wiki/Pueblo_Bonito

6.   Lekson. Pg. 128.

7.   Michael Coren. *Growing Crops With No Water, The Old Fashioned Way.* Retrieved from: www.fastcoexist.com/1680477/growing-crops-with-no-water-the-old-fashioned-way.

8.   Lekson. Pg 154

9.   Ibid. Pg. 329

10.   Information on the Hohokam came from the compilation of the following sources:

David R. Abbott. (2003). *Centuries of Decline During the Hohokam Archaic Period at Pueblo Grande.* University of Arizona Press: Tucson, AZ.

Steven Dominguez & Kenneth E. Kolm. (2005). *Beyond Water Harvesting: A Soil Hydrology Perspective on Traditional Southwestern Agricultural Technology.* American Antiquity 70(4) pp. 732-765.

David E. Doyel (2008*) Irrigation, Production, and Power in Phoenix Basin Hohokam Society.in The Hohokam Millennium Edited by Fish, Suzanne K. and Fish, Paul R.* School for Advanced research Press: Santa Fe, NM

Suzanne Fish; Paul R. Fish; John R. Madsen; editors. (1992). *The Marana Community in the Hohokam World.* University of Arizona Press: Tucson, AZ.

Hunt, Robert C. Hunt; David Guillet; James,Bayman; Paul Fish; Suzanne Fish; Keith Kintigh; & James A. Neeley. (2005). *Plausible Ethnographic Analogies for the Social Organization of Hohokam Canal Irrigation.* American Antiquity 70(3) pp. 433-456.

Scott Ingram. (2008). *Streamflow and Population Change in the Lower Salt River Valley of Central Arizona, ca A.D.775 to 1450.* American Antiquity, 73(1), pp. 136-165

Stephen Lekson (2008)

W. Bruce Masse. (1981). *Prehistoric Irrigation Systems in the Salt River Valley, Arizona* Science. 214(23). Pp. 408-416.

Paul Minnis. (1995).*Social Adaptation to Food Stress: A Prehistoric Southwestern Example.* University of Chicago Press: Chicago. IL.

Stephen Plog. (2008). *Ancient Peoples of the American Southwest. Second Edition.* Thames & Hudson. NYC:NY

J. J. Reid & B. K. Montgomery. (1998). The Brown and the Gray: Pots and Population Movement in East-central Arizona. Journal of Anthropological Research 54, 447–459.

Miriam Stark, Jeffry J. Clark & Mark D. Elson. (1995). *Causes and Consequences of Migration in the 13th Century Tonto Basin.* Journal of Anthropological Archaeology 14(2): pp. 212-246.

Hoski Schaafsma & John M. Briggs. (2007). *Hohokam Field Building: Silt Fields in the Northern Phoneix Basin.* The Kiva. 72(4), pp. 431-455.

J. Homer Thiel & Michael W. Diehl.(2006) *Final Report: Rio Nuevo Archaeology, 2000-2003.* Chapter 3: *Cultural History of the Tucson Basin and the Project Area.* Center for Desert Archaeology. Tucson AZ.

Henry D. Wallace & James P. Holmlund. (1984). *The Classic Period in the Tucson Basin.* Kiva 49(3/4) pg. 167-194

Henry D. Wallace; James M.Heidke and William H. Doelle. (2009). *Hohokam Origins.* Kiva 75(2). Pp. 289-295

Michael R. Waters and John C. Ravesloot. (2001). *Change and the Cultural Evolution of the Hohokam along the Middle Gila River and Other River Valleys in South-central Arizona.* American Antiquity, 66(2), pp. 285-299.

Stephanie M. Whittlesey. (1995). *The Mogollon, Hohokam and O'Otam: Rethinking the Early Formative Period in Southern Arizona*Kiva 60(4). Pp. 465-498

Michelle L.Wienhold.(2013). *Prehistoric Land Use and Hydrology: A Multi-scalar Spatial Analysis in Central Arizona.* Journal of Archeological Science. Vol. 40. Pp. 250-259.

11. Lekson. Pg. 82

12. Ibid. pg. 121

13. Hunt et al, pg 452.

     W. Bruce Masse. Pg 414.

14. Reisner. Pg. 256

15. Hoski Schaafsma. Pg 431.

16. Ingram, Scott. (2008).

     Lekson. pg 205

17. Reisner. Pg 459.

18. Lynn H. Gamble. (2005). *Culture and Climate: Reconsidering the Effects of Paleoclimatic Variability Among Southern California Hunter-Gatherer Societies* World Archaeology. 37(1). pp. 92-108.

19. Ibid. pg 93-95.

20. Joshua Fischman. (1996). *The California Social Climbers: Low Water Prompts High Status.* Science. 272.5263. Retrieved from:http://dml.regis.edu/login?url=http://go.galegroup.com/ps/i.do?id=GALE%7CA18311917&v=2.1&u =regis&it=r&p=GRGM&sw=w&asid= 051b80ab311f774fa4ecaf5e6fbe8397. Pg 812.

21. Jeanne E. Arnold; Michael R. Walsh; & Sandra E. Hollimon. (2004). *The Archaeology of California.* Journal of Archaeological Research Vol 12. No 1, pp. 99 1-75. Pg. 8

22. Jeanne E. Arnold & Terisa M. Green.(2002). *Comments: Mortuary Ambiguity: The Ventureno Chumash Case.* American Antiquity, 67(4). pp. 760-771.

    Lynn Gamble; Phillip L. Walker; & Glenn S. Russell.(2002). *Further Considerations On the Emergence of Chumash Chiefdoms.* American Antiquity, 67(4). pp. 772-777.

    Lambert. P.M. Lambert & P.L. Walker.(1991). *Physical Anthropological Evidence for the Evolution of Social Complexity in Coastal Southern California.* Antiquity. 65:963-973.

23. Gamble, Lynn. Pg 97.

    Jones, Terry L. & Al Schwitalla. (2008). *Archaeological Perspectives on the Effects Of Medieval Drought in Prehistoric California.* Quaternary International. 188. Pp.54

24. Patricia M. Lambert.(1993). *Health in Prehistoric Populations of the Santa Barbara Channel Islands* American Antiquity 58(3). Pp. 509-525.

25. A compilation of the following sources contributed to the information on the Native Americans in the Central and Owens Valley

    Hundley, Norris, Jr. (2001). *The Great Thirst – Californians and Water: A History.* University of California Press: Berkeley, CA

    Terry Jones, Terry L. & Al Schwitalla.(2008).

    Terry L. Jones & Kathryn A. Klar, Editors. (2007). *California Prehistory: Colonization, Culture and Complexity.* AltaMira Press: Lanham, MD.

    Harry W. Lawton; Philip J. Wilke ; Mary DeDecker; & William M. Mason. (1976).&Journal of California Anthropology. 3(1). pp. 13-50.

26. Information on agriculture and the Paiute came from,

    Hundley. (2001). Pg 19

    Harry W, Lawton, et. al. pg. 18

    Worldmark Encyclopedia of Cultures and Daily Life. (2009)Ed Timothy L. Gall and Heneen Hobby Vol 2. Americas. 2nd ed. Detroit: Gale pp 424- 432.

    This reading provides a brief review of the history of the Northern Paiutes.

27. Hundley.(2001). pg. 16.

28. Paul E. Minnis.(1995).*Social Adaptation to Food Stress: A Prehistoric Southwestern Example.* University of Chicago Press: Chicago. IL.

Minnis discusses how prehistoric cultures adapted to food stress.

29. Sarah F. Bates; David H. Getchens; Lawrence MacDonnell; & Wilkinson, Charles F. (1993). *Searching Out The Headwaters: Change and Rediscovery in Western Water Policy.* Island Press: Washington D.C.pg. 200.

Chapter 3 Notes – "Build It and They Will Come"
Recorded History

1. Information on methods used in the Southwest came from numerous sources; however, two that provided a good overview included,

    William E. Doolittle. (1992). *Agriculture in North America on the Eve of Contact: A Reassessment.* Annals of the Association of American Geographers. 82(3). Pp 386-401.

    Alvin R. Sunseri. (1973). *Agricultural Techniques in New Mexico at the Time of the Anglo-American Conquest.* Agricultural History, 47(4), pp. 329-337).

2. Marc Reisner.pg 24.

3. Zebulon Pike. (1810). *Account of the Expedition to the Sources of the Mississippi and Through the Western Parts of Louisiana to the Sources of the Arkansaw, Kans, La Platte and Pierre Juan, Rivers.* Philadelphia, PA:C & A Conrad & Co. pg. 525

4. Edwin James. (1823). *An Account of an Expedition from Pittsburgh to the Rocky Mountains, Performed in the Years 1819, 1820American Journeys Collection:* London: Longman, Hurst, Orme and Brown. pp. 236-237.

5. Kathleen A. Miller.(2001). *Climate and Water Resources in the West: Past and Future.* Journal of the West. 40(3), pp. 39-47.

6. John Wesley Powell. (1879). *Report on the Lands of the Arid Region of the United States: Second Edition.* Washington, D.C.: Government Printing Office. Pg 9.

7. David Wisart. (2004). The Great Plains Region. In: Encyclopedia of the Great Plains: University Press. Pp x111-xv111. Retrieved from: https:://enwikipedia.org/wiki/GreatPlains.

8. Elwyn B Robinson. *(1974). An Interpretation of the History of the Great Plains.* North Dakota History. 41(2), pg. 6

9. Jeffrey Jacobs. (2011). *The Sustainability of Water Resources in the Colorado River Basin.* Pp 6-12. The Bridge. National Academy of Engineering. 41(4).

10. John Wesley Powell. (1897). Pg. 1

11. Donald Worster. (1995). *Rivers of Empire: Water, Aridity, and the Growth of the American West.* New York, New York: Oxford University Press. (pg. 133)

12. Thadis H. Box. (1977). *The Arid Lands Revisited, 100 Years After John Wesley Powell.* Utah State University Honors Lectures dated May 1, 1977.

13. Cary J. Mock.(2000). *Rainfall in the Garden of the United States Great Plains, 1870-1889.* Climatic Change. 44(1-2), pp. 173-195.

    James D. Bennett. (1967). *Oasis Civilization in the Great Plains.* Great Plains Journal. 7(1), pg. 28.

14. James D. Bennett. Pg. 29

15. Cynthia Barnett. (2011). *Blue Revolution: Unmaking America's Water Crisis.* Boston, MA: Beacon Press. Pg 90.

16. James D. Bennett.pg.32

17. Kelly C. Harper. (1974). *The Mormon Role in Irrigation Beginnings and Diffusion in the Western States: A Historical Geography*. Retrieved from: http://scholarsarchive.byu.edu/etd/4764/

18. Donald Worster. Pg 102.

19. Theodore Roosevelt. (1901). *First Annual Message to Congress. December 3, 1901*. Para. 65. Retrieved from: http://www.presidency.ucsb.edu/ws/?pid=29542

20. Frederick Jackson Turner. (1903). *Contribution of the West to American Democracy*. Atlantic Monthly, January 1903, pg. 90

21. Reclamation Act/Newlands Act of 1902. Retrieved from:http://www.ccrh.org/comm/umatilla/primary/newlands.htm

22. Donald Worster. Pg 173.

23. Marc Reisner. Pg 134

24. The USBR's adoption of huge projects is expressed in:

    Norris Hundley,Jr. (2001). *The Great Thirst: Californians and Water: A History. Revised edition.* University of California Press: Berkeley: CA.

    Norris Hundley, Jr. (2009). *Water and the West: The Colorado River Compact and the Politics of Water in the Americans West. Second edition.* Los Angeles: University of California Press.

    Hundley, Norris, Jr. (1996). *Water in the West in Historical Imagination: Part 1.* The Western Historical Quarterly. vol. 27 (1). Pp. 4-31.

    Hundley, Norris, Jr. (1996). *Water in the West in Historical Imagination: Part Two - A Decade Later Part 2.* The Historian. vol. 66 (3). pp. 455-490.

Mark Reisner. 1993

Donald Worster. (1995).

25. Reisner.(pg. 54)

26. Information on the Owens River water grab came from

   Norris Hundley, Jr. (2001)

   Norris Hundley, Jr. (2009)

   Marc Reisner. (1993)

   Donald Worster. (1995.)

27. Ted Knudson. (2014). *Outrage in Owens Valley a Century After L.A. Began Taking Its Water.* Sacramento Bee. January 5, 2014. Retrievedfrom: http://www.sacbee.com/news/investigations/the-public-eye/ article2588151.html#storylink=cpy

28. Marc Reisner. pg. 102

29. Background on the Colorado River Compact came from the compilation of numerous sources that included:

   Norris Hundley, Jr. (2001).

   Norris Hundley, Jr. (2009).

   Mark Reisner. (1993)

   George Sibley (2013). *Water Wranglers: The 75 Year History of the Colorado River District: A Story About the Embattled Colorado River and the Growth of the West.* Colorado River District.

   Elliot West. (2012). *The Essential West: Collected Essays by Elliot West.* Norman, OK: University of Oklahoma Press

   Donald Worster (1995).

30. Information on the Central Valley Project came from the following sources:

Norris Hundley, Jr. (2001).

Norris Hundley, Jr. (2009).

Lawrence B. Lee. (1985). *California Water Politics: Depression Genesis of the Central Valley Project, 1933-1944.* Journal of the West. 24 (4). Pp. 63-81.

Marc Reisner. (1993).

Eric A. Stene *Central Valley Project: Overview.* United States Bureau of Reclamation.

Donald Worster. (1995)

United States Bureau of Reclamation. *Managing Water in the West: Central Valley Project.* Retrieved from: http://www.usbr. gov/projects/Project.jsp?proj_Name=Central+Valley+Projects

31. Devin Galloway & Frances S. Riley. (1999). *San Joaquin Valley, California: Largest Human Alteration of the Earth's Surface.* United States Geological Survey: Menlo Park, CA. Retrieved from: http://pubs.usgs.gov/circ/circ1182/pdf/06SanJoaquinValley.pdf

32. USGS.(2015). *USGS Water Science School: Land Subsidence.* Retrieved from: http://water.usgs.gov/edu/earthgwland subside.html

33. Bettina Boxall. (2015). *Overpumping of Central Valley Groundwater Creating a Crisis, Experts Say.* L.A. Times. March 18, 2015. Retrieved from: http://www.latimes.com/local/ california/la-me-groundwater-20150318-story.html

Devin Galloway & Frances S. Riley. (1999).

J.F. Poland; B.E. Lofgren; R.L. Ireland; & R.G. Pugh. (1975). *Land Subsidence in San Joaquin Valley, California as of 1972.* U.S. Geological Survey Professional Papers – 437H. Retrieved from: http://pubs.usgs.gov/pp/0437h/report.pdf

This very technical report provides data on land subsidence in various areas of the San Joaquin Valley between 1947 and 1972.

34. Background on the California State Water Project (CSWP) came from:

Norris Hundley, Jr. (2001)

Norris Hundley, Jr. (2009)

Ronnie Cohen; Barry Nelson; & Gary Wolff. (2004). *Energy Down the Drain: The Hidden Costs of California's Water Supply.* Natural Resources Defense Council and Pacific InstituteRetrieved from: http://www.nrdc.org/water/conservation/edrain/execsum.as

Marc Reisner. (1993).

State of California: Department of Water Resources. (2015). *California State Water Project Overview.*Retrieved from: http://www.water.ca.gov/swp/

Donald Worster. (1995)

35. Marc Reisner (1993). (pg 9).

36. Background information on the Central Arizona Project (CAP) came from:

Arizona Department of Water Resources. *Securing Arizona's Water Future: Overview of Arizona's Groundwater Management Code*

Norris Hundley, Jr. (2001).

Norris Hundley, Jr. (2009)

Hanemann, Michael.(2002). *The Central Arizona Project.* Department of Agricultural and Resource Economics, UCB: CUDARE Working Papers: Paper 937.

Reisner, Marc. (1993).

Worster, Donald. (1995)

37. Reisner, Marc. (1993).

38. Michael Hanemann.(2002). Pg. 6.

39. Donald Worster. Pg 155.

40. Herbert Hoover. (1929). Quoted in Glennon, Robert. (2002). *Water Follies: Groundwater Pumping and the Fate of America's Fresh Water.* Island Press: Washington, D.C.

41. Rachel Carson. (2002). *Silent Spring: 40th Anniversary Edition.* Houghton Mifflin Harcourt: New York, NY

42. U.S. Bureau of Reclamation. (2015) *Bureau of Reclamation: About US: Fact Sheet.* Retrieved from: www.usbr.gov/main/about/fact.html

43. Aldo Leopold. (1949. *A Sand County Almanac: And Sketches Here and There.* Oxford University Press: Oxford, England

Chapter 4 Notes – Taming the Wild River
Colorado River History

1. Mark Reisner (1993). pg. 130

2. Oskin, Becky. (2012). *New Clues Emerge in Puzzle of Grand Canyon's Age.* Live Science, dated November 29, 2012. Retrieved from: livescience.com/25123-grand-canyon-old-age.html.

3. Ives, John C. ; Newberry, J.S.; and Baird, Spencer Fullerton. (1861). *Report Upon the Colorado River of the West: Explored in*

1857 and 1858 by Lieutenant Joseph C. Ives. United States Army Corps of Topographical Engineers.(pg. 110)

4. Powell, John Wesley. (1875). *Exploration of the Colorado River of the West and Its Tributaries: Explored in 1869, 1870, 1871 and 1872.* Government Printing Office: Washington D.C. pg. 80

5. Information on the settling of the West came from the expected sources.

   Hundley, Morris, Jr. (2001)

   Hundley, Morris, Jr. (2009)

   Reisner, (1993)

   Sibley, George. (2012). *The 75-Year History of the Colorado River District: A Story About the Embattled Colorado River and the Growth of the West.* Silt, CO: Wolverine Publishing

   Worster, Donald. (1995)

6. United States Bureau of Reclamation. (2015). *Colorado River Basin Water Supply and Demand Study.*

7. Basics on prior appropriation came from

   Hundley. (2001)

   Hundley. (2009)

   Sibley (2012)

   Worster, (1995)

8. Gopalakrishnan, Chennat. (1973). *The Doctrine of Prior Appropriation and Its Impact on Water Development: A Critical Survey.* American Journal Of Economics & Sociology, 32(1), 61-72.

9. Hundley.(2001). Pg. 167

Reisner. Pg. 102

10. Reisner. (1993).

11. McCaffrey, Stephen C. (1996). *The Harmon Doctrine: One Hundred Years Later: Buried, Not Praised.* Natural Resources Journal. Vol. 36, pp. 549-590.

12. Sherow, James E. (1990). *The Contest for the "Nile of America": Kansas v. Colorado (1907).* Great Plains Quarterly, 10(1), pg 59.

13. Tyler, Daniel. (1996). *Delph E. Carpenter and the Principle of Equitable Apportionment.* Western Legal History: The Journal of the Ninth Judicial Circuit Historical Society. 9(1), pp. 34-53.

14. Hundley, Jr., Norris. (1982). *The 'Winters' Decision and Indian Water Rights: A Mystery Reexamined.* The Western Historical Quarterly, 13(1), pp. 17- 42.

15. Shurts, John Lytle. (1997). *Winters Doctrine: Origin and Development of the Indian Reserved Rights Doctrine in Its Social and Legal Context, 1880s-1930s.* A dissertation presented to Department of History & Graduate School of the University of Oregon. Ann Arbor, MI.pg. 5

16. Background on the Colorado River Compact was derived from the following:

     Hundley. (2009). Pg. x.

     Libecap, Gary D. (2007). *The Assignment of Property Rights on the Western Frontier: Lessons for Contemporary Environmental Resource Policy.* Journal of Economic History 67(2), pg. 285.

     Limerick, Patricia Nelson and Hanson, Jason L. (2012). *A Ditch in Time: The City, the West and Water.* Golden, CO: Fulcrum Publishing.

     Reisner. Pg 121

17. Background on development of Imperial Valley and formation of the Salton Sea is found in:

    Hundley. (2001)

    Hundley. (2001)

    Reisner. (1993)

    Worster. (1995)

18. United States Bureau of Land Management. *Take It Outside: Lake Cahuilla.* Retrieved from:http://www.blm.gov/ca/st/en/fo/ elcentro/recreation/ohvs/isdra/dunesinfo/tio_ohv/travel_dune. print.htm.

19. Wikipedia. (2015). *Salton Sea.* Retrieved from: https://en.wikipedia.org/wiki/Salton_Sea#/media/ File:Saltonseadrainagemap.jpg

20. Information on the Colorado Compact came from:

    Hundley. (2001)

    Hundley. (2009)

    Limerick & Hanson. (2012)

    Reisner. (1993)

    Sibley. (2012).

    United States Bureau of Reclamation. (1922). *Colorado River Compact, 1922.* Retrieved from: https://www.usbr.gov/lc/ region/pao/pdfiles/crcompct.pdf

    Worster. (1995)

21. Hundley. (2009). Pg. 301.

22. Upper Colorado River Basin Compact (1948). Retrieved from: https://www.usbr.gov/lc/region/pao/pdfiles/ucbsnact.pdf

23. Background on Arizona v. California came from

Arizona v. California 373 U.S. 546 (1963). Retrieved from: https://supreme.justia.com/cases/federal/us/373/546/

Haber, David. (1964). *Arizona v. California – A Brief Review.* Natural Resources Journal. Vol. 4. (pp. 17-28).

Hundley. (2001).

Hundley. (2009).

MacDonnell, Lawrence J. (2012).*Arizona v. California Revisited.* Natural Resources Journal. Vol. 52. (pp. 363-420)

Shurtz. (1997)

Trelease, Frank J. (1963). *Arizona v. California: Allocation of Water Resources to People, States and Nation.* The Supreme Court Review. Vol. 1963, pp. 158-205

Worster, Donald. (1995).

24. Background information and the resulting issues on the Colorado River Compact and is found in

Hundley. (2001)

Hundley. (2009)

Limerick & Hanson. (2012)

Newkirk, Barrett. (2013). *Quantification Settlement Agreement Upheld by Judge.* Desert Sun. June 5, 2013. Retrieved from: http://www.mydesert.com/article/20130605/NEWS0701/ 306050002/Quantification-Settlement-Agreement- ruling-Salton-Sea.

Reisner. (1993)

Sibley. (2012)

Water Education Foundation. (2014). *Quantification Settlement Agreement.* Retrieved from:http://www.watereducation.org/aquapedia/quantification-settlement-agreement

Worster. (1995)

25. U.S. Bureau of Reclamation. (2012). *Colorado River Basin: Water Supply and Demand Study: Technical Report B – Water Supply Assessment.* Pg. B-31.Retrieved from: http://www.usbr.gov/lc/region/programs/crbstudy/finalreport/Technical%20Report%20B%20-%20Water%20Supply%20Assessment/TR-B_Water_Supply_Assessment_FINAL.pdf pg. B-22

26. Information on the Colorado River Storage Project (CRSP) obtained from:

Glen Canyon Dam Adaptive Management Program. (2014). *Colorado River Storage Project.* Retrieved from: http://www.gcdamp.gov/fs/CRSP.pdf

Hundley. (2001)

Hundley. (2009)

Limerick & Hanson. (2012)

Reisner. (1993)

Sibley. (2012).

West, Elliot. (2012). *The Essential West: Collected Essays by Elliot West.* Norman, OK: University of Oklahoma Press

Worster. (1995)

U. S. Department of Reclamation.(2008). *Upper Colorado Region: Colorado River Storage Project.* Retrieved from: http://www.usbr.gov/uc/rm/crsp/

27. Reisner. Pg. 281

28. Eggert, Charles; Litton, Martin and Clark Nathan. (1953). *The Wilderness River Trail video.* Sierra Club: Retrieved from: https://www.youtube.com/watch?v=JfyFC8CX1Nc

29. Brower, David. (1955). *Two Yosemites.* Sierra Club. Retrieved from: https://archive.org/details/cubanc_000041

30. Stegner, Wallace. (1955). *This is Dinosaur: Echo Park and Its Magic Rivers.* Alfred A. Knopf: New York, NY.

31. Harvey, Mark. (1995). *The Battle for Dinosaur: Echo Park Dam and the Birth of the Modern Wilderness Movement.* Montana: The Magazine of Western History.

32. Porter, Elliot. ((1966). *The Place That No One Knew. Foreward by David Brower.* Sierra Club

33. Information on the Quantification Settlement Agreement came from:

    Newkirk, Barrett. (2013). *Quantification Settlement Agreement Upheld by judge.*

    Desert Sun. June 5, 2013. Retrieved from: http://www.mydesert.com/ article/20130605/NEWS0701/306050002/ Quantification- Settlement-Agreement-ruling-Salton-Sea.

    San Diego County Water Authority. (2015). Quantification Settlement Agreement for the Colorado River. Retrieved from: http://www.sdcwa.org/sites/default/files/qsa-fs.pdf

    Water Education Foundation. (2014). *Quantification Settlement Agreement.* Retrieved from:http://www.watereduction.org/ aquapedia quantification-settlement-agreement

    Williams, Matt. (2013). *Judge Upholds 2003 Quantification Settlement Agreement.* Association of California Water Agencies. Retrieved from: http://www.acwa.com/news/water-supply-challenges/judge-upholds-2003-colorado-river-quantification-settlement-agreement

34. U.S. Bureau of Reclamation. (2012). Reclamation: Managing Water in theWest: The Colorado River Basin Water Supply and Demand Study. Pg.8

35. U.S. Bureau of Reclamation. (2007). *Record of Decision: Colorado River Interim Guidelines for Lower Basin Shortages and the Coordinated Operations for Lake Powell and Lake Mead.*

36. Information on interstate issues derived from:

Hundley, Norris Jr. (2001)

Hundley, Norris Jr. (2009)

Limerick, & Hanson. (2012)

Reisner. (1993)

Sibley. (2012).

Worster. (1995)

37. Colorado Division of Water Resources. (2005). *Transbasin Diversions.* Retrieved from: http://water.state.co.us/SurfaceWater/SWRights/WaterDiagrams/Pages/TransbasinDiversions.aspx

38. Information on the Colorado Big Thompson Project (C-BT) compiled from:

Robert Autobee. (1996), *Colorado-Big Thompson Project.* Bureau of

Reclamation: Washington, D.C.

Hundley. (2001)

Hundley. (2009)

Limerick & Hanson L. (2012)

Reisner. (1993)

Sibley. (2012).

Worster. (1995)

United States Department of the Interior: Bureau of Reclamation. (2012a).*Colorado River Basin: water supply and demand study: executive summary.* Retrieved from: http://www.usbr.gov/lc/region/programs/crbstudy/finalreport/Executive%20Summary/CRBS_Executive_Summary_FINAL.pdf

39. Sibley, George. (2012). Pg. 46

40. Winchester, John N. (2012). *A Historical View: Transmountain Diversion Development in Colorado.* United States Committee on Irrigation and Drainage Report: Denver CO.

41. NASA.(). *Visible Earth: Water Level Changes in Lake Mead.* Retrieved from:http://visibleearth.nasa.gov/view.php?id=45945

42. Glen Canyon Institute.(). *Lake Powell Reservoir: A Failed Solution.* Retrieved from: http://www.glencanyon.org/glen_canyon/failed.

43. Solomon, Steven. (2011). *Water: The Epic Struggle for Wealth, Power and Civilization.* Harper Perennial: New York. NY. Pg. 332

44. Glennon. (2002)

45. Worster. (1995). Pg 322

46. Colorado River Basin Salinity Control Forum. (2011). *Water Quality Standards for Salinity: Colorado River System.* Retrieved from: http://www.crb.ca.gov/Salinity/2011/2011%20REVIEWOctober%20Final.pdf

47. Reisner. Pg. 120

48. Solomon, Steven. (2002). Pg. 332

49. Glen Canyon Institute. *FAQ: How Much Sediment is Deposited in the Reservoir by the Colorado River?* Retrieved from: GlenCanyon. org

50. Reisner. Pg. 474.

51. Wikipedia.(2016). *Ogallala Aquifer.* Retrieved from: https:// en.wikipedia.org/wiki/Ogallala_Aquifer

52. Worster. (pg. 313)

53. Glennon, Robert. (2002). Pg 124

54. Barnett. pg. 7.

55. Reisner. Pg 438

56. Glennon, Robert. (2009) pg 305

57. Glennon. (2002)

    Reisner. Pg 439

58. First presented in a lecture in 1833, the Tragedy of the Commons pointed out the issues resulting from Adam Smith's "Invisible Hand"where rational decisions are made by individuals that often impact the common good negatively. Two sources were used.

    Lloyd, William Forster (1833).*Two Lectures on the Checks of Population.* England: Oxford University.

    Hardin, Garrett. (1968). *The Tragedy of the Commons.* Science. 162(3859. Pp. 1243-1248

59. Egan, Timothy. (2006). *The Worst Hard Time.* NYC, NY: Mariner Books. Pg 311.

60. Weather Channel. (2015). *Dust Storm Covers Phoenix.* Retrieved from: http://www.weather.com/news/news/phoenix-arizona-dust-storm

61. Knudson, Ted. (2014). *Outrage in Owens Valley a Century After L.A. Began Taking Its Water.* Sacramento Bee. January 5, 2014

Chapter 5 Notes – 'California Dreamin'
California Today

1. John Phillips & Michelle Phillips.(1963)*California Dreamin'.* On "If You Can Believe Your Eyes and Ears" Los Angeles, CA: Dunhill Records. Release date March 1966.

2. Jan Null. (2015). *4-Year Rainfall Deficits Look Daunting.* Golden Gate Weather Services: Weather and Climate Blog dated April, 6, 2015.

3. U.S. Department of Agriculture. (2015). National Drought Monitor. Retrieved from: http://www.drought.gov/drought/area/ca

4. John Erdman. (2015). *California's Snowpack at Record Early-April Low: Sierra Snow Survey Finds Bare Ground.* Retrieved from: http://www.weather.com/climate-weather/drought/news/california-sierra-snowpack-record-low-april-2015#/!

5. California Department of Water Resources.(2016). *Snow Water Equivalents (inches).* Dated March 25, 2016. Retrieved from: http://cdec.water.cagov/cdecapp/snowapp/sweq.action

6. U.S. Department of Agriculture. (2016). National Drought Monitor. Retrieved from: http://droughtmonitor.unl.edu/Home/StateDrought Monitor.aspx?CA

7. California Department of Water Resources. (August 5, 2015). *California Data Exchange Center – Reservoirs.* Retrieved from: http://www.water.ca.gov/waterconditions/waterconditions.cfm

8. NASA. (2014). *NASA Analysis: 11 Trillion Gallons to Replenish California Drought.* NASA Science News.Dated December 16, 2014.

9. Amanda Zamora; Lauren Kirchner; & Abrahm Lustgarten. (2015). *Killing the Colorado: The Truth Behind the Water Crisis in the West: California's Drought is Part of a Much Bigger Water Crisis.* ProPublica dated June 25, 2015.

10. Matt Stevens & Chris Megerian. (2015). *Southern California Lags Behind in Water Conservation.* LA Times dated April 7, 2015.

11. Rob Kuznia. (2015). *Rich Californians Balk at Limits: 'We're not all equal when it comes to water.'* Washington Post dated June 13, 2015.

12. State of California (2015). *Executive Order B-29-19.*

13. California Department of Water Resources.(2015). *California State Water Project.* Retrieved from: http://www.water.ca.gov/swp/

14. California Department of Water Resources. (2015). *News Release dated March 2, 2015.* Retrieved from: http://www.water.ca.gov/news/newsreleases/2015/030215allocation.pdf

15. Information on the Quantification Settlement Act came from:

    Barrett Newkirk. (2013). *Quantification Settlement Agreement Upheld by Judge.* Desert Sun. June 5, 2013. Retrieved from: http://www.mydesert.com/article/20130605/NEWS0701/

306050002/Quantification-Settlement-Agreement-ruling-Salton-Sea.

Matt Williams. (2013). *Judge upholds 2003 Colorado River Quantification Settlement Agreement.* Association of California Water Agencies. Retrieved from: http://www.acwa.com/news/water-supply-challenges/ judge-upholds-2003-colorado-river-quantification- settlement-agreement

San Diego County Water Authority. *Quantification Settlement Agreement for the Colorado River.* Retrieved from: http://www.sdcwa.org/sites/default/files/qsa-fs.pdf

U.S. Bureau of Reclamation. (2012). Reclamation: Managing Water in the West: The Colorado River Basin Water Supply and Demand Study. Pg 8

16. Gary Polakovic. *Runoff: It's an Ongoing Challenge.* San Diego State University: The Salton Sea. Retrieved from: http://www.sci.sdsu.edu/salton/FarmRunoff.html

17. Henry Brean. (2013). *As Lake Mead Shrinks, California Uses More Than Its Share of Water.* Las Vegas Review Journal dated May 24, 2013.

18. Michael Cohen. (2014). *Hazard's Toll: The Costs of Inaction at the Salton Sea.* Pacific Institute: Boulder, CO.

19. Dana Goodyear. (2015). *The Dying Sea: What Will California Sacrifice to Survive the Drought?* New Yorker, May 4, 2015 issue.

20. Michael Cohen. (2014).

21. San Diego County Water Authority. (2015). *San Diego County's Water Sources.* Retrieved from: http://www.sdcwa.org/san-diego-county-water-sources

22. San Diego County Water Authority (2015). *Seawater Desalination: The Carlsbad Desalination Project. Fact Sheet.* Retrieved from: http://www.sdcwa.org/sites/default/files/desal-carlsbad-fs-single.pdf

23. Paul Rogers. (2014). *Nation's Largest Ocean Desalination Plant Goes Up Near San Diego; Future of the California Coast?* San Jose Mercury News. Dated May 29, 2014.

24. San Diego Water Authority. (2015).

25. Paul Rogers. (2014)

26. Erik Anderson. (2015). *Eyes Look to Carlsbad's Desalination Plant.* KPBS Radio News. July 27, 2015. Retrieved from: http://www.kpbs.org/news/2015/jul/27/eyes-look-carlsbad-desalination-plant/

27. Paul Rogers. (2014).

28. Hiltzik, Michael. (2015). *Desalination Plants Aren't A Good Solution for California Drought.* LA Times. April 24, 2105

29. Hamilton, Matt. (2015). *Santa Barbara to Spend $55 million on Desalination Plant As Drought 'Last Resort'.* LA Times. Dated July 22, 2015.

30. Michael Young & James C. McColl.(2009). *Double Trouble: The Importance of Accounting for Obtaining Water Entitlements Consistent with Hydrological Realities.* The Australian Journal of Agricultural and Resource Economics. 54. pp. 19-35.

31. City of Santa Barbara. (2016). *Drought Information.* Retrieved from: http://www.santabarbaraca.gov/gov/depts/pw/resources/system/docs/ default.asp?utm_source=WaterConservation&utm_medium=Drought&utm_campaign=QuickLink

32. KSBY News (2016). *Lake Cachuma water Levels Could Reach Historic Low By End of 2016.* Retrieved from: http://www.ksby.com/story/31906634/lake-cachuma-water-level-could-reach-historic-low-by-end-of-2016

33. Anna R. Schecter & Matthew De Luca. (2015).*In Palm Springs, America's 'Oasis' Grapples with Drought.* NBC News. Retrieved from: www.nbcnews.com/storyline/california-drought/palm-springs-oasis-grapples-drought-n337371

34. California Department of Food and Agriculture. (2015). *California Agricultural Production Statistics for 2013.* Retrieved from: http://www.cdfa.ca.gov/Statistics/

35. Michael Cohen; Juliet Christian-Smith; & John Berggren. (2013). *Water to Supply the Land: Irrigated Agriculture in the Colorado River Basin.* Pacific Institute. Oakland, CA

36. Articles detailing California and the production of almonds included:

    Robin Abcarian.(2015). *Almonds, the Demons of Drought? Frustrated Growers Tell Another Story.* LA Times. April 6, 2015. Retrieved from: http://www.latimes.com/local/abcarian/la-me-0417-abcarian-almonds-demons-20150417-column.html

    James Hamblin. (2014). *The Dark Side of Almond Use.* The Atlantic. August 24, 2014.

37. Kim Kyle, Jon Schleuss, & Priya Krishnakumar. (2015). *XXX Gallons of Water Went to Make This Plate.* LA Times. April 7, 2015. Retrieved from:http://graphics.latimes.com/food-water-footprint/

38. Information regarding alfalfa production in California was derived from: Alliance for Water Efficiency. (2010). *Flood Irrigation*

Introduction. Retrieved from: http://allianceforwaterefficiency. org? flood_Irrigation_Introduction.aspx

Blaine R. Hanson; Khaled M. Bali; & Blake L. Sanden. (2008). *Irrigated Alfalfa Management for Mediterranean and Desert Zones. Chapter7: Irrigating Alfalfa in Arid Regions.* University of California: Davis: Division of Agriculture and Natural Resources.

Daniel H. Putnam; Charles G. Summers; & Steve B. Orloff. (2007). *Irrigated Alfalfa Management for Mediterranean and Desert Zones. Chapter 1: Alfalfa Production Systems in California.* University of California: Division of Agriculture and Natural Resources

39. Blaine Hanson. *Irrigation of Agricultural Crops in California. University of California Davis.* Retrieved from: http://www.arb. ca.gov/fuels/lcfs/workgroups/lcfssustain/hanson.pdf

40. California Department of Food and Agriculture (2015). *California Agricultural Production Statistics.* Retrieved from: www.cdfa.ca.gov/statistics.

41. Noel Brinkerhoff. (2014). *Could California Drought Be Ended by Stopping Alfalfa Exports to China?* Retrieved from: http:// www.allgov.com/news/us-and-the-world/could-california- drought-be-ended-by-stopping-alfalfa-exports-to-china- 140222?news=852504

42. Numerous books and articles discuss how inexpensive water is and the subsidies the federal government has extended. Some of these include:

Charles Fishman. (2012).Pg. 267

Robert Glennon.(2009). Pg. 223

Eduardo Porto. (2014). *The Risks of Cheap Water.* NY Times dated October 14, 2014

43. Eduardo Porter. (2014).

44. Jay Famiglietti. (2014). *The Groundwater Crisis.* Nature Climate Change. Vol. 4. Retrieved from: http://web.mit.edu/12.000/ www/ m2018/pdfs/ groundwatercrisis.pdf pg. 946

Tom Philpott. (2014). *These Maps of California's Water Shortage Are Terrifying.* Mother Jones dated October 30, 2014.

45. NASA Jet Propulsion Laboratory. (2014). *NASA Data Reveal Major Groundwater Loss in California.* California Institute of Technology. Retrieved from: http://www.jpl.nasa.gov/news/ news.php?release=2009-194

46. Adam Volland (2014). *Earth's Disappearing Ground Water.* NASA. Retrieved from: http://earthobservatory.nasa.gov/blogs/ earthmatters/files/2014/11/nclimate2425-f1.jpg

47. California Department of Water Resources. (2015). *Groundwater.* Retrieved from:http://www.water.ca.gov/groundwater/

48. CBS News. (2014). *Depleting the Groundwater: Report by Leslie Stahl for 60 Minutes: Dated November 16, 2014.* Retrieved from: http://www.cbsnews.com/news/depleting-the-water/

49. Jeremy Miller. (2014). *California's Sweeping Groundwater Regulation.* High Country News. Dated November 10, 2014. Retrieved from: http://www.hcn.org/issues/46.19/californias-sweeping-new-groundwater-regulations

50. State of California: Department of Water Resources. (2015). *Most Significant Droughts: Comparing Historical and Recent Conditions.*State of California.

51. United States Bureau of Reclamation. (2016). *Managing water in the West: lower Colorado River Operations: archives of Daily Reservoir and River Conditions.*

52. Summit Technologies, Inc.(2016). *Lake Powell Water Database.* Retrieved from: http://lakepowell.water-data.com

53. Gene Cubbison.(2014). *Running Dry: Drought in California: San Diego Approves $3.5B Recycled Water Project.* NBC San Diego: dated November 18, 2014

54. Jeff Daniels. (2015). *LA Considers $1 Billion 'Toilet to Tap' Water Program.*CNBC dated October, 22, 2105.

55. Ted Grantham & Joshua Viers. (2014a). *100 years of California's Water Rights Systems: Patterns, Trends and Uncertainties.* Environmental Research Letters 9. Pp. 1-10. doi:10.1088/1748-9326/9/8/084012

    Ted Grantham & Joshua Viers. (2014b). *California Water Rights: You Can't Manage What You don't Measure.* UC Davis Center of Watershed Sciences. Retrieved from: http://californiawaterblog. com/2014/   08/20/california-water-rights-you-cant-manage-what-you-dont-measure/

56. Jason Dearen & Garance Burke. (2014). *California Drought: State's Flawed Water System Can't Track Usage.* Associated Press. Retrieved from: http://www.huffingtonpost.com/2014/05/27/california-drought_n_5395501.html

57. Grantham and Viers. (2014a). pg.1

58. Jenny Choy; Geoff McGhee; & Melissa Rohde. (2014). *Water in the West: Understanding California's Groundwater: Recharge Groundwater's Second Act.* Stanford Woods Institute for the Environment.

59. Ibid.

60. UC Davis. Center for Watershed Science. (2015). *Water Storage: Myth: We can build our way out of California's water problems with new dams.* Retrieved from: https://watershed.ucdavis.edu/myths/

61. California Department of water Resources. (2016). *2016 Drought Contingency Plan CVP and SWP Operations February – November 2016.*(Submitted January 15, 2016).

62. Ibid. (2016). Pg 11.

63. Ibid. (2016). Pg 12.

Chapter 6 Notes
"Drought Does Not Mean a Water Shortage"
Arizona Today

1. Arizona Municipal Water Users Association. (2014). *Drought Does Not Equal A Water Shortage.* One for Water - October 23, 2014 meeting. Retrieved from: http://www.cap-az.com/documents/meetings/10-23-2014/Drought%20Does%20Not%20 Equal%20A%20Water%20Shortage-1pg.pdf

2. Background information on the Groundwater Management Act of 1980 came from:

   Arizona Department of Water Resources. *Securing Arizona's Future Overview of the Arizona Groundwater Management Code.* Retrieved from: http://www.azwater.gov/AzDWR/WaterManagement/documents/Groundwater_Code.pdf

   Arizona Department of Water Resources.(2010). *Water Atlas: Volume 8: Active Management Areas Water Atlas.* Retrieved from:

http://www.azwater.gov/azdwr/StatewidePlanning/WaterAtlas/ActiveManagementAreas/documents/Volume_8_final.pdf

Hanemann, Michael. (2002). *The Central Arizona Project*. University of California, Berkeley: Department of Agricultural Resource Economics. CUDARE Working Papers # 937.

Megdal, Sharon B. (2012). *The Water Report: Arizona Groundwater Management*. Water Resources Research Center, University of Arizona.

3. U.S. Bureau of Reclamation. (2007). *Record of Decision: Colorado River Interim Guidelines for Lower Basin Shortages and the Coordinated Operations for Lake Powell and Lake Mead Guidelines*.

4. Arizona Department of Water Resources. *Securing Arizona's Future Overview of the Arizona Groundwater Management Code*. Hanemann, Michael. (2002). *The Central Arizona Project*. University of California, Berkeley: Department of Agricultural Resource Economics. CUDARE Working Papers # 937.

5. Several sources provided information on the issues Tucson experienced as CAP became operational.

McKinnon, Shaun. (2012). *Arizona Canal Project and Uphill Journey*. The Republic. Retrieved from: http://archive.azcentral.com/arizonarepublic/news/articles/20121125arizona-canal-project0an-uphill-journey.html

Water Research Center, College of Agricultures, University of Arizona (1999). *The Rise and Fall of CAP: In Water in the Tucson Area: A Status report*. Arizona Daily Star dated July 11,1999.

6. Central Arizona Project. (2015). *CAP: Your Water Your Future: Recharge Program*. Retrieved from http://www.cap-az.com/departments/recharge-program/recharge-in-arizona

Choy, Jenny, McGhee, Geoff and Rohde, Melissa. (2014). *Water in the West: Understanding California's Groundwater: Recharge Groundwater's Second Act.* Stanford Woods Institute for the Environment Megdal, Sharon B. (2012).

This report addresses both recharge and water banking in Arizona.

7. Central Arizona Project. (2015). *CAP: Your Water Your Future: Recharge Program.* Retrieved from: http://www.cap-az.com/departments/recharge-program/recharge-in-arizona

   City of Tucson. (2015). *Recharged Water.* Retrieved from: https://www.tucsonaz.gov/water/recharged-water

8. Ferris, Kathleen. (2015). *Leadership: Water Brings Phoenix and Tucson Together.* One for Water. Arizona Municipal Water Users Association. April 20, 2015. Retrieved from: https://amwua.wordpress.com/2015/04/20/leadership-water-brings-phoenix-and-tucson-together/

   Central Arizona Project. (2015). *CAP: Your Water Your Future: Recharge Program.* Retrieved from: http://www.cap-az.com/departments/recharge-program.

9. O'Donnell, Michael and Colby, Bonnie. (2010). *Water Banks: A Tool for Enhancing Water Supply Reliability.* Department of Agricultural and Resource Economics, University of Arizona. pg.2

10. Arizona Water Banking Authority (AWBA). (2013). Arizona Water Banking Authority: Annual Report 2013.

11. Arizona Department of Water Resources. (2015). *Securing Arizona's Water Future: Supply and Demand.* Retrieved from: http://www.azwater.gov/AzDWR/PublicInformationOfficer/documents/supplydemand.pdf

12. Arizona Municipal Water Users Association. (2014). *Drought Does Not Equal A Water Shortage.* One for Water. October 23, 2014 meeting. Retrieved from: http://www.cap-az.com/documents/meetings/10-23-2014/Drought%20Does%20Not%20Equal%20A%20Water%20Shortage-1pg.pdf

13. Jayne Belnap & D.H. Campbell. (2011), Effects of climate change and land use on water resources in the Upper Colorado River Basin: U.S. Geological Survey Fact Sheet.

14. Pamela Packard. (2014). *Colorado River Shortages Could Occur By 2016 or 2017.* Arizona Capitol News dated March 3, 2014.

15. Carefree Water Company: *Brief History of Carefree Water Company.* Retrieved from: http://www.carefreewaterco.com/watercompanyhistory.html

16. Boston Water Sewer Commission. (2015). *Rates: 2015 Water and Sewer Rates.*Retrieved from: http://www.bwsc.org/services/rates/ rates.asp

    City of Phoenix. (2015). *Water and Sewer Rates.* Retrieved from: https://www.phoenix.gov/waterservices/customerservices/rateinfo

17. deBuys, William. (2011). *A Great Aridness: Climate Change and the Future of the American Southwest.* Oxford University Press: NYC, NY. p. 171.

18. Arizona Department of Water Resources. (2015). *Securing Arizona's Water Future: Supply and Demand.* Retrieved from: http://www.azwater.gov/AzDWR/PublicInformationOfficer/documents/supplydemand.pdf

    Cohen, Michael; Christian-Smith, Juliet; and Berggren, John. (2013). *Water to Supply the Land: Irrigated Agriculture in the Colorado River Basin.* Pacific Institute. Oakland, CA. pg 39

19. Cohen, Michael. et. al. (2013). (pg. 43)

20. Abraham Lustgarten & Naveena Sadasivam. (2015). *Holy Crop: How Federal Dollars are Financing the Water Crisis in the West.* ProPublica. Retrieved from: https://projects.propublica.org/killing-the-colorado/story/arizona-cotton-drought-crisis

21. Michael Gunther. (2013). *The Impact of a Cotton T-Shirt: How Smart Choices Can Make A Difference in Our Water and Energy Footprint.* World Wild Life Fund.

22. Joseph Heller. (1955). *Catch 22.* Simon and Schuster: New York, NY. pg. 86.

23. Lustgarten and Sadasivam, (2015)

24. Cohen et al. (2013) (pg. 64 & 65)

25. Ibid. (pg. 62)

26. Eric Holthaus. (2015). *Dry Heat: As Lake Mead Hits Record Lows and Water Shortages Loom, Arizona Prepares for the Worst.* Science. Retrieved from: http://www.slate.com/articles/health_and_science/science/2015/05/arizona_water_shortages_loom_the_state_prepares_for_rationing_as_lake_mead.single.html

    Brandon Loomis. (2015).*As the River Runs Dry: The Southwest's Water Crisis.* The Republic. Retrieved from: http://www.azcentral.com/story/news/arizona/investigations/2015/02/27/southwest-water-crisis-part-one/24011053/

    Packard, Pamela (2014).

Chapter 7 Notes -
What Happens in Las Vegas Does NOT Stay in Las Vegas
Las Vegas Today

1. Bureau of Land Management, Nevada. *Prehistoric Cultural Resources*. Rhttp://www.blm.gov/nv/st/en/fo/lvfo/blm_programs/lvfo_recreation/prehistoric_cultural.print.html

2. Mary Manning & Andy Samuelson. (2008). *A Gamble in the Sand: How Las Vegas Transformed Itself from a Railroad Watering Hole to the 'Entertainment Capital of the World'*. Las Vegas Sun. dated May 15, 2008.

3. Charles Fishman. (2011). *The Big Thirst: The Secret Life and Turbulent Future of Water*. Free Press: New York, NY. pp. 51-53

   Fishman goes into a great deal of detail on the fountains and

   Otherwater features along the strip, especially the Bellagio.

4. Circle of Blue Water News. (2012). *Q & A: Pat Mulroy on Las Vegas and the Journey to Water Efficiency*. Interview on October 12, 2012. Retrieved from: *Dam Nation: How Water Shaped the West and Will Determine Its Future*. Retrieved from: http://www.circleofblue.org/waternews/2012/world/qa-pat-mulroy-on-las-vegas-and-the-journey-to-water-efficiency/

   Fishman, (2011). Pg. 58

5. Fishman, (2011). Pg. 58.

6. Ibid. pg. 66-69

7. Charles Fishman. (2010). *The Big Thirst: Nothing's Quite So Thirsty as a Las Vegas Golf Course*. Retrieved from: http://www.fastcompany.com/1749643/big-thirst-nothing's-quite-so-thirsty-las-vegas-golf-course

8. Ibid

9.   Fishman. 2011. Pg. 66

10. Fishman. (2010).

11. Circle of Blue. (2015). *Price of water 2015: Up 6%in 30 Major Cities.* Retrieved from: http://www.circleofblue.org/2015/world/price-of-water-2015-up-6-%-in-30-major-u-s-cities-41-%-rise-since-2010/

12. Circle of Blue. (2012).

     Henry Brean. (2015). *Exit Interview: Mulroy Talks About Her Life As Las Vegas' Water Chief.* Las Vegas Review-Journal. February 1, 2014

13. Las Vegas Sun. (2015). *Utilities dated October 25, 2015.*Retrieved from: http://lasvegassun.com/guides/move-in/utilities/

14. Abraham Lustgarten. (2015). *The Water Witch.* ProPublica dated June 2, 2015. Retrieved from: https://projects.propublica.org/killing-the-colorado/story/pat-mulroy-las-vegas-water-witch

15. Robert Glennon. (2009). *Unquenchable: America's Water Crisis and What to Do About It.* Island Press. Washington D.C.pg. 15

16. Henry Brean (a). (2015). *Return Flows Deserve All Credit for Las Vegas' Water Supply.* Las Vegas Review-Journal dated June 13, 2015.

17. Henry Brean (b). (2015). *Exit Interview: Mulroy Talks About Her Life As Las Vegas' Water Chief.* Las Vegas Review-Journal. February 1, 2014.

     Emily Greene. (2008). *Quenching Las Vegas' Thirst.* Las Vegas Sun. Retrieved from: http://lasvegassun.com/news/topics/water/

William deBuys, (2011). *A Great Aridness: Climate Change and the Future of the American Southwest.* Oxford University Press: NYC.NY pg. 150

18. Jeremy Hobson. Host. (2014). *Nevada's Former Water Czar Shares Lessons Learned.* Public Radio: here and Now dated May 29 2014. Retrieved from: http://hereandnow.wbur.org/2014/05/29/nevada-water-lessons

19. Matt Jenkins. (2015). *The Water Czar Who Reshaped Colorado River Politics.* High Country News dated March 2, 2105.

Southern Nevada Water Authority. (2015). *Water Banking.* Retrieved from: http://www.snwa.com/ws/future_banking.html

20. Doug Kenny and Jeff Lukas. (2013). *Challenges of the Colorado River Basin presentation.* Retrieved from: http://www.slideshare.net/LearnMoreAboutClimate/climate-change-and-water-in-the-west-the-colorado-river-basin

21. Casey Coates Danson. (2013). *Dwindling Colorado River Forces First-Ever Cuts in Lake Powell Water Releases.* DaGlobal Possibilities date august 21, 2013. Retrieved from: http://www.globalpossibilities.org/dwindling-colorado-river-forces-first-ever-cuts-in-lake-powell-water-releases/

22. Numerous articles on the Third Straw included:

Eric Holthaus. (2014). *Lake Mead: Before and After the Epic Drought.* Slate.

Kaylee Thompson. (2014). *The Last Straw: How the Fortunes of Las Vegas Will Rise or Fall With Lake Mead.* Popular Science dated June 22,2014.

Walker, Alissa. (2015). *Lake Mead Is Now Lower Than Ever, But Las Vegas Has a Crazy Survival Plan.* Gizmodo. Retrieved from:

http://gizmodo.com/this-giant-straw-will-suck-vegass-water-from-the-dese-1590135681/1700743879

Anne VanderMey. (2015). *Las Vegas: City of Gambling, Tech Conferences and Water Crises.* Fortune dated January 9, 2015.

23. deBuys, (2011). *Pg. 157*

24. Henry Brean (b). (2015).

25. Jenkins. (2015).

Chapter 8 Notes – "The Trouble I'm In"
Colorado River Today

1. Rossdale, Gavin. (2008). *The Trouble I'm In.* On Wanderlust. BMG Rights Management U.S., LLC

2. USGS. (2015), *Current Conditions of Colorado River Streamflow.* Retrieved from: http://www.usgs.gov/water/

3. Cynthia Barnett. (2011). *Blue Revolution: Unmaking America's Water Crisis.* Boston, MA: Beacon Publishing.

4. Marc Reisner. (1993). *Cadillac Desert: The American West and Its Disappearing Water, Revised Edition.* NYC, NY: Penguin Books.

5. Charles Fishman. (2011). *The Big Thirst: The Secret Life and Turbulent Future of Water.* Free Press: New York, NY

6. Robert Glennon(2009). *Unquenchable: America's Water Crisis and What To Do About It.* Washington, D.C.: Island Press

Robert Glennon. (2002). *Water Follies: Groundwater Pumping and the Fate of America's Fresh Water.* Island Press: Washington, D.C.

7. Norris Hundley, Jr.. (2009). *Water and the West: The Colorado River Compact and the Politics of Water in the American West. Second Edition.* Los Angeles: University of California Press.

8. Steven Solomon. (2011). *Water: The Epic Struggle for Wealth, Power, and Civilization.* Harper Perennial: New York, NY

9. Donald Worster (1995). *Rivers of Empire: Water, Aridity, and the Growth of the American West.* New York, New York: Oxford University Press.

10. All population numbers, both historical and as of 2010 was obtained from the U.S. Census Bureau. Retrieved from: http://www.census.gov

11. Michael Cohen; Juliet Christian-Smith; & John Berggren. (2013). *Water to Supply the Land: Irrigated Agriculture in the Colorado River Basin.* Pacific Institute. Oakland, CA (pg. 56 and pg. 61)

12. Ibid. (pg. 73)

13. Ibid.pg. 60

14. Imperial County Department of Agriculture. (2014). *Imperial County: Agricultural Crop & Livestock Report: 2013.* Retrieved from: http://www.co.imperial.ca.us/ag/crop_&_livestock_reports/Crop_&_Livestock_Report_2013.PDF

    Oldham County Water District. *Interesting Water Facts.* Retrieved from: http://www.oldhamcountywater.com/interesting-water-facts.html

15. Andres Thompson. (2015). *2015 May Just Be Hottest Year on Record.* Scientific American. August 2015.

16. USDA. (2015). Drought Monitor. Retrieved from: http://droughtmonitor.unl.edu/Home/RegionalDroughtMonitor.aspx?west

17. Paul Rogers. (2014). *California Drought: Past Dry Periods Have Lasted More Than 200 Years, Scientists Say.* San Jose Mercury News dated January 25, 2014. Retrieved from: http://www.mercurynews.com/science/ ci_24993601/california-drought-past-dry-periods-have-lasted-more

    Glen M. MacDonald. (2007). *Severe and Sustained drought in Southern California and the West: Present conditions and insights from the past on causes and impacts.* Quaternary International.173-174. Pp. pg. 95

18. Chris Mooney. (2015). *The Pacific Ocean May Have Entered a New Warm Phase – and the Consequences Could Be Dramatic.* Washington Post dated April 10, 2015.

19. William K. Stevens.(1994). *Severe Ancient Droughts: A Warning to California.* New York Times dated July 19, 1994. Scott Stine indicated in the articles:

20. Stephanie L. Castle: Brian F. Thomas; John T. Reager; Matthew Rodell; Sean C. Swenson; & James S. Famiglietti(2014). *Groundwater Depletion During Drought Threatens Future Water Security of the Colorado River Basin.* Geophys. Research Letters., 41, pp. 5904–5911, doi:10.1002/2014GL061055.

21. USBR. *Lower Colorado Water Supply Report.* Retrieved from: http://www.usbr.gov/lc/region/g4000/weekly.pdf

22. Ibid

23. Rong-Gong Lin & Rosana Xia. (2015). *Water Managers Dodge Bullet With 'May Miracle' Rains.* LA Times dated July 17, 2015

24. United States Bureau of Reclamation. (2015). *Glen Canyon Dam/Lake Powell: Current Status.* Retrieved from: http://www.usbr.gov/uc/water/crsp/cs/gcd.html

25. Colorado Water Conservation Board. (2015). *Colorado Water Plan: Final 2015.* Retrieved from: http://coloradowaterplan.com

26. U.S. Bureau of Reclamation. (2012). *Colorado River Basin Water Supply and Demand Study: Executive Summary.*

27. James S. (Jay) Famiglietti. (2014). *Satellite Study Reveals Parched U.S. West Using Up Underground Water.* NASA News Release dated July 24, 2014. Retrieved from: http://www.nasa.gov/press/2014/july/satellite-study-reveals-parched-us-west-using-up-underground-water/#.VeS3WOm_e0s

28. Sandra Postel. (2014). *Groundwater Depletion in Colorado River Basin Poses Big Risk to water Security.* National Geographic: Water Currents

29. Stephanie L. Castle; Brian F. Thomas.; John T. Reager; Matthew Rodell; Sean C. Swenson; & James S. Famiglietti. (2014). *Groundwater Depletion During Drought Threatens Future Water Security of the Colorado River Basin.* Geophys. Research Letters., 41, pp. 5904–5911, doi:10.1002/2014GL061055.

30. Postel, (2014)

31. Braxton Little. (2009). *The Ogallala Aquifer: Saving a Vital U.S. Water Source.* Scientific American. March 2009.

32. Reisner, . (1993) (pg.10)

33. James S. Famiglietti (Jay).(2014). *The Global Groundwater Crisis: Groundwater Depletion the World Over Poses a Greater Threat to*

Global Water Security Than Is Currently Acknowledged. Nature Climate Change. vol. 4. Pp. 945-949.

34. Ibid. (pg. 649)

35. Colorado Water Conservation Board (2015). *Colorado Climate Plan: Policies and Strategies to Mitigate and Adapt: Executive Summary.* Retrieved from: http://cwcbweblink.state.co.us/ WebLink/ 0/doc/196541/Electronic.aspx?searchid=243b8969-739b-448c-bd2d-699af9b7aea0. Pg 2

36. National Research Council. (2007). *Colorado River Basin Water Management: Evaluating and Adjusting to Hydroclimatic Variability.* Washington, D.C.: National Academies Press.

    Stephen Saunders; Charles Montgomery; & Tom Easley.(2008). *Hotter and Drier: The West's Changed Climate.* Rocky Mountain Climate Organization and Natural Resources Defense Council. Pg. 1v.

37. National Oceanic and Atmospheric Administration (NOAA). (2014). *Future Temperature and Precipitation Change in Colorado.* Climate.Gov. Retrieved from: https://www.climate.gov/news-features/featured-images/future-temperature-and-precipitation-change-colorado

38 U.S.G.S.(2011) *Effects of Climate Change and Land Use on Water Resources in the Upper Colorado River Basin.* Retrieved from: http://pubs.usgs.gov/fs/2010/3123/pdf/FS10-3123.pdf

    Kathleen A. Miller (2001).

39. National Research Council. (2007). *Colorado River Basin Water Management: Evaluating and Adjusting to Hydroclimatic Variability.* Washington, D.C.: National Academies Press.

40. De Buys. 2011). Pg.26.

41. Jonathan Overpeck & Bradley Udall. (2010). *Dry Times Ahead.* Science 328 (June 25, 2010). Pp 1642

    Richard Seager; Mingfang Ting; Isaac Held; Yochanan Kushnir; Jian Lu; Gabriel Vecchi; Huei-Ping Huang; Nili Harnik; Ants Leetma, Ngar-Cheung Lau; Jennifer Velez; & Naomi Niak. (2007). *Modeled Projections of an Imminent Transition to a More Arid Climate in Southwestern North America.* Science 316. (May 25, 2007). pp. 1181

42. Julie Vano, Bradley Udall, Daniel Cayan Jonathan Overpeck, Levi Brekke, Tapahs Da, Holly Hartmann, Hugo Hidalgo, Martin Hoerling, Gregory McCabe, Kiyomi Morino, Robert Webb, Kevin Werner & Dennis Lettenmaier.(2014). *Understanding Uncertainly in Future Colorado River Streamflow.* American Meteorological Society.pg 59-77)

43. Tim Barnett; Robert Malone; William Pennell; Detlet Stammer; Bert Semtner; & Warren Washington. (2004). *The Effects of Climate Change on Water Resources in the West.: Introduction and Overview.* Climate Change. Vol 62. Pg.7.

44. Kathleen A. Miller (2001). *Climate and Water Resources in the West: Past and Future.* Journal of the West. 40(3), pp. 39-47

    U.S.G.S.. (2010). *Effects of Climate Change and Land Use on Water Resources in the Upper Colorado River Basin.* Retrieved from: http://pubs.usgs.gov/fs/2010/3123/pdf/FS10-3123.pdf

    U.S. Bureau of Reclamation. (2012). *Colorado River Basin Water Supply and Demand Study: Executive Summary.* Pg. ES-6

45. Jeffrey Jacobs.(2011). *The Sustainability of water Resources in the Colorado River Basin.* The Bridge.vol.41(4). p.11. National Academy of Engineering: Washington, D.C.

46. Denver Water. (2015.) *Inside City 2015 Rates.* Retrieved from: http://www.denverwater.org/BillingRates/RatesCharges/2015-rates/inside-city/

47. Charles Fishman. (2011). Pg. 275

    Robert Glennon. (2009). (Pg. 223)

48. State of Colorado. (2013). *Executive Order D 2013-005: Directing the Colorado water Conservation Board to Commence Work on the Colorado water Plan.* Retrieved from: http://cwcbweblink. state. co.us/WebLink/ElectronicFile.aspx?docid=171100&searchid=c 428f27e-6b83- 4a97-908c-31bb6996cf74&dbid=0

49. Ibid

50. Ibid

51. Donald Worster. (1995). (pg. 22)

52. Colorado Water Conservation Board. (2004). *Statewide WaterSupply Initiative Report (SWSI). Executive Summary. Pg 1.*Retrieved from: http://cwcb.state.co.us/publicinformation/ publications/Pages/StudiesReports.aspx

53. Abraham Lustgarten. (2015). *Use It or Lose It: Across the West, Exercising One's Right to Water.* ProPublica date June 9, 2015.

54. Colorado Water Conservation Board. (2015). *Colorado's Water Plan: Final- 2015.* Retrieved from: http://coloradowaterplan. com. Pg. 9-13

    "The State of Colorado Demand will continue to uphold the prior appropriation doctrine." (pg. 9-3).

55. Colorado Constitution. amend. XVI, § 6.

56. Serageldin, Ismall. (2009). *Water: Conflicts Set to Arise Within As Well As Between States.* 459(7244):163. DOI:10.1038/459163b

57. Colorado Basin Roundtable. (2015). *Colorado Basin Implementation Plan: Collaborating on Colorado's Water Plan.*

58. Lawrence J. MacDonnell; Reed Benson; Bonnie Colby; Robert Glennon; Bradley Udall; & Charles Wilkinson. (2015). *Navigating a Pathway Toward Colorado's Water Future: A Review and Recommendations on Colorado's Draft Water Plan.* Center for Natural Resources, Energy and the Environment.

59. Colorado Water Conservation Board. (2015). Colorado Water Plan: Final 2015. Pg. 3-23

60. Ibid. pg. 8-13.

   "However, the Framework cannot take the place of specific negotiations and agreements."

61. Ibid. pg. ES-10

62. Ibid. pg. 6-131

63. Ibid. Metro Basin Roundtable and South Platte Basin Roundtable (2015). Pg. S-12.

64. Colorado Water Conservation Board. Statewide Water Supply Initiative (2011). Pg. 1-13

   Colorado Water Conservation Board. (2015). ES-%

65. Ibid. (2015).

66. Ibid. (2015). Pg. 6-18

67. Charles Fishman. (2011). P.165

68. Stahl, Lesley. (2014). *Depleting the Groundwater.* CBS News. 60 Minutes. Dated November 16, 2014. Retrieved from: http://www.cbs.news.com/news/depleting-the-groundwater/

69. Colorado Water Conservation Board. (2015). *Colorado's Water Plan: Final – 2015.* (pg. 7-15)

70. Ibid.

71. Eric Balken. (2015). *It's Time to Let Lake Powell Go.* High Country News. December 1,2105

72. McBride, Pete (Producer, Director and Writer.(2013). *I Am Red.* (Documentary). United States: American Rivers.org Retrieved from: http://www.petemcbride.com/MOTION/i-am-red/1

Chapter 9 Notes-What Do You Pay for Water? The Price of Water

1. Toronto Globe and Mail. (1998). *Editorial dated 23 May 1998.*

2. Charles Fishman (2012). *The Big Thirst: The Secret Life and Turbulent Future of Water.* Free Press: New York, NY

3. Ibid. pg. 269.

   Robert Glennon. *Unquenchable: America's Water Crisis and What To Do About It.*(2009). Island Press. Washington D.C. pg. 225

4. Las Vegas Valley Water District. *Water Rates and Usage Thresholds.* Retrieved from: http://www.lvvwd.com/custserv/billing_rates_thresholds.html

5. Imperial Irrigation District (IID). 2015. *About IID Water.* Retrieved from: http://www.iid.com/water/about-iid-water

6. James, Ian. (2015). *Nestle Says It Will Use Less Water at California Plants.* Mother Jones dated May 14, 2015.

   Lobosco, Katie. (2015). *Drought Turns Californians Against Water Bottling Companies.* CNN Money dated May 26, 2015. Retrieved from: http://money.cnn.com/ 2015/05/26/news/companies/california-bottled-water-drought/

7. Denver Water. (2015). *Inside City 2015 Rates.* Retrieved from: http://www.denverwater.org/BillingRates/RatesCharges/2015-rates/inside-city/

8. City of Santa Fe: Water Division. Retrieved from: www. Santafenm.gov/ water division

9. Mark Oswald. (2015). *Santa Fe Water Rates Among Highest, Surveys Show, But Usage is Low.* Retrieved from: http://www. abqjournal.com/577825/ news/rates-are-high-but-usage-is-low. html

   Nelson Schwartz. (2015). *The Parched West: Water Pricing in Two Thirsty Cities: In One Guzzlers Pay More, and Use Less.*N.Y Times. Dated May 6, 2015.

10. Brian Melley. (2015). *Appeals Court Rules Against Higher Water Rates for Big Users.* Fresno Bee dated April 20, 2015. Retrieved from: http://www.fresnobee. Com/news/state/california/water-and-drought/article19667244.html#

    Storylink=cpy

    Stevens, Matt. (2015). *In a Blow to Water Conservation, Court Rejects San Juan Capistrano's Tiered Rates .* LA Times . Dated April 20, 2015.

11. Anthony Pura. (2013). *Fresno's Water Rates to Nearly Double by 2016.* ABC Action News: KFSN: Fresno. Retrieved from: http://abc30.com/ archive/9207745/

12. George Hostetter. (2014). *Fresno Council Repeals Water Rate Increases, Avoids Ballot Fight.* Fresno Bee dated July 31,2014. Retrieved from: http://www.fresnobee.com/news/politics-government/election/ article19522851.html

13. Glennon.(2012). Pg. 223

14. Ryan Lillis. (2015). *Sacramento To Speed Up Water Meter Installations.* The Sacramento Bee, dated February 23, 2015.

"Sacramento has more unmetered properties than any other city in California. While Sacramento leaders had fought for decades to avoid installing meters on homes, most other communities around the state are entirely served by water meters.

15. Robert Glennon. (2012). Pg 223.

16. Fresno Bee. (2015). *All Cities Must Put In water Meters. Editorial.* Dated June 22, 2105. Retrieved from: http://wwww. fresnobee.com/opinion/editorials/ article25197094.html

17. Hans Poschman. *Water Usage in the West.* Council of State Governments. Retrieved from: http://www.csgwest.org/policy/ WesternWaterUsage.aspx

18. City of Fresno: Public Utilities: Water Division. (2015). Important Documents: Proposed Water Rate Increases Fact Sheet. Retrieved from: http://www.fresno.gov/Government/ DepartmentDirectory/PublicUtilities/Watermanagement/ waterrates.htm

19. Charles Fishman. (2012). Pg. 269

Robert Glennon & Gary Libecap. (2014). *The West Needs a Water Market to Fight Drought..* Wall Street Journal dated October 23, 2014.

20. Lucinda Sue Crosby.(2012). *Water in the West: An Overview and an Environmental Essay.* Morris Publishing: Kearney, Nebraska

21. Maude Barlow & Tony Clarke. (2003). *Blue Gold: The Battle Against Corporate Theft of the World's Water.* McClelland and Stewart: Toronto, Ontario

22. Charles Fishman. (2012). Pg 280

     Robert Glennon. (2009). Pg. 307

23. Robert Glennon. (2009). Pg. 229

     Fishman, Charles. (2012).pg. 275

24. Marc Reisner. (1993. (pg. 516)

25. Charles Fishman. (2012). Pg 223

26. Robert Glennon. (2009). Pg. 229

27. Smith, Adam (1882). *Inquiry Into the Nature and Causes of the Wealth of Nations. Vol.1.* pg. 42. London: G. Walker, J. Akerman, E Edwards; Thomas Tegg: G. and J. Robinson, Liverpool: E. Thompson, Manchester; J. Noble Hull; J. Wilson, Berwick; W. Whyte & Co. Edinburgh; and R. Griffin and Co. Glasgow. Retrieved from: http://books.google.com/books?id =viZBAAAA IAAJ&printsec= frontcover&dq=in+wealth+of+nations+volume+1&hl= en&sa=X&ei=kMXeUpDGFGSyAHe14DoCg&ved= 0CC8Q6AEwA A#v= onepage&q=in%20wealth% 20of%20nations%20volume%201&f=false

28. City of Scottsdale, AZ. (2015). *City of Scottsdale Water and Sewer Rate Report:* Retrieved from: http://www.scottsdaleaz. gov/Assets/Public+Website/water/Rates+$!26+Fees/ FY15WaterWastewaterRateRpt.pdf

29. Robert Glennon. (2009). Pg.201.

30. Ibid. (pg. 198)

31. Charles Fishman. (2012).

32. Fishman, Charles Fishman. 2012). Pg. 269

33. Ibid. pg. 109and pg 303

34. Caitlin Owens; James Queally; & Emily Alpert Reyes. (2014). *UCLA-Area Water Main Break Spews Millions of Gallons.* LA Times dated July 29, 2014.

35. Chris Roberts. (2014). *Leaks Contribute To Drought, But Water Conservation to be the 'New Normal' for California.* The Examiner dated August 12, 2014.

    Lisa Krieger. (2014). *California Drought: Bay Area Loses Billions of Gallons to Leaky Pipes.* San Jose Mercury News dated August 16, 2014.

36. American Society of Civil Engineers. (2016). *2013 Report Card for America's Infrastructure.*

37. Cynthia Barnett. (2014). *Hey, America: It's Time to Talk About the Price of Water.* ENSIA dated October 6, 2104.

38. Circle of Blue. (2015). *Price of Water: 2010-2015: A Survey of water Prices for Households in 30 Major U.S. Cities.* Retrieved from: http://www.circleofblue.org/2015/world/price-of-water-2015-up-6-percent-in-30-major-u-s-cities-41-percent%-rise-since-2010/

39. Cynthia Barnett. (2014).

Chapter 10 Notes– "Teach Your Children Well"
Lessons Learned From Other Countries

1. Information on water management in Israel was found in:

Seth M. Siegel. (2015). *Let There Be Water: Israel's Solution for a WaterStarved World.* St. Marten's Press: New York, New York.

Christopher Woody; (2015). *Israel's Revolutionary Water Management Methods Aren't Going Aren't Going To Be Enough to Solve California's Devastating Drought.* Business Insider. dated June 15, 2015.

Palestinian Water Authority. (2012). *Annual Status Report on Water Resources, Water Supply, and wastewater in the Occupied State of Palestine – 2011.* Palestinian Water Authority: Ramallah. Pg. 28

Sharon Udasin. (2015). *Israeli, Jordanian Officials Signing Historic Agreement on Water Trade.* The Jerusalem Post dated February 26, 2015.

Yaakov Lappin. (2015). *Israel to Double Amount of Water Entering Gaza.* The Jerusalem Post dated March 4, 2015.

Israel Water Authority. (2012). *Master Plan for the National Water Sector.* Retrievedfrom: http://www.water.gov.il/Hebrew/ProfessionalInfoAndData/2012/09-Israel-Water-Sector-Master-Plan-2050.pdf

Israel Water Authority. (2015). *Water Sector in Israel: IWRM Model.* Retrieved from: http://www.water.gov.il/Hebrew/ProfessionalInfoAndData/2012/02-Israel%20Water%20Sector%20%20IWRM%20Model.pdf

Christopher Woody. (2015). *Israel's Revolutionary Water Management Methods Aren't Going Aren't Going To Be Enough to Solve California's Devastating Drought.* Business Insider. dated June 15, 2015.

Isabel Kershner. (2015).*Aided By the Sea, Israel Overcomes An Old Foe: Drought.* The New York Times dated May 29, 2015

2. Central Bureau of Statistics. (2009). *Israel in Statistics: 1948-2007.* Central Bureau of Statistics: Jerusalem.March 5, 2009).

3. Central Bureau of Statistics (2014). *Israel's Population on the Eve of Independence Day.* Central Bureau of Statistics: Jerusalem. May 1, 2014.

4. Seth M. Siegel. (2015). Pg. 240

5. Seth M. Siegel. (2015). In an interview with Oded Fixler, Deputy General Manager of the Israel Water and Sewage Authority. Pg 45.

6. Ibid. (pg.45)

7. Ibid. (pg. 238)

8. Ibid. (2015). Pg 64

9. Ibid. (2015). Pg.88

10. Israel Water Authority. (2012). *Long –Term Master Plan for the National Water Sector: Part A- Policy Document: version 4.* Water Authority Planning Division.

11. Siegel. (2015). Pg 91

12. Woody. (2015)

13. Information on Singapore's water management system came from: Barnett, Cynthia. (2011). *Blue Revolution: Unmaking America's Water Crisis.*Boston, MA: Beacon Press.

    Meera Senthilingam. (2014). *Drinking Sewage: Solving Singapore's Water Problem.* CNN News. Retrieved from: http://www.cnn.com/2014/09/23/ living/newater-singapore/

PUB, Singapore's Water Agency. (2016). *Overview_ Four National Taps Provide Water for All.*Retrieved from: http://www. pub.gov.sg/water/ Pages/default.aspx

14. Information on Chile's water management system came from:

Carl J Bauer. (2005). *In The Image of the Market: The Chilean Model of Water Resources Management.* International Journal of Water 3(2). Pp. 146-165

Bauer, Carl J. (2008). *The Experience of Chilean water Markets.* Presentation at Expo Zaragoza, 2008.

Joe Mentor, Jr. (2001). *Trading Water, Trading Places: Water Marketing in Chile and the Western United States.* AWRA/IWLRI-University of Dundee International Specialty Conference: August 6-8, 2001.

Maria de la Luz Domper. (2009). *Chile: A Dynamic Water Market.* World Bank: World Development Indicators Online.

R. Quenton Grafton; Clay Landry; Gary D. Libecap: Sam McGlennon; and Robert O'Brien. (2010). *An Integrated Assessment of Water Markets in Australia, Chile, China , South Africa, and the USA.*National Bureau of Economic Research: Working Paper 16203. Retrieved from: http://www.nber.org/ papers/ w16203

15. Carl J. Bauer. (2005). Pg. 150

16. Mentor. (2001). Pg 4

17. Ibid. (2001). Pg. 7

18. Grafton. Et. al. (2010).pg 24.

19. Mentor. (2001). Pg 7.

20. Bauer. (2005). Pg. 154

21. Bauer.(2008).

22. Bauer. (2005). (p. 161)

23. Humberto Pena. *Chiles Experiences on water Reform.* Retrieved from:http://siteresources.worldbank.org/EXTWAT/ Resources/4602122-1213366294492/ 51062201213649450319/3.1.1_Chiles_Experiences_ on_Water_Reform.pdf

24. Information on the water sharing and trading system is a synthesis of the following sources:

    Australia Government. (2010). *Guide to the Proposed Basin Plan: Volume 1.* Commonwealth of Australia. pp. 1-223.

    Brett Walton. (2014). '*Transformational' Water Reforms, Though Wrenching, Helped Australia Endure Historic Drought, Experts Say.* Circle of Blue dated March 10, 2014.

    Commonwealth of Australia. (2011). *Water Markets in Australia: A Short History.* National Water Commission: Canberra, Australia

    Commonwealth of Australia. (2010). *The Impacts of Water Trading in the Southern Murray-Darling Basin: An Economic, Social and Environmental Assessment.* National Water Commission; Canberra, Australia. (pg. 28)

    Charles Fishman (2012). *The Big Thirst: The Secret Life and Turbulent Future of Water.* Free Press: New York, NY

    Michael D. Young and James C. McColl. (2005). *Defining Tradable Water Entitlements and Allocations: A Robust System.* Canadian Water Resources Journal 30(1). Pp. 65-72.

    Michael D. Young & James C, McColl. (2009). *Double Trouble: The Importance of Accounting For and Defining Water Entitlements*

Consistent With Hydrological Realities. The Australian Journal of Agricultural and Resource Economics, 53, pp. 19–35.

Michael D. Young. (2011). *Evaluating Economic Policy Instruments for Sustainable Water Management in Europe: WP6 IBE Ex-post Case Studies: The Role of the Unbundling Water Rights in Australia's Southern Connected Murray Darling Basin.* Environmental Progress Inc. Lexington, South Carolina

Michael D. Young. (2010). *Managing Water Scarcity: Lessons from Australia Presentation.* Water for Food International Conference, May 2-5, 2010.Video available from: http://waterforfood. nebraska.edu/2010/ video.php?ID=8b

Michael D. Young & J.C. McColl. (2008). *Water Trading in the MDBC: How well is the market functioning?* Paper presented at the Australian Agricultural and Resource Economics Society 52nd Annual Conference.

Michael D. Young. (2011). *The Role of Unbundling Water Rights in Australia's Southern Connected Murray Darling Basin.*EPI Water: Evaluating Economic Policy Instruments for Sustainable Water Management in Europe.

Michael D. Young. (2015). *Unbundling Rights: A Blueprint for the Development ofRobust Water Allocation Systems for the Western United States.* Nicholas Institute for Environmental Policy Solutions: Duke University.

Mike D. Young.(2005). *Designing Water Entitlement Regimes for and Ever-Changing and Ever-Varying Future.* Agricultural Water Management 145 (November). Pp. pg.32-38

Mike D. Young. (2016). Correspondence between the author and Professor Young

25. Australia Government. (2010). *Guide to the Proposed Basin Plan: Volume 1.* Commonwealth of Australia. pp. 1-223.

26. Michael Young. (2011). *The Role of Unbundling Water Rights in Australia's Southern Connected Murray Darling Basin. EPI* Water: Evaluating Economic Policy Instruments for Sustainable Water Management in Europe.

   Michael D. Young & James C, McColl. (2009). Double Trouble: The Importance of Accounting For and Defining Water Entitlements Consistent With Hydrological Realities. The Australian Journal of Agricultural and Resource Economics, 53, pp. 19–35.

27. Michael D. Young.(2005). *Designing Water Entitlement Regimes for and Ever-Changing and Ever-Varying Future.* Agricultural Water Management 145 (November). Pp. pg.2

   Michael D. Young & James C, McColl. (2009). Double Trouble: The Importance of Accounting For and Defining Water Entitlements Consistent With Hydrological Realities. The Australian Journal of Agricultural and Resource Economics, 53, pp. 19–35.

28. Michael Young and James C. McColl,. (2005). *Defining Tradable Water Entitlements and Allocations: A Robust System.* Canadian Water Resources Journal 30(1). Pp. p. 66

29. Young and McColl. (2009). Pg 20

30. Commonwealth of Australia. (2010). *The Impacts of Water Trading in the Southern Murray-Darling Basin: An Economic, Social and Environmental Assessment.* National Water Commission; Canberra, Australia. pg. 3

31. Charles Fishman. (2012). Pg 283

Michael D.Young. (2010). *Managing Water Scarcity: Lessons from Australia Presentation.* Water for Food International Conference, May 2-5, 2010.Video available from: http://waterforfood. nebraska.edu/2010/ video.php?ID=8b

32. Commonwealth of Australia. (2011). *Water Markets in Australia: A Short History.* National Water Commission: Canberra, Australia. pg. 52.

    Australia Government. (2010). *Guide to the Proposed Basin Plan: Volume 1.* Commonwealth of Australia. pg. 4.

33. Commonwealth of Australia. (2010). *The Impacts of Water Trading in the Southern Murray-Darling Basin: An Economic, Social and Environmental Assessment.* National Water Commission; Canberra, Australia. pg. 3

34. Michael D. Young. (2011). *Evaluating Economic Policy Instruments for Sustainable Water Management in Europe: WP6 IBE Ex-post Case Studies: The Role of the Unbundling Water Rights in Australia's Southern Connected Murray Darling Basin.* Environmental Progress Inc. Lexington, South Carolina. Pg 3

35. Commonwealth of Australia. (2010). *The Impacts of Water Trading in the Southern Murray-Darling Basin: An Economic, Social and Environmental Assessment.* National Water Commission; Canberra, Australia.pg. 28

36. Commonwealth of Australia. (2011). *Water Markets in Australia: A Short History.* National Water Commission: Canberra, Australia. pg. 106

37. Commonwealth of Australia. (2010). *The Impacts of Water Trading in the Southern Murray-Darling Basin: An Economic, Social and Environmental Assessment.* National Water Commission; Canberra, Australia. pg. 28

38. Commonwealth of Australia. (2011). *Water Markets in Australia: A Short History.* National Water Commission: Canberra, Australia. pg. 109.

39. Commonwealth of Australia. (2010). *The Impacts of Water Trading in the Southern Murray-Darling Basin: An Economic, Social and Environmental Assessment.* National Water Commission: Canberra, Australia. (pg. 28)

40. Michael D. Young. (2016). Correspondence between the author and Professor Young

41. Commonwealth of Australia. (2010). *The Impacts of Water Trading in the Southern Murray-Darling Basin: An Economic, Social and Environmental Assessment.* National water Commission: Canberra, Australia. Pg. 28

42. Michael D. Young & J.C. McColl. (2008). *Water Trading in the MDBC: How well is the market functioning?* Paper presented at the Australian Agricultural and Resource Economics Society 52nd Annual Conference. Pg XXX.

43. Commonwealth of Australia. (2011). *Water Markets in Australia: A Short History.* National Water Commission: Canberra, Australia. pg.80

44. Brett Walton. (2014). *'Transformational' Water Reforms, Though Wrenching, Helped Australia Endure Historic Drought, Experts Say.* Circle of Blue dated March 10, 2014.

45. Commonwealth of Australia. (2011). *Water Markets in Australia: A Short History.* National Water Commission: Canberra, Australia. pg.47

46. Woody. (2015)

47. Michael D. Young. (2015). *Unbundling Rights: A Blueprint for the Development ofRobust Water Allocation Systems for the Western United States.* Nicholas Institute for Environmental Policy Solutions: Duke University.

48. Interview with Michael Young (2016)

49. Ibid.(2016).

50. Commonwealth of Australia. (2010). *The Impacts of Water Trading in the Southern Murray-Darling Basin: An Economic, Social and Environmental Assessment.* National water Commission: Canberra, Australia. pg. 28

Chapter 11 Notes – "Something's Gotta Give"
A New Water Ethic

1. Johnny Mercer. (1955). *Something's Gotta Give*

2. Sarah Tory. (2016). *In Utah, A Massive Water Project Is Gaining Ground.* High Country News dated February 28, 2016

3. New Mexico Environmental Law Center. (2015). *Issues.* Retrieved from: http://nmelc.org/issues

4. State of California. (2015). Executive Order B-29-15. Retrieved from: http://gov.ca.gov/docs/4.1.15_Executive_Order.pdf

5. Charles Fishman(2011). *The Big Thirst: The Secret Life and Turbulent Future of Water.* Free Press: New York, NY

6. Frank Shyong, Hailey Branson-Potts & Matt Stevens. (2015). *California's Wealthy Lagging in Water Conservation.* LA Times dated April 5, 2015.

7. Wallace Stegner. (1955). *This is Dinosaur: Echo Park Country and Its Magic Rivers.* Alfred A. Knopf: New York, NY

8. Aldo Leopold. (1949. *A Sand County Almanac: And Sketches Here and There.* Oxford University Press: Oxford, England

9. Ibid.

10. David Groenfeldt (2013-10-01). *Water Ethics: A Values Approach to Solving the Water Crisis.* Earthscan Water Text. Taylor and Francis.

11. Kate Galbraith. (2012). *Push Comes To Shove Over Water Restrictions.* New York Times, March 17,2012. Retrieved from: http://www.nytimes.com/2012/03/18/us/in-west-texas-push-comes-to-shove-over-water-restrictions.html?pagewanted=all&_r=0

12. John Rawls.(1971). *A Theory of Justice.* Belknap Press: Cambridge MA

13. U.S Declaration of Independence. para 2. (1776)

14. Jie Liu; Amarbayasgalan Dorjderem; Jinhua Fu: & Xiaohui Lei. (2011:*Water Ethics and Water Resource Management.* UNESCO Bangkok.

Chapter 12 Notes
"Whisky is for drinking, water is for fighting"
The Future

1. Andrew Blankstein. (2015). *Tom Selleck Settlement Accepted in California water Right.* NBC News. Retrieved from: http://www.nbcnews.com/storyline/california-drought/tom-selleck-settlement-accepted-california-water-dispute-n392896

2. Dale Kasler & Phillip Reese. (2015). *California Farmers In Line for More Drought Cutbacks.* Sacramento Bee dated May 11, 2015.Matt Stevens. (2015). *In a Blow to Water Conservation,*

Court Rejects San Juan Capistrano's Tiered Rates . LA Times . Dated April 20, 2015.

3. Tom Havens. (2015). *California Passing From Water Crisis to Water Collapse.* The Desert Review: Letters to the Editor, dated May 11, 2105.

4. Amanda Zamora; Lauren Kirchner; &Abrahm Lustgarten. (2015). *Killing the Colorado: The Truth Behind the Water Crisis in the West: California's Drought is Part of a Much Bigger water Crisis.* ProPublica dated June 25, 2015.

5. United States Department Bureau of Reclamation. (2012b).*Colorado River Basin: Water Supply and Demand Study: Appendix F4: Option Characterization – Importation.* Retrieved from: http://www.usbr.gov/lc/region/ programs/ crbstudy/finalreport/Technical%20Report%20F%20%20 Development%20of%20Options%20and%20Stategies/ TR-F_Appendix4_FINAL.pdf

6. Cook, Benjamin; Ault, Toby R. & Smerdon, Jason E. (2015). *Unprecedented 21st Century Drought Risk in the Americans Southwest and Central Plains.* Science Advances. Vol. 1 (1) doi:12.1126/scladv.1400082

7. Jay Famiglietti,(2014). *How Much Water Does California Have Left?*L.A. Times Op Ed,July 8,2014.

8. Dylan Thomas. (1952). *Do Not Go Gentle Into That Good Night.* New Directions Publishing: NYC.NY.

9. Paul Rogers. (2014). *California Drought: Past Dry Periods Have Lasted More Than 200 Years, Scientists Say.* San Jose Mercury News dated January 25, 2014.

10. Colorado Water Conservation Board. (2015). *Colorado Water Plan: 2nd Draft.* pg 2. Retrieved from:https://www.colorado.

gov/pacific/Cowaterplan/july-2015-second-draft-colorados-water-plan

11. Rogers. (2014).

12. John M. Glionna. (2015). *Lake Mead Water Level; Falls to a New Low, and Is Likely To Get Worse.* LA Times dated April 29, 2015.

13. Poh-Ling Tan & Sue Jackson. (2013). *Impossible Dreaming – Does Australia's Water Law and Policy Fulfil Indigenous Aspirations.* Environmental and Planning Law Journal, Vol. 30, pp. 132-149.Retrieved from: https://www.griffith.edu.au/__data/assets/pdf_file/0010/ 491374/Tan-Jackson-2013-EPLJ.pdf

14. Colorado Water Conservation Board. (2015). *Colorado Water Plan – Final -2015.* (pg. 6-123).

15. Ibid. (pg. 6-120).

16. Glennon, Robert. (2016)/ Interview with author on March 11, 2016.

17. John F. Kennedy.(1959). *Remarks at the Convocation of the United Negro College Fund, Indianapolis, Indiana, April 12, 1959.* John F. Kennedy Presidential Library and Museum. Retrieved from: http://www.jfklibrary.org/Research/Research-Aids/JFK-Speeches/ Indianapolis-IN_19590412.aspx

18. Interview with Tony Blair by Matt Hussey. (2010) Retrieved from: http://www.shortlist.com/entertainment/tony-blair-versus-shortlist

19. Sarah F. Bates; David H. Getchens; Lawrence MacDonnell; & Charles F. Wilkinson. (1993). *Searching Out The Headwaters: Change and Rediscovery in Western Water Policy.* Island Press: Washington D.C.p. 202.

Bibliography

Abbott, David R. (2003). *Centuries of Decline During the Hohokam Archaic Period at Pueblo Grande.* University of Arizona Press: Tucson, AZ.

Abcarian, Robin.(2015). *Almonds, the Demons of Drought? Frustrated Growers Tell Another Story.* LA Times. April 6, 2015. Retrieved from: http://www.latimes.com/local/abcarian/la-me-0417-abcarian-almonds-demons-20150417-column.html

Ahlstrom, Richard V.N.; Van West, Carla; & Dean, Jeffrey S. (1995). *Environmental and Chronological Factors in Mesa Verde-Northern Rio Grande Migration.* Journal of Anthropological Archaeology. 14. Pp. 125-142

Allen, Cain. (2007). *'Boils, swell and whorl pool': The Historical Landscape of the Dalles-Celilo Reach of the Columbia River.* Oregon Historical Quarterly. Vol. 108(4).

Allen, J.L. (1978). *Division of the Waters: Changing Conception of the Continental Divide,1804-44.* Journal of Historical Geography. Vol. 4(4). pg. 357-370

American Society of Civil Engineers. (2016). *2013 Report Card for America's Infrastructure.* Retrieved from: http://www.infrastructurereportcard.org/grades/

Anderson, Erik. (2015). *Eyes Look to Carlsbad's Desalination Plant.*

KPBS Radio News. July 27, 2015. Retrieved from: http://www.kpbs.org/news/2015/jul/27/eyes-look-carsbad-desalination-plant/

Arizona Municipal Water Users Association. (2014). *Drought Does Not Equal A Water Shortage.* One for Water - October 23, 2014 meeting.

Retrieved from: http://www.cap-az.com/documents/ meetings/10-23-2014/Drought%20Does%20Not%20Equal%20 A%20Water%20 Shortage-1pg.pdf

Arizona Department of Water Resources. *Securing Arizona's Water Future: Overview of Arizona's Groundwater Management Code.* Retrieved from: http://www.azwater.gov/AzDWR/ WaterManagement/documents/Groundwater_Code.pdf

Arizona Department of Water Resources. (2015). *Securing Arizona's Water Future: Supply and Demand.* Retrieved from: http://www.azwater. gov/AzDWR/PublicInformationOfficer/documents/supplydemand. pdf

Arizona Department of Water Resources. (2010). *Water Atlas: Volume 8: Active Management Areas Water Atlas.* Retrieved from: http://www.azwater.gov/azdwr/StatewidePlanning/WaterAtlas/ ActiveManagementAreas/documents/Volume_8_final.pdf.

Arizona Water Banking Authority (AWBA). (2013). Arizona Water Banking Authority: Annual Report 2013.

Arnold, Jeanne E. & Green, Terisa M. (2002). *Comments: Mortuary Ambiguity: Ventureno Chumash Case.* American Antiquity, 67(4). pp. 760-771.

Arnold, Jeanne E. , Walsh, Michael R. & Hollimon, Sandra E. (2004). *The Archaeology of California.* Journal of Archaeological Research vol. 12. No 1,(99) 1-75.

Bacigalupi. Paulo. (2015). *The Water Knife.* Alfred A. Knopf. Alfred A Knopf. NYC, NY.

Bibliography

Balken, Eric. (2015). *It's Time to Let Lake Powell Go.* High Country News. December 1,2105

Barber, K., & Fisher, A. H. (2007, Winter). *From Coyote to the Corps of Engineers: Recalling the History of The Dalles-Celilo Reach.*

Oregon Historical Quarterly, *108*(4), 520.

Barlow, Maude and Clark, Tony. (2003). *Blue Gold: The Battle Against Corporate Theft of the World's Water.* McClelland and Stewart: Toronto, Ontario

Barnett, Cynthia. (2011). *Blue Revolution: Unmaking America's water Crisis.* Boston, MA: Beacon Press.

Barnett, Cynthia. (2014). *Hey, America: It's Time to Talk About the Price of Water.* ENSIA dated October 6, 2104.Retrieved from: http://ensia.com/features/hey-america-its-time-to-talk-about-the-price-of-water/

Barnett, Tim, Malone, Robert, Pennell, William, Stammer, Detlet, Semtner, Bert, and Washington, Warren. (2004). *The Effects of Climate Change on Water Resources in the West.: Introduction and Overview.* Climate Change. Vol 62. Pp. 1-11.

Bates, Sarah F.; Getchens, David H; MacDonnell, Lawrence; & Wilkinson, Charles F. (1993). *Searching Out The Headwaters: Change and Rediscovery in Western Water Policy.* Island Press: Washington D.C.

Bauer, Carl J. (2005). *In The Image of the Market: The Chilean Model of Water Resources Management.* International Journal of Water 3(2). Pp. 146-165

Bauer, Carl J. (2008). *The Experience of Chilean water Markets.* Presentation at Expo Zaragoza, 2008.

Belnap, Jayne, and Campbell, D.H., 2011, Effects of climate change and land use on water resources in the Upper Colorado River Basin: U.S. Geological Survey Fact Sheet.

Bennett, James D. (1967). *Oasis Civilization in the Great Plains.* Great Plains Journal.7(1), pp. 26-32.

Benson, Larry & Berry, Michael S. (2009). *Climate Change and Cultural Response in Prehistoric American Southwest.* U.S. Geological Survey – Published Research. Paper 725.

Benson, L.V.; Ramsey, D.K.; Stahle, D.W.; & Petersen, K.L. (2013). *Some Thoughts on the Factors that Controlled Prehistoric Maize Production in the Southwest with Application to Southwestern Colorado.* Journal of Archeological Science 40, pp. 2869-2880.

Benson, L.V.; Griffin, E.R.; Stein, J.R.; Friedman, R.A.; & Andrae, S.W. (2014). *Mummy Lake: An Unroofed Ceremonial Structure Within a Large Ritual Landscape. Journal of Archaeological Science44. pp. 164-179.*

Bentham, Jeremy. 1776. *Fragment on Government; Being an Examination of What Is Delivered, on the Subject of Government in General in the Introduction to Sir William Blackstone's Commentaries. Paragraph 2 Retrieved from:* http://www.efm.bris.ac.uk/het/bentham/government.htm

Blair, Tony. (2010). Interview by Matt Hussey. Retrieved from: http://www.shortlist.com/entertainment/tony-blair-versus-shortlist

Blankstein, Andrew. (2015). *Tom Selleck Settlement Accepted in California Water Right.* NBC News. Retrieved from: http://www.nbcnews.com/storyline/california-drought/tom-selleck-settlement-accepted-california-water-dispute-n392896

Boston Water Sewer Commission. (2015). *Rates: 2015 Water and Sewer Rates.* Retrieved from: http://www.bwsc.org/services/rates/rates.asp

John Wesley Powell. Utah State University Honors Lectures dated
May 1, 1977. Retrieved from: http://digitalcommons.usu.edu/
cqui/viewcontent.cqui?article=1019&context=honor lectures&
seiredir=1&referer=http%3A%2F%2Fwww.google.com%2Furl%
3Fsa%3Dt% 26rct%3Dj%26q%3Djohn%2520wesley%
2520 powell%2520report%2520on%2520the%2520lands%2
520of%2520the%2520arid2520region%2520%281878%29%
26source%3 Dweb%26cd%3D5%26ved%3D0CE-
MQFjAE%26url%3D
http%253A%252F%252Fdigitalcommons.usu.edu%252Fc-
gi%252Fviewcontent.cgi%253Farticle%253D1019%2526contex-
t%253Dhonor_lectures%26ei%3
DSUyZUZ_TNsq9yQG0pYHIBA%26usg%3DAFQjCNHnznzk-
b8c0HM8BtFRrusUXJeiljA% 26sig2%3
DjLVPP qqKiQgx9sd7AXyZdw%26bvm%3D-
bv.46751780%2Cd.a
Wc#search=%22john%20wesley%20powell%20report%20
lands%20arid%20region%20%281878%29%22

Boxall, Bettina. (2015). *Over pumping of Central Valley Groundwater
Creating a Crisis, Experts Say.* L.A. Times. March 18, 2015.
Retrieved from: http://www.latimes.com/local/california/la-me-
groundwater-20150318- story.html

Brean, Henry. (2013). *As Lake Mead Shrinks, California Uses More
Than Its Share of Water.* Las Vegas Review Journal dated May 24,
2013. Retrieved from: http://www.reviewjournal.com/news/water-
environment/lake-mead-shrinks-california-uses-more-its-share-
water

Brean, Henry. (2015). *Exit Interview: Mulroy Talks About Her Life as Las
Vegas' Water Chief.* Las Vegas Review-Journal. February 1, 2014.

Brinkerhoff, Noel. (2014). Could California Drought Be Ended by Stopping Alfalfa Exports to China? Retrieved from: http://www.allgov.com/news/us-and-the-world/could-california-drought-be-ended-by-stopping- alfalfa-exports-to-china-140222?news=852504

Bureau of Land Management, Nevada. *Prehistoric Cultural Resources.*

Retrieved from: http://www.blm.gov/nv/st/en/fo/lvfo/blm_programs/lvfo_recreation/prehistoric_cultural.print.html

Butler, Virginia L.. *Relic Hunting, Archaeology, and Loss of Native American Heritage at The Dalles.* (2007). Oregon Historical Quarterly. Winter 2007. (624).

California Department of Food and Agriculture. (2015). *California Agricultural Production Statistics.*

California Department of Water Resources. (August 5, 2015).

California Data Exchange Center – Reservoirs. Retrieved from: http://cdec.water.ca.gov/cdecapp/resapp/getResGraphsMain.action

California Department of Water Resources.(2015). *California State Water Project.* Retrieved from: http://www.water.ca.gov/swp/

California Department of Water Resources. (2015). *Groundwater.* Retrieved from: http://www.water.ca.gov/groundwater/

California Department of Water Resources. (2015). *News Release dated March 2, 2015.* Retrieved from: http:/www,water.ca.gov/news/newsreleases/2015/030215allocation.pdf

California Department of Water Resources. (2016). *2016 Drought Contingency Plan CVP and SWP Operations February – November 2016.*(Submitted January 15, 2016). Retrieved from: http://www.water.ca.gov/waterconditions/

Cameron, Catherine. (1995). *Migration and Movement of Southwestern Peoples.* Journal of Anthropological Archaeology. 14. pp. 104-124

Carefree Water Company: *Brief History of Carefree Water Company.* Retrieved from: http://www.carefreewaterco.com/ watercompanyhistory.html

Carson, Rachel. (2002). *Silent Spring: 40th Anniversary Edition.* Houghton Mifflin Harcourt: New York

CBS News. (2014). *Depleting the Groundwater: Report by Leslie Stahl for 60 Minutes: Dated November 16, 2014.* Retrieved from: http://www. cbsnews.com/news/depleting-the-water/

Castle, Stephanie L.: Thomas, Brian F.; Reager, John T.; Rodell, Matthew; Swenson, Sean C.; and Famiglietti, James S. (2014). *Groundwater Depletion During Drought Threatens Future Water Security of the Colorado River Basin.* Geophys. Research Letters., 41, pp. 5904–5911, doi:10.1002/2014GL061055.

Central Arizona Project. (2015). *CAP: Your Water Your Future: Recharge Program.* Retrieved from http://www.cap-az.com/departments/ recharge-program/recharge-in-arizona

Central Bureau of Statistics. (2009). *Israel in Statistics: 1948-2007.*

Central Bureau of Statistics: Jerusalem. March 5, 2009).

Central Bureau of Statistics (2014). *Israel's Population on the Eve of Independence Day.*

Central Bureau of Statistics: Jerusalem. May 1, 2014.

Childs, Craig. (206). *House of Rain: Tracking a Vanished Civilization Across the American Southwest.* Little Brown and Co: New York, New York

Choy, Janny, McGhee, Geoff and Rohde, Melissa. (2014). *Water in the West: Understanding California's Groundwater: Recharge Groundwater's Second Act.* Stanford Woods Institute for the Environment. Retrieved from: http://waterinthewest.stanford.edu/groundwater/recharge/

Churchill, Melissa J.; Potter, James M.; & Wilshusen, Richard H. "Prehistoric Reservoirs and Water Basins in the Mesa Verde Region: Intensification of Water Collection Strategies during the Great Pueblo period." *American Antiquity* 62.4 (1997): 664+. *Academic One File*. Web. 25 Apr. 2015.

Circle of Blue. (2015). *Price of Water: 2010-2015: A Survey of water Prices for Households in 30 Major U.S. Cities.* Retrieved from: http://www.circleofblue.org/waternews/wpcontent/uploads/201/04/*WaterPricing2015gaphs*.pdf

Circle of Blue Water News. (2012). *Q & A: Pat Mulroy on Las Vegas and the Journey to Water Efficiency.* Interview on October 12, 2012. Retrieved from: *Dam Nation: How Water Shaped the West and Will Determine Its Future.* Retrieved from: http://www.circleofblue. org/waternews/2012/world/qa-pat-mulroy-on-las-vegas-and-the-journey-to-water-efficiency/

City of Fresno: Public Utilities: Water Division. (2015). Important Documents: Proposed Water Rate Increases Fact Sheet. Retrieved from: http://www.fresno.gov/Government/DepartmentDirectory/PublicUtilities/Watermanagement/waterrates.htm

City of Phoenix. (2015). *Water and Sewer Rates.* Retrieved from: https://www.phoenix.gov/waterservices/customerservices/rateinfo

City of Santa Barbara. (2016).*Drought Information.* Retrieved from: http://www.santabarbaraca.gov/gov/depts/pw/resources/system/ docs/default.asp?utm_source=WaterConservation&utm_medium=Drought&utm_campaign=QuickLink

City of Santa Fe: Water Division. Retrieved from: www.Santafenm.gov/water division

City of Scottsdale, AZ. (2015). *City of Scottsdale Water and Sewer Rate Report*. Retrieved from: http://www.scottsdaleaz. gov/Assets/Public+Website/water/Rates+$!26+Fees/ FY15WaterWastewaterRateRpt.pdf

City of Tucson. (2015). *Recharged Water.* Retrieved from: https://www. tucsonaz.gov/water/recharged-water

Cohen, Michael. (2014). *Hazard's Toll: The Costs of Inaction at the Salton Sea.* Pacific Institute: Boulder, CO.

Cohen, Michael; Christian-Smith, Juliet; and Berggren, John. (2013). *Water to Supply the Land: Irrigated Agriculture in the Colorado River Basin.* Pacific Institute. Oakland, CA.

Cohen, Ronnie; Nelson, Barry; and Wolff, Gary. (2004). *Energy Down the Drain: The Hidden Costs of California's Water Supply.* Natural Resources Defense Council and Pacific Institute. Retrieved from: http://www.nrdc.org/water/conservation/edrain/execsum.asp

Colorado Constitution. amend. XVI, § 6. Colorado Basin Roundtable. (2015). *Colorado Basin Implementation Plan: Collaborating on Colorado's Water Plan.* Retrieved from: coloradowaterplan.com

Colorado Water Conservation Board (2015). *Colorado Climate Plan: Policies and Strategies to Mitigate and Adapt: Executive Summary.* Retrieved from: http://cwcbweblink.state.co.us/WebLink/0/ doc/196541/Electronic.aspx?searchid=243b8969-739b-448c-bd2d-699af9b7aea0

Colorado Water Conservation Board. (2015). *Colorado's Water Plan: 2nd Draft.*

Colorado Water Conservation Board. (2015). *Colorado Water Plan: Final 2015.* Retrieved from: http://coloradowaterplan.com

Colorado Water Conservation Board. (2004). *Statewide Water Supply Initiative Report(SWSI). Executive Summary. Pg. 1.* Retrieved from: https://cwcb.state.co.us/http://cwcb.state.co.us/publicinformation/publications/Pages/StudiesReports.aspx

Colorado Water Conservation Board. (2011). Statewide Water Supply Initiative: 2010.

Commonwealth of Australia. (2010). *Guide to the Proposed Basin Plan: Volume 1.* National Water Commission: Canberra, Australia. pp. 1-223.

Commonwealth of Australia. (2010). *The Impacts of Water Trading in the Southern Murray-Darling Basin: An Economic, Social and Environmental Assessment.*

Commonwealth of Australia. (2011). *Water Markets in Australia: A Short History.* National Water Commission: Canberra, Australia. pg. 1-155.

Cook, Benjamin; Ault, Toby R. & Smerdon, Jason E. (2015). *Unprecedented 21st Century Drought Risk in the Americans Southwest and Central Plains.* Science Advances. Vol. 1 (1) doi:12.1126/scladv.1400082.

Cook, Edward R., Woodhouse, Connie A., Eakin, C. Mark, Meko, David M. & Stahle, David W.(2004).*Long-term Aridity Changes in the Western United States.* Science 306(5). pp 1015-1018.

Cook, Edward, Seager, Richard. Hiem, Richard, Jr., Vose, Russell S., Herweijer, Celine, and Woodhouse, Connie (2009). *Mega droughts in North America: placing IPCC projections of hydroclimatic change in a long-term palaeoclimate context.* Journal of Quaternary Science 25(1) pp 48-61. DOI: 10.1002/jqs.1303

Cordell, Linda S.; & Plog, Fred. (1979).*Escaping the Confines of Normative Thought: A Reevaluation of Puebloan Prehistory.* American Antiquity. 44(3). Pp 405-429

Coren, Michael. *Growing Crops With No Water, The Old Fashioned Way.* Retrieved from: www.fastcoexist.com/1680477/growing-crops-with-no-water-the-old-fashioned-way.

Crosby, Lucinda Sue (2012). *Water in the West: An Overview and an Environmental Essay.* Morris Publishing: Kearney, Nebraska

Cubbison, Gene .(2014). *Running Dry: Drought in California: San Diego Approves $3.5B Recycled Water Project.* NBC San Diego: dated November 18, 2014. Retrieved from: http://www.nbc sandiego. com/news/politics/San-Diego-Eyes-Recycled-Water-Project-in-Drought- Conditions-283058261.html

Daniels, Jeff. (2015). *LA Considers $1 Billion 'Toilet to Tap' Water Program.* CNBC dated October, 22, 2105. Retrieved from: http:// www.cnbc.com/2015/10/22/la-considers-1-billion-toilet-to-tap-water-program.html

Danson, Casey Coates. (2013). *Dwindling Colorado River Forces First-Ever Cuts in Lake Powell Water Releases.* Global Possibilities date august 21, 2013. Retrieved from: http://www.globalpossibilities. org/dwindling-coloradoriver-forces-first-ever-cuts-in-lake-powell-water-releases/

deBuys, William, (2011). *A Great Aridness: Climate Change and the Future of the American Southwest.* Oxford University Press: Oxford, U.K.

de la Luz Domper, Maria. (2009). *Chile: A Dynamic Water Market.* World Bank: World Development Indicators Online.

Diamond, Jared. *Collapse: How Societies Choose to Fail or Succeed.* (2005). NYC, NY: Viking Press. Pg. 137

Dearen, Jason and Burke, Garance. (2014). *California Drought: State's Flawed Water System Can't Track Usage.* Associated Press. Retrieved from: http://www.*Huffingtonpost*.com?2014/05/27/California-drought_n_5395501.html

Denver Water. (2015.) *Inside City 2015 Rates.* Retrieved from: http://www.denverwater.org/BillingRates/RatesCharges/2015-rates/inside-city/

Dominguez, Steven & Kolm, Kenneth E. (2005). *Beyond Water Harvesting: A Soil Hydrology Perspective on Traditional Southwestern Agricultural Technology.* American Antiquity 70(4) pp. 732-765.

Doolittle, William E. (1992). *Agriculture in North America on the Eve of Contact: A Reassessment.* Annals of the Association of American Geographers. 82(3). Pp 386-401.

Doyel, David E. (2008*) Irrigation, Production, and Power in Phoenix Basin Hohokam Society.in The Hohokam Millennium Edited by Fish, Suzanne K. and Fish, Paul R.* School for Advanced research Press: Santa Fe, NM

Erdman, John. (2015). *California's Snowpack at Record Early-April Low: Sierra Snow Survey Finds Bare Ground.*

Euler, Robert C., George J. Gumerman, Thor N. V. Karlstrom, Jeffrey S. Dean, and Richard H. Hevly. (1979). The Colorado Plateaus: Cultural Dynamics and Paleo environment. Science 205:1089–1101

Ezzo, Joseph A & Price, T. Douglas (2002), *Migration, Regional Reorganization, and Spatial Group Composition at Grasshopper Pueblo, Arizona.* Journal of Archaeological Science: 29, pg. 499-520

Fagan, Brian. (2011). *Elixir: A History of Water and Humankind.* Bloomsbury Press: New York, NY.

Famiglietti, Jay. (2014). *How Much Water Does California Have Left?* L.A. Times Op Ed, July 8,2014. Retrieved from: http://www. latimes.com/opinion/op-ed/la-oe-famiglietti-drought-california-20150313-story. html

Famiglietti, James S. (2014). *The Global Groundwater Crisis: Groundwater Depletion the World Over Poses a Greater Threat to Global Water Security Than Is Currently Acknowledged.* Nature Climate Change. vol. 4. Pp. 945-949.

Famiglietti, Jay. (2014). *The Groundwater Crisis.* Nature Climate Change. Vol. 4.Retrieved from: http://web.mit.edu/12.000/www/m2018/pdfs/groundwatercrisis.pdf

Famiglietti, James S.(Jay). (2014). *Satellite Study Reveals Parched U.S. West Using Up Underground Water.* NASA News Release dated July 24, 2014. Retrieved from: http://www.nasa.gov/press/2014/july/satellite-study-reveals-parched-us-west-using-up-underground-water/#.VeS3WOm_e0s

Ferris, Kathleen. (2015). *Leadership: Water Brings Phoenix and Tucson Together.* One for Water. Arizona Municipal Water Users Association. April 20, 2015. Retrieved from: https://amwua.wordpress.com/2015/04/20/leadership-water-brings-phoenix-and-tucson-together/

Fish, Suzanne; Fish, Paul R.; Madsen, John R. editors. (1992). *The Marana Community in the Hohokam World.* University of Arizona Press: Tucson, AZ

Fischman, Joshua. (1996). *The California Social Climbers: Low Water Prompts High Status.* Science. 272.5263. Retrieved from: http://dml.regis.edu/login?url=http://go.galegroup.com/ps/i.o?id=GALE%7CA18311917&v=2.1&u=regis&it=r&p=GRGM&sw=w&asid=051b80ab311f774fa4ecaf5e6fbe8397.

Fishman, Charles. (2010). *The Big Thirst: Nothing's Quite So Thirsty as a Las Vegas Golf Course.* Retrieved from: http://www.fastcompany.com/1749643/big-thirst-nothing's-quite-so-thirsty-las-vegas-golf-course

Fishman, Charles. (2011). *The Big Thirst: The Secret Life and Turbulent Future of Water.* Free Press: New York, NY.

Fresno Bee. (2015). *All Cities Must Put In water Meters. Editorial.* Dated June 22, 2105. Retrieved from: http://www.fresnobee.com/opinion/editorials/article25197094.html

Galbraith, Kate. (2012). *Push Comes To Shove Over Water Restrictions.* New York Times, March 17,2012. Retrieved from: http://www.nytimes.com/2012/03/18/us/in-west-texas-push-comes-to-shove-over-waterrestrictions.html?pagewanted=all&_r=0

Galloway, Devin and Riley, Frances S. (1999). *San Joaquin Valley, California: Largest Human Alteration of the Earth's Surface.* United States Geological Survey: Menlo Park, CA. Retrieved from: http://pubs.usgs.gov/circ/ circ1182/pdf/06San JoaquinValley.pdf

Gamble, Lynn H. (2005). *Culture and Climate: Reconsidering the Effects of Paleoclimatic Variability Among Southern California Hunter-Gatherer Societies* World Archaeology. 37(1). pp. 92-108.

Gamble, Lynn: Walker, Phillip L.; and Russell, Glenn S. (2002). *Further Considerations On the Emergence of Chumash Chiefdoms.* American Antiquity, 67(4).pp . 772-777.

Glennon, Robert. (2009). *Unquenchable: America's Water Crisis and What To Do About It.* Island Press. Washington D.C.

Glennon, Robert. (2002). *Water Follies: Groundwater Pumping and the Fate of America's Fresh Water.* Island Press: Washington, D.C. (pg.47)

Glennon, Robert and Libecap, Gary(2014). *The West Needs a Water Market to Fight Drought.*. Wall Street Journal dated October 23, 2014.

Glionna, John M. (2015). *Lake Mead Water Level; Falls to a New Low, and Is Likely To Get Worse.* LA Times dated April 29, 2015. Retrieved from: http://www.latimes.com/nation/la-na-lake-mead-low-20150429-story. html

Gold, P.C. *The Long Narrows: The Forgotten Geography and Cultural Wonder.* (2007). Oregon Historical Quarterly. 108(4).

Goodyear, Dana. (2015). *The Dying Sea: What Will California Sacrifice to Survive the Drought?* New Yorker, May 4, 2015 issue.

Gorbachev, Mikhail. Foreward of Water: The Drop of Life: Perils of Pollution. (2001) written by Peter Swanson. Northwood Press: Woodstock, ON, Canada.

Grace, Stephen. (2013). *Dam Nation: How Water Shaped the West and Will Determine Its Future.* Globe Pequot Press: Guilford, CT

Graham Clark. *World Prehistory: New Perspectives. Third edition.* (1977). Cambridge University Press: Cambridge, Great Britain

Grafton, R. Quenton: Landry, Clay; Libecap, Gary D.; McGlennon, Sam; & O'Brien, Robert. (2010). *An Integrated Assessment of Water Markets in Australia, Chile, China , South Africa, and the USA.* National Bureau of Economic Research: Working Paper 16203. Retrieved from: http://www.nber.org/papers/w16203

Grantham , Ted and Viers, Joshua. (2014a). *100 years of California's Water Rights Systems: Patterns, Trends and Uncertainties.* Environmental Research Letters 9. Pp. 1-10. doi:10.1088/1748-9326/9/8/084012

Grantham , Ted and Viers, Joshua. (2014b). *California Water Rights: You Can't Manage What You Don't Measure.* UC Davis Center of

Watershed Sciences. Retrieved from: http://californiawater blog. com/2014/08/20/california-water-rights-you-cant-manage-what-you-dont-measure/

Greene, Emily. (2008). *Quenching Las Vegas' Thirst.* Las Vegas Sun. Retrieved from: http://lasvegassun.com/news/topics/water/

Groenfeldt, David (2013-10-01). *Water Ethics: A Values Approach to Solving the Water Crisis.* Earthscan Water Text. Taylor and Francis.

Gunther, Michael. (2013). *The Impact of a Cotton T-Shirt: How Smart Choices Can Make A Difference in Our Water and Energy Footprint.* World Wild Life Fund.

Hamilton, Matt. (2015). *Santa Barbara to Spend $55 million on Desalination Plant As Drought 'Last Resort'.* LA Times. Dated July 22, 2015.

Hamblin, James, (2014). *The Dark Side of Almond Use.* The Atlantic. August 24, 2014.

Hanemann, Michael.(2002). *The Central Arizona Project.* Department of Agricultural and Resource Economics, UCB: CUDARE Working Papers: Paper 937.

Hanson, Blaine R.; Bali, Khaled M.; Sanden, Blake L.(2008). *Irrigated Alfalfa Management for Mediterranean and Desert Zones. Chapter7: Irrigating Alfalfa in Arid Regions.* University of California: Division of Agriculture and Natural Resources

Hanson, Blaine. *Irrigation of Agricultural Crops in California. University of California Davis.*

Harper, Kelly C. (1974). *The Mormon Role in Irrigation Beginnings and Diffusion in the Western States: A Historical Geography.*

Havens, Tom. (2015). *California Passing From Water Crisis to Water Collapse.* The Desert Review: Letters to the Editor, dated May 11,

2105. Retrieved from: http://www.thedesertreview.com/california-passing-from- water-crisis-to-water-collapse/

Heller, Joseph. (1955). *Catch 22*. Simon and Schuster: New York, NY

Hiltzik, Michael. (2015). *Desalination Plants Aren't A Good Solution For California Drought*. LA Times. April 24, 2105

Hobson, Jeremy. Host. (2014). Nevada's Former Water Czar Shares Lessons Learned. Public Radio: here and Now dated May 29 2014. Retrieved from: http://hereandnow.wbur.org/2014/05/29/nevada-water- lessons

Hodge, Adam. (2012). *In Want of Nourishment to Keep Them Alive: Climate Fluctuations, Bison Scarcity, and the Smallpox Epidemic of 1780-82 on the Northern Great Plains*. Environmental History, Vol 17 (April) pp.365-403. doi: 10.1093/envhist/ emr153.

Holthaus, Eric. (2015). *Dry Heat: As Lake Mead Hits Record Lows and Water Shortages Loom, Arizona Prepares for the Worst*. Science. Retrieved from: http://www.slate.com/articles/health_and_science/ science/2015/05/arizona_water_shortages_loom_the_state_ prepares_for_rationing_as_lake_mead.single.html

Holthaus, Eric. (2014). *Lake Mead: Before and After the Epic Drought*. Slate. Retrieved from: http://www.slate.com/articles/technology/ future_tense/2014/07/lake_mead_before_and_after_colorado_ river_basin_losing_water_at_shocking.html

Hoover, Herbert. (1929). Quoted in Glennon, Robert. (2002). *Water Follies: Groundwater Pumping and the Fate of America's Fresh Water*. Island Press: Washington, D.C.

Hostetter, George, (2014). *Fresno Council Repeals Water Rate Increases, Avoids Ballot Fight*. Fresno Bee dated July 31,2014. Retrieved from: article19522851.html

Hundley, Norris. Jr. (2001). The Great Thirst – Californians and Water: A History. University of California Press: Berkeley, CA

Hundley, Norris, Jr. (2009). *Water and the West: The Colorado River Compact and the Politics of Water in the Americans West. Second edition.* Los Angeles: University of California Press.

Hundley, Norris, Jr. (1996). *Water in the West in Historical Imagination: Part 1.* The Western Historical Quarterly. vol. 27 (1). Pp. 4-31.

Hundley, Norris, Jr. (1996). *Water in the West in Historical Imagination: Part Two - A Decade Later Part 2.* The Historian. vol. 66 (3). pp. 455-490.

Hunt, Robert C.; Guillet, David; Bayman, James; Fish, Paul; Fish, Suzanne; Kintigh, Keith; & Neely, James A. (2005). *Plausible Ethnographic Analogies for the Social Organization of Hohokam Canal Irrigation.* American Antiquity 70(3) oo. 433-456.

Imperial County Department of Agriculture. (2014). *Imperial County: Agricultural Crop & Livestock Report: 2013.* Retrieved from: http://www.co.imperial.ca.us/ag/crop_&_livestock_reports/Crop_&_Livestock_Report_2013.PDF

Imperial Irrigation District (IID). 2015. *About IID Water.* Retrieved from: http://www.iid.com/water/about-iid-water

Ingram, Scott. (2008). *Streamflow and Population Change in the Lower Salt River Valley of Central Arizona, ca A.D.775 to 1450.* American Antiquity, 73(1), pp. 136-165

Institute for the Environment. (2013). *Assessment of Climate Change in the Southwest United States.* Island Press: Washington, D.C.

Israel Water Authority. (2012). *Master Plan for the National Water Sector.* Retrieved from: http://www.water.gov.il/Hebrew/

ProfessionalInfoAndData/2012/09-Israel-Water-Sector-Master-Plan-2050.pdf

Israel Water Authority. (2012). *Long –Term Master Plan for the National Water Sector: Part A- Policy Document: version 4.*Water Authority Planning Division.

Israel Water Authority. (2015). *Water Sector in Israel: IWRM Model.*

Retrieved from: http://www.water.gov.il/Hebrew/Professional InfoAndData/2012/02Israel%20Water%20Sector%20-%20 IWRM%20Model.pdf

Jacobs, Jeffrey. (2011). *The Sustainability of Water Resources in the Colorado River Basin.* Pp 6-12. The Bridge. National Academy of Engineering. 41(4).

James, Edwin. (1823). *An Account of an Expedition from Pittsburgh to the Rocky Mountains, Performed in the Years 1819, 1820American Journeys Collection:* London: Longman, Hurst, Orme and Brown. pp. 236- 237.

James, Ian. (2015). *Nestle Says It Will Use Less Water at California Plants.* Mother Jones dated May 14, 2015. Retrieved from: http://www. usatoday.com/story/money/business/2015/05/14/nestle-bottled-water/27296813/

Jenkins, Matt. (2015). *The Water Czar Who Reshaped Colorado River Politics* High Country News dated March 2, 2105. Retrieved from: http://www.hcn.org/issues/47.4/the-water-czar-who-reshaped-colorado-river-politics

Jones, Terry L.; Brown, Gary M.; Raab, L. Mark; McVickar, Janet L.; Spaulding, W. Geoffrey; Kennett, Douglas J.; York, Andres; and Walker, Phillip L. (1999). *Environmental Imperative Reconsidered: Demographic Crises During the Medieval Climatic Anomaly.* Current Anthropology Vol. .40, No. 2

Jones, Terry L. and Klar, Kathryn A. Editors. (2007). *California Prehistory: Colonization , Culture and Complexity.* AltaMira Press: Lanham, MD.

Jones. Terry L.; and Schwitalla, Al. (2008). *Archaeological Perspectives on the Effects of Medieval Drought in Prehistoric California.* Quarternary International 188. Pp. 41-58.

Kant, Immanuel. *Fundamental principles of the metaphysics of morals.* (trans. 1949). New York: Liberal Arts Press. Retrieved from: http://etext.lib.Virginia.toccernew2?id=KanFund. xml&images=images/modeng&data=/texts/english/modeng/ parsed&tag=public&part=1&division=div2.

Kasler, Dale & Resese, Phillip. (2015). *California Farmers In Line for More Drought Cutbacks.* Sacramento Bee dated May 11, 2015.

Kennedy, John F. (1959). *Remarks at the Convocation of the United Negro College Fund, Indianapolis, Indiana, April 12, 1959.* John F. Kennedy Presidential Library and Museum. Retrieved from: http://www. jfklibrary.org/ Research/Research-Aids/JFK-Speeches/ Indianapolis-IN_19590412.aspx

Kenny, Doug and Lukas, Jeff. (2013). *Challenges of the Colorado River Basin presentation.* Retrieved from: http://www.slideshare.net/Learn MoreAboutClimate/climate-change-and-water-in-the-west-the-colorado-river- basin

Kershner, Isabel. (2015).*Aided By the Sea, Israel Overcomes An Old Foe: Drought.* The New York Times dated May 29, 2015. Retrieved from: nytimes.com/2015/05/30/world/middleeast/water-revolution-in-israel-overcomes-any-threat-of-drought.html?_r=1&referrer=

Knudson, Ted. (2014). *Outrage in Owens Valley a Century After L.A. Began Taking Its Water.* Sacramento Bee. January 5, 2014.Retrieved from:

sacbee.com/news/investigations/the-public-eye/article2588151.html#storylink=cpy

Krieger, Lisa. (2014). *California Drought: Bay Area Loses Billions of Gallons to Leaky Pipes.* San Jose Mercury News dated August 16, 2014. Retrieved from: http://www.mercurynews.com/drought/ci_26350962/californiadrought-bay-area-loses-billions-gallons-leaky

Kuckelman. Kristin A. (2010). *The Depopulation of Sand Canyon Pueblo, A Large Ancestral Pueblo Village in Southwestern Colorado.* American Antiquity 75(3).pg. 497-525

Kyle, Kim, Schleuss, Jon, and Krishnakumar, Priya. (2015). *XXX Gallons of Water Went to Make This Plate.* LA Times. April 7, 2015. Retrieved from: http://graphics.latimes.com/food-water-footprint/

Lambert, Patricia M. (1993). *Health in Prehistoric Populations of the Santa Barbara Channel Islands* American Antiquity 58(3). Pp. 509-525.

Lambert. P.M.& Walker, P.L. (1991). *Physical Anthropological Evidence for the Evolution of Social Complexity in Coastal Southern California.* Antiquity. 65:963-973.

Lang, William. (2007). *The Meaning of Falling Water: Celilo Falls and The Dalles in Historical Literature.* Oregon Historical Quarterly. Winter 2007

Lappin, Yaakov. (2015). *Israel to Double Amount of Water Entering Gaza.* The Jerusalem Post dated March 4, 2015.

Las Vegas Sun. (2015). *Utilities dated October 25, 2015.*Retrieved from: http://lasvegassun.com/guides/move-in/utilities/

Las Vegas Valley Water District. *Water Rates and Usage Thresholds.* Retrieved from: http://www.lvvwd.com/custserv/billing_rates_thresholds.html

Lavigne, Franck; Degeai, Jean-Philippe; Komorowski, Jean-Christophe; Guillet, Sebastien; Robert, Vincent; Lahitte, Pierre; Oppenheimer Clive; Stoffel Markus; Vidal, Celine M.; Surono; Praromo, Indyo; Wassmer, Patrick; Hajdas, Irka; Hadmoko, Danang Sri; andde Belizal, Edouard. (2013) *Source of the Great A.D. 1257 Mystery Eruption Unveiled, Samalas Volcano, Rinjani Volcanic Complex, Indonesia.* PNAS 110(42) pp. 16742-16747. doi/10.1073/pnas.1307520110

Lawton, Harry W.; Wilke, Philip J. ; DeDecker, Mary; Mason, and William M.(1976). *Agriculture Among the Paiute of Owens Valley.* Journal of California Anthropology. 3(1). pp. 13-50.

Lee, Lawrence B. (1985). *California Water Politics: Depression Genesis of the Central Valley Project, 1933-1944.* Journal of the West. 24 (4). Pp. 63-81.

Leigh, Mitch (music) and Darion, Joe (lyrics). *To Dream the Impossible Dream (1972).*

Lekson, Stephen H. (2008). *A History of the Ancient Southwest.* School for Advanced Research: Santa Fe, NM

Lekson, Stephen H. (1995).*Introduction.* Journal of Anthropological Archaeology. 14. Pp 99-103

Lekson, Stephen H. ; & Cameron, Catherine. (1995). *The Abandonment of Chaco Canyon, the Mesa Verde Migration and the Reorganization of the Pueblo World.* Journal of Anthropological Archaeology 14, pp 184-202.

Lekson, Stephen H.; Windes, Thomas C.; Stein, Jorh R.; & Judge, W. James. (1988). *The Chaco Canyon Community.* Scientific American. July. pp. 100-109

Leopold, Aldo. (1949. *A Sand County Almanac: And Sketches Here and There.* Oxford University Press: Oxford, England

Bibliography

Lillis, Ryan. (2015). *Sacramento To Speed Up Water Meter Installations.* The Sacramento Bee, dated February 23, 2015.

Limerick, Patricia Nelson and Hanson, Jason L. (2012). *A Ditch in Time: the City, the West and Water.* Golden, CO: Fulcrum Publishing. Kindle Edition.

Lin, Rong-Gong and Xia, Rosana. (2015). *Water Managers Dodge Bullet With 'May Miracle' Rains.* LA Times dated July 17, 2015

Lipe, William D. (1995). *The Depopulation of the Northern San Juan: Conditions in the Turbulent 1200s.* Journal of Anthropological Archaeology. 14 pp. 142-`69

Little, Jane Braxton. (2009). *The Ogallala Aquifer: Saving a Vital U.S. Water Source.* Scientific American. March 2009.

Liu, Jie; Dorjderem, Amarbayasgalan; Fu, Jinhua: and Lei, Xiaohui. (2011_: *Water Ethics and Water Resource Management.* UNESCO Bangkok

Lobosco, Katie. (2015). *Drought Turns Californians Against Water Bottling Companies.* CNN Money dated May 26, 2015. Retrieved from: http://money.cnn.com/2015/05/26/news/companies/California-bottled-water-drought/

Loomis, Brandon. *As the River Runs Dry: The Southwest's Water Crisis.* The Republic. Retrieved from: http://www.azcentral.com/story/news/arizona/investigations/2015/02/27/southwest-water-crisis-part- one/24011053/

Lustgarten, Abrahm and Sadasivam, Naveena. (2015). *Holy Crop: How Federal Dollars are Financing the Water Crisis in the West.* ProPublica. Retrieved from: https://projects.propublica.org/killing-the-colorado/story/arizona-cotton-drought-crisis

Lustgarten, Abrahm. (2015). *The Water Witch.* ProPublica dated June 2, 2015. Retrieved from: https://projects.propublica.org/killing-the-colorado/ story/pat-mulroy-las-vegas-water-witch

Lustgarten, Abrahm. (2015). *Use It or Lose It: Across the west, Exercising One's Right to Water.* ProPublica date June 9, 2015.

MacDonald, Glen M. *(2007). Severe and Sustained Drought in Southern California and the West: Present conditions and Insights From the Past on Causes and Impacts.* QuaternaryInternational.173-174. pp. 87-100

MacDonald, Glen M.; Krementetski, Constantine V.; & Hidalgo, Hugo G. (2008). *Southern California and the Perfect Drought: Simultaneous prolonged Drought in Southern California and the Sacramento and Colorado River Systems.* Quaternary International 199. pp. 11-23.

MacDonnell, Lawrence J.; Benson, Reed; Colby, Bonnie; Glennon, Robert; Udall, Bradley; and Wilkinson, Charles. (2015). *Navigating a Pathway Toward Colorado's Water Future: A Review and Recommendations on Colorado's Draft Water Plan.* Center for Natural Resources, Energy and the Environment.

Manning, Mary. And Samuelson, Andy. (2008). *A Gamble in the Sand: How Las Vegas Transformed Itself From a Railroad Watering Hole to the 'Entertainment Capital of the World'.* Las Vegas Sun. dated May 15, 2008.

Masse, W. Bruce. (1981). *Prehistoric Irrigation Systems in the Salt River Valley, Arizona* Science. 214(23). Pp. 408-416

McGlade, Caitlin. (2015). *Lake Mead Sinks to Record Low, Risking Water Shortages.* USA Today dated June 24, 2015.

McKinnon, Shaun. (2012). *Arizona Canal Project and Uphill Journey.* The Republic. Retrieved from: http://archive.azcentral.com/arizona

republic/news/articles/20121125arizona-canal-project-an-uphill-journey. html

Megdal, Sharon B. (2012). *The Water Report: Arizona Groundwater Management.* Water Resources Research Center, University of Arizona.

Meko, David M., Woodhouse, Connie A., Baisan, Christopher A., Knight, Troy. Lukas, Jeffrey J., Hughes, Malcolm K., and Salzer, Matthew W. (2007) *Medieval Drought in the Upper Colorado River Basin. AGU Publications.* DOI: 10.1029/2007GL029988

Melley, Brian. (2015). *Appeals Court Rules Against Higher Water Rates for Big Users.* Fresno Bee dated April 20, 2015. Retrieved from: http://www.fresnobee.Com/news/state/california/water-and-drought/article19667244.html#storylink=cpy

Mentor, Joe Jr. (2001). *Trading Water, Trading Places: Water Marketing in Chile and the Western United States.* AWRA/IWLRI-University of Dundee International Specialty Conference: August 6-8, 2001.

Metro Basin Round table and South Platte Basin Round table. (2015). *South Platte Basin Implementation Plan.* Retrieved from: coloradowaterplan.com

Mill, John Stuart. (1863). *Utilitarianism.* Retrieved from: https://www.utilitarianism.com/mill1.htm

Miller, Jeremy. (2014). *California's Sweeping Groundwater Regulation.* High Country News. Dated November 10, 2014. Retrieved from: http://www.hcn.org/issues/46.19/californias-sweeping-new-groundwater- regulations

Miller, Kathleen A. (2001). *Climate and Water Resources in the West: Past and Future.* Journal of the West. 40(3), pp. 39-47.

Minnis, Paul E. (1995).*Social Adaptation to Food Stress: A Prehistoric Southwestern Example.* University of Chicago Press: Chicago. IL

Mock, Cary J. (2000). *Rainfall in the Garden of the United States Great Plains, 1870-1889.*Climatic Change. 44(1-2), pp. 173-195

Mooney, Chris. (2015). *The Pacific Ocean May Have Entered a New Warm Phase – and the Consequences Could Be Dramatic.* Washington Post dated April 10, 2015.

Moore, Jerry D. (1999). *Archaeology in the Forgotten Peninsula: Settlement and Subsistence in Northern Baja California.* Journal of California and Great Basin Anthropology. 21(1). Pp. 17-44.

NASA. (2014). *NASA Analysis: 11 Trillion Gallons to Replenish California Drought.* NASA Science News. Dated December 16, 2014.

NASA Jet Propulsion Laboratory. (2014). *NASA Data Reveal Major Groundwater Loss in California.* California Institute of Technology. Retrieved from: http://www.jpl.nasa.gov/news/news.php?release=2009-194

National Research Council. (2007). *Colorado River Basin Water Management: Evaluating and Adjusting to Hydroclimatic Variability.* Washington, D.C.: National Academies Press.

Newkirk, Barrett. (2013). *Quantification Settlement Agreement Upheld by Judge.* Desert Sun. June 5, 2013. Retrieved from: http://www.mydesert.com/article/20130605/NEWS0701/306050002/Quantification-Settlement-Agreement-ruling-Salton-Sea.

National Oceanic and Atmospheric Administration (NOAA). (2014). *Future Temperature and Precipitation Change in Colorado.* Climate. Gov. Retrieved from: https://www.climate.gov/news-features/featured-images/future-temperature-and-precipitation-change-colorado

Nerburn, Kent. (2006). *Chief Joseph & the Flight of the Nez Perce: The Untold Story of an American Tragedy. Reprint Edition.* Harper One: San Francisco, CA

New Mexico Environmental Law Center. (2015). *Issues.* Retrieved from: http://nmelc.org/issues

Null, Jan. (2015). *4-Year California Rainfall Deficits: 2011-12 to 2014: Update June 23, 2015.* Golden Gate Weather Services. Retrieved from: http://ggweather.com/4-year_deficit.htm

O'Donnell, Michael and Colby, Bonnie. (2010). *Water Banks: A Tool For Enhancing Water Supply Reliability.* Department of Agricultural and Resource Economics, University of Arizona.

Oldham County Water District. *Interesting Water Facts.* Retrieved from: http://www.oldhamcountywater.com/interesting-water-facts.html

Owen, David, (2015). *Where the River Runs Dry: The Colorado and America's Water Crisis.* The New Yorker dated May 25, 2015.

Owens, Caitlin, Queally, James and Reyes, Emily Alpert. (2014). *UCLA-Area Water Main Break Spews Millions of Gallons.* LA Times dated July 29, 2014.

Overpeck, Jonathan. And Udall, Bradley. (2010). *Dry Times Ahead.* Science 328 (June 25, 2010). pp 1642-1643

Packard, Pamela. (2014). *Colorado River Shortages Could Occur By 2016 or 2017.* Arizona Capitol News dated March 3, 2014.

Palestinian Water Authority. (2012). *Annual Status Report on Water Resources, Water Supply, and Wastewater in the Occupied State of Palestine – 2011.* Palestinian Water Authority: Ramallah.

Philpott, Tom. (2014). *These Maps of California's Water Shortage Are Terrifying.* Mother Jones dated October 30, 2014. Retrieved from:

http://www.motherjones.com/tom-philpott/2014/10/caliifornia-groundwater-withdrawal-china-india-middle-east

Pike, Zebulon. (1810). *Account of the Expedition to the Sources of the Mississippi and Through the Western Parts of Louisiana to the Sources of the Arkansaw, Kans, La Platte and Pierre Juan, Rivers.* Philadelphia, PA: C & A Conrad & Co

Plog, Stephen E. (2008). *Ancient Peoples of the American Southwest. Second Edition.* Thames & Hudson. NYC:NY

Plog, Stephen E. and Heitman, Carrie. (2010). *Hierarchy and Social Inequality in the American Southwest, A.D. 800-1200.* Proceedings of the National Academy of Sciences. Vol. 107(46). Pp. 19619-19626.

Polakovic, Gary. *Runoff: It's an Ongoing Challenge.* San Diego State University: The Salton Sea. Retrieved from: http://www.sci.sdsu.edu/salton/FarmRunoff.html

Poland, J.F; Lofgren, B.E.; Ireland, R.L.; and Pugh, R.G. (1975). *Land Subsidence in San Joaquin Valley, California as of 1972.* U.S. Geological Survey Professional Papers – 437H. Retrieved from: http://pubs. usgs.gov/pp/0437h/report.pdf

Porter, Eduardo. (2014). *The Risks of Cheap Water.* NY Times dated October 14, 2014.

Poschman, Hans. *Water Usage in the West.* Council of State Governments. Retrieved from: http://www.csgwest.org/policy/WesternWaterUsage.aspx

Postel, Sandra. (2014). *Groundwater Depletion in Colorado River Basin Poses Big Risk to Water Security.* National Geographic: Water

Powell, John Wesley. (1879). *Report on the Lands of the Arid Region of the United States: Second Edition.* Washington, D.C.: Government Printing Office

Bibliography

PUB, Singapore's Water Agency. (2016). *Overview_ Four National Taps Provide Water for All.* Retrieved from: http://www.pub.gov.sg/water/ Pages/ default.aspx

Pura, Anthony. (2013). *Fresno's Water Rates to Nearly Double by 2016.* ABC Action News: KFSN: Fresno. Retrieved from: http://abc30. com/archive/9207745/

Putnam, Daniel H.; Summers, Charles G.; and Orloff, Steve B. (2007). *Irrigated Alfalfa Management for Mediterranean and Desert Zones. Chapter 1: Alfalfa Production Systems in California.* University of California: Division of Agriculture and Natural Resources.

Raab, L. Mark; and Larson, Daniel O.;. (1997). *Medieval Climatic Anomaly and Punctuated Cultural Evolution in Coastal Southern California.* American Antiquity. 62 (2). pp. 319-336.

Rand, Ayn. (1957).*Atlas Shrugged.* Random House: New York, NY

Rawls, John.(1971). *A Theory of Justice.* Belknap Press: Cambridge MA

Reclamation Act/Newlands Act of 1902. Retrieved from: http://www. ccrh.org/comm/Umatilla/primary/newlands.htm

Reid, J. J. & Montgomery, B. K. (1998). The Brown and the Gray: Pots and Population Movement in East-central Arizona. Journal of Anthropological Research 54, 447–459.

Reisner. Marc. (1993). *Cadillac Desert: The American West and Its Disappearing Water. Revised and updated edition.* Penguin Books: NYC, NY.

Ritterbush, Lauren W. (2002) *Drawn by the Bison: Late Prehistoric Native Migration into the Central Plains.* Great Plains Quarterly. Fall 22, pp.259-270

Roberts, Chris. (2014). *Leaks Contribute To Drought, But Water Conservation to be the 'New Normal' for California.* The Examiner dated

August 12, 2014. Retrieved from: http://archives.sf examiner.com/
sanfrancisco/leaks-contribute-to-drought-but-water-conservation-
to-be-new-normal-for-california/Content?oid =2871609

Robinson, Elwyn B. (1974). *An Interpretation of the History of the Great
Plains,* North Dakota History. 41(2), pp. 5-19

Rogers, Paul. (2014). *California Drought: Past Dry Periods Have Lasted
More Than 200 Years, Scientists Say.* San Jose Mercury News dated
January 25, 2014. Retrieved from: http://www.mercurynews.com/
science/ci_24993601/california-drought-past-dry-periods-have-
lasted-more

Rogers, Paul. (2014). *Nation's Largest Ocean Desalination Plant Goes Up
Near San Diego; Future of the California Coast?* San Jose Mercury
News. Dated May 29, 2014.

Romm, Joe. (2014). *NASA Bombshell: Global Groundwater Crisis
Threatens Our Food Supplies Our Security.* Climate. Retrieved from:
http://thinkprogress.org/climate/2014/10/31/3586561/global-
groundwater-crisis/34/

Roosevelt, Theodore. (1901). *First Annual Message to Congress. December
3, 1901.* Para. 65. Retrieved from: http://www.presidency. ucsb.edu/
ws/pid=29542

Salzer, Matthew W. & Kipfmueller, Kurt F. 2005. *Reconstructed
Temperature and Precipitation of Southern Colorado Plateau.* Climatic
Change 70:465-487 DOI: 10.1007/s10584-005-5922-3

San Diego County Water Authority. (2015). *San Diego County's Water
Sources.* Retrieved from: http://www.sdcwa.org/san-diego-county-
water- sources

San Diego County Water Authority (2015). *Seawater Desalination: The
Carlsbad Desalination Project. Fact Sheet.* Retrieved from: http://
www.sdcwa.org/ sites/default/files/desal-carlsbad-fs-single.pdf

San Diego County Water Authority. *Quantification Settlement Agreement for the Colorado River.* Retrieved from: http://www.sdcwa.org/sites/default/files/qsa-fs.pdf

Saunders, Stephen; Montgomery, Charles; and Easley, Tom. (2008). *Hotter and Drier: The West's Changed Climate.* Rocky Mountain Climate Organization and Natural Resources Defense Council

Schaafsma, Hoski. (2007). *Hohokam Field Building.* The Kiva. 72(4), pp. 431-455.

Schecter, Anna R. and DeLuca, Matthew. (2015).*In Palm Springs, America's 'Oasis' Grapples with Drought.* NBC News. Retrieved from:www.nbc.news.com/storyline/California-drought/palm-springs-oasis-grapples-drought-n337371

Schwartz, Nelson. (2015). *The Parched West: Water Pricing in Two*

Thirsty Cities: In One Guzzlers Pay More, and Use Less. N.Y Times. Dated May 6, 2015.

Seager, Richard; Ting, Mingfang; Held, Isaac; Kkkushnir, Yochanan; Lu, Jian; Vecchi, Gabriel; Huang, Huei-Ping; Harnik, Nili; Leetmaa, Ants, Lau, Ngar-Cheung; Velez, Jennifer; and Niak, Naomi. (2007). *Modeled Projections of an Imminent Transition to a More Arid Climate in Southwestern North America.* Science 316. (May 25, 2007). pp. 1181-1184

Senthilingam, Meera. (2014). *Drinking Sewage: Solving Singapore's Water Problem.* CNN News. Retrieved from: http://www.cnn.com /2014/09/23/living/newater-singapore/

Shyong. Frank; Branson-Potts, Hailey; & Stevens, Matt. (2015). *California's Wealthy Lagging in Water Conservation.* LA Times dated April 5, 2015. Retrieved from: http://www.latimes. com/local/lanow/la-me-ln-wealthy-cities-lag-in-conservation-20150404-story.html#page=1

Sibley, George (2013). *Water Wranglers: The 75 Year History of the Colorado River District: A Story About the Embattled Colorado River and the Growth of the West.* Colorado River District.

Siegel, Seth M. (2015). *Let There Be Water: Israel's Solution for a Water Starved World.* St. Marten's Press: New York, New York.

Smith, Adam (1882). *Inquiry Into the Nature and Causes of the Wealth of Nations. Vol.1.* pg. 42. London: G. Walker, J. Akerman, E Edwards; Thomas Tegg: G. and J. Robinson, Liverpool: E. Thompson, Manchester; J. Noble Hull; J. Wilson, Berwick; W. Whyte & Co. Edinburgh; and R. Griffin and Co. Glasgow.

Solomon, Steven. (2011). *Water: The Epic Struggle for Wealth, Power, and Civilization.* Harper Perennial: New York, NY

Southern Nevada Water Authority. (2015). *Water Banking.* Retrieved from: http://www.snwa.com/ws/future_banking.html

Stark, Miriam; Clark, Jeffry J.; & Elson, Mark D. (1995). *Causes and Consequences of Migration in the 13*th *Century Tonto Basin.* Journal of Anthropological Archaeology 14. Pp. 212-246.

State of California: Department of Water Resources. (2015). *California State Water Project Overview.* State of California. Retrieved from: http://www.water.ca.gov/swp/

State of California: Department of Water Resources. (2015). *Most Significant Droughts: Comparing Historical and Recent Conditions.* State of California. Retrieved from: http://www.water.ca.gov/water conditions/docs/California_Signficant_Droughts_2015_small.pdf

State of California. (2015). Executive Order B-29-15. Retrieved from: http://gov.ca.gov/docs/4.1.15_Executive_Order.pdf

State of Colorado. (2013). *Executive Order D 2013-005: Directing the Colorado Water Conservation Board to Commence Work on the*

Colorado water Plan. Retrieved from: http://cwcbweblink.state. co.us/WebLink/ElectronicFile.aspx?docid=171100&searchid=c428f 27e-6b83-4a97- 908c-31bb6996cf74&dbid=0

Stegner, Wallace. (1955). *This is Dinosaur: Echo Park Country and Its Magic Rivers.* Alfred A. Knopf: New York, NY

Stene, Eric A. *Central Valley Project: Overview.* United States Bureau of Reclamation.

Stephen Sills. (1967). *For What It's Worth* lyrics

Stevens, Matt. (2015). *In a Blow to Water Conservation, Court Rejects San Juan Capistrano's Tiered Rates* . LA Times . Dated April 20, 2015.

Stevens, Matt and Megerian, Chris. *Southern California Lags Behind in Water Conservation.* L.A. Times, April , 2015

Stevens, William K. (1994). *Severe Ancient Droughts: A Warning to California.* New York Times dated July 19, 1994.

Stine, Scott. 1994. Extreme and Persistent Drought in California and Patagonia During Mediaeval Time. Nature 369, pp. 546–549.

Summit Technologies. *Water Data Facts.* Retrieved from: http:// lakepowell.water-data,com

Sunseri, Alvin R. (1973). *Agricultural Techniques in New Mexico at the Time of the Anglo-American Conquest.* Agricultural History, 47(4), pp. 329-337).

Tan, Poh-Ling & Jackson, Sue. (2013). *Impossible Dreaming – Does Australia's Water Law and Policy Fulfil Indigenous Aspirations.* Environmental and Planning Law Journal, Vol. 30, pp. 132-149. Retrieved from: https://www.griffith.edu.au/__data/assets/ pdf_file/0010/491374/Tan-Jackson-2013-EPLJ.pdf

Thiel, J. Homer & Diehl, Michael W. (2006) *Final Report: Rio Nuevo Archaeology, 2000-2003.* Chapter 3: *Cultural History of the Tucson*

Basin and the Project Area. Center for Desert Archaeology. Tucson AZ.

Thomas, Dylan. (1951). *Do Not Go Gentle Into That Good Night.*

Thompson, Andres. (2015). *2015 May Just Be Hottest Year on Record.* Scientific American. August 2015.

Thompson, Kaylee. (2014). *The Last Straw: How the Fortunes of Las Vegas Will Rise or Fall With Lake Mead.* Popular Science dated June 22,2014. Toronto Globe and Mail. (1998). *Editorial dated 23 May 1998.*

Tory, Sarah. (2016). *In Utah, A Massive Water Project Is Gaining Ground.* High Country News dated February 28, 2016

Turner, Frederick Jackson. (1903). *Contribution of the West to American Democracy.* Atlantic Monthly, January 1903

UC Davis. Center for Watershed Science. (2015). *Water Storage: Myth: We can build our way out of California's water problems with new dams.* Retrieved from: https://watershed.ucdavis.edu/myths/water+storage/#2

Sharon Udasin. (2015). *Israeli, Jordanian Officials Signing Historic Agreement on Water Trade.* The Jerusalem Post dated February 26, 2015.

United States Bureau of Reclamation. (2015) *Bureau of Reclamation: About US: Fact Sheet.* Retrieved from: www.usbr.gov/main/about/fact.html

United States Bureau of Reclamation. (2012). *Colorado River Basin Water Supply and Demand Study: Executive Summary.*

United States Bureau of Reclamation.(2012b). *Colorado River Basin: Water Supply and Demand Study: Appendix F4: Option Characterization – Importation.* Retrieved from: http://www.

usbr.gov/lc/region/programs/crbstudy/finalreport/Technical%20 Report%20F%20 %20Development%20of%20Options%20 and%20Stategies/ TR-F_Appendix4_FINAL.pdf

United States Bureau of Reclamation. (2015). *Glen Canyon Dam/Lake Powell: Current Status.* Retrieved from: http://www.usbr.gov/uc/ water.crsp/gcd.html

United States Bureau of Reclamation: Lower Colorado River Operations. Retrieved from: http://www.usbr.gov/lc/region/g4000/ hourly/mead-elv. html.

United States Bureau of Reclamation. *Managing Water in the West: Central Valley Project.*

United States Bureau of Reclamation. (2016). *Managing Water in the West: lower Colorado River Operations: archives of Daily Reservoir and River Conditions.* Retrieved from: http://www.usbr.gov/lc/region/ g4000/levels_archive.html

United States Bureau of Reclamation. (2012). Reclamation: Managing Water in The West: The Colorado River Basin Water Supply and Demand Study.

United States Bureau of Reclamation. (2007). *Record of Decision: Colorado River Interim Guidelines for Lower Basin Shortages and the Coordinated Operations for Lake Powell and Lake Mead Guidelines*

United States Bureau of Reclamation: Upper Colorado Region. Retrieved from: http://www.usbr.gov/uc/water/rsvrs/ops/crsp_40_ gc.html

United States Census Bureau. Retrieved from: http://www.census.gov

United States Declaration of Independence. para 2. (1776).

United States Department of Agriculture. (2015). National Drought Monitor. Retrieved from: http://www.drought.gov/drought/area/ca

U.S.G.S.. (2010). *Effects of Climate Change and Land Use on Water Resources in the Upper Colorado River Basin.* Retrieved from: http://pubs.usgs.gov/fs/2010/3123/pdf/FS10-3123.pdf

USGS. (2014). *Colorado River Basin Area Study.* Retrieved from: http://water.usgs.gov/watercensus/colorado.html

USGS. (2015), *Current Conditions of Colorado River Streamflow.* Retrieved from: http://www.usgs.gov/water/

USGS. *Water Basics.* http://water.usgs.gov/edu/mwater.html.

USGS. *The Water Cycle.* http://water.usgs.gov/edu/watercycle.html

USGS.(2015). *USGS Water Science School: Land Subsidence.* Retrieved from: http://water.usgs.gov/edu/earthgwlandsubside.html

USGS. (2015). *The World's Water: Distribution of Earths Water.* Retrieved from: http://water.usgs.gov/edu/earthwherewater.html

VanderMey, Anne. (2015). *Las Vegas: City of Gambling, Tech Conferences and Water Crises.* Fortune dated January 9, 2015.

Vano, Julie A., Udall, Bradley, Cayan, Daniel R., Overpeck, Jonathan T., Brekke, Levi D., Das, Tapash, Hartmann, Holly C., Hidalgo, Hugo G., Hoerling, Martin, McCabe, Gregory J., Morino, Kiyomi, Webb, Robert S., Werner, Kevin, and Lettenmaier, Dennis P. (2013). *Understanding Uncertainties in Future Colorado River Stream Flow.* Bulletin of the American Meteorological Society. December 2103. pp. 59-78. DOI: 10.1175/BAMS-D-12-00228.1

Walker, Alissa. (2015). *Lake Mead Is Now Lower Than Ever, But Las Vegas Has a Crazy Survival Plan.* Gizmodo. Retrieved from: http://gizmodo.com/this-giant-straw-will-suck-vegass-water-from-the-dese-1590135681/1700743879

Wallace, Henry D. and Holmlund, James P. (1984). *The Classic Period in the Tucson Basin.* Kiva 49(3/4) pg. 167-194

Walton, Brett. (2014). *'Transformational' Water Reforms, Though Wrenching, Helped Australia Endure Historic Drought, Experts Say.* Circle of Blue dated March 10, 2014. Retrieved from: http://www.circleofblue.org/waternews/2014/world/transformational-water-reforms-though-wrenching-helped-australia-endure-historic-drought-experts-say/

Water Research Center, College of Agricultures, University of Arizona (1999). *The Rise and Fall of CAP: In Water in the Tucson Area: A Status report.* Arizona Daily Star dated July 11,1999.

Waters, Michael R. and Ravesloot, John C. (2001). *Change and the Cultural Evolution of the Hohokam along the Middle Gila River and Other River Valleys in South-central Arizona.* American Antiquity, 66(2), pp. 285- 299.

West, Elliot. (2012). *The Essential West: Collected Essays by Elliot West.* University of Oklahoma Press: Norman, OK

Whittlesey, Stephanie M. (1995). *The Mogollon, Hohokam and O'Otam: Rethinking the Early Formative Period in Southern Arizona* Kiva 60(4). Pp. 465-498

Wienhold, Michelle L. (2013). *Prehistoric Land Use and Hyrdrology: A Multi-scalar Spatial Analysis in Central Arizona.* Journal Of Archeological Science. Vol. 40. Pp. 250-259

Williams, Matt. (2013). *Judge upholds 2003 Colorado River Quantification Settlement Agreement.* Association of California Water Agencies. Retrieved from: http://www.acwa.com/news/water-supply-challenges/judge-upholds-2003-colorado-river-quantification-settlement-agreement

Wills, W.H.; and Dorshow, Wetherbee Bryan. (2012). *Agriculture and Community In Chaco Canyon: Revisiting Pueblo Alto.* Journal of Anthropological Archaeology. 31. pp 138-155.

Woodhouse, Connie A.; Meko, David M.; Macdonald, Glen M.; Stahle, Dave W.; & Cook, Edward R. (2010).*A 1200-Year Perspective of 21st Century Drought in Southwestern North America.* Proceedings of the National Academy of Sciences. 107(50). Pg. 21283-21288. DOI:10.1073/pnas.091197107

Worldmark Encyclopedia of Cultures and Daily Life. (2009)Ed Timothy L. Gall and Heneen Hobby Vol 2. Americas. 2nd ed. Detroit: Gale pp 424- 432.

Woody, Christopher. (2015). *Israel's Revolutionary Water Management Methods Aren't Going To Be Enough to Solve California's Devastating Drought.* Business Insider. dated June 15, 2015.

Worster, Donald (1995). *Rivers of Empire: Water, Aridity, and the Growth of the American West.* New York, New York: Oxford University Press.

Young, Michael. (2010). *Managing Water Scarcity: Lessons from Australia Presentation.* Water for Food International Conference, May 2-5, 2010. Video available from: http://waterforfood.nebraska.edu/2010/video.php?ID=8b

Young, Michael. (2015). *Unbundling Rights: A Blueprint for the Development of Robust Water Allocation Systems for the Western United States.* Nicholas Institute for Environmental Policy Solutions: Duke University.

Young, Michael and McColl, James C. (2005). *Defining Tradable Water Entitlements and Allocations: A Robust System.* Canadian Water Resources Journal 30(1). Pp. 65-72.

Young, Michael and McColl, James C. (2009). *Double Trouble: The Importance of Accounting for Obtaining Water Entitlements Consistent with Hydrological Realities.* The Australian Journal of Agricultural and Resource Economics. 54. pp. 19-35.

Young, Michael D. (2011). *Evaluating Economic Policy Instruments for Sustainable Water Management in Europe: WP6 IBE Ex-post Case Studies: The Role of the Unbundling Water Rights in Australia's Southern Connected Murray Darling Basin.* Environmental Progress Inc: Lexington, South Carolina.

Young, Mike.(2005). *Designing Water Entitlement Regimes for and Ever-Changing and Ever-Varying Future.* Agricultural Water Management 145 (November).

Zamora, Amanda; Kirchner, Lauren; & Lustgarten, Abrahm. (2015). *Killing the Colorado: The Truth Behind the Water Crisis in the West: California's Drought is Part of a Much Bigger Water Crisis.* ProPublica dated June 25, 2015.

Acknowledgements

ONE CANNOT WRITE A BOOK like this without relying on those who came before to ensure a solid understanding of the background and all the relevant issues. This clearly applies here. The "Water Canon" comprised of books written by Marc Reisner, Donald Worster, Morris Hundley, Jr., Robert Glennon and Charles Fishman provided both history and an appreciation of the complex world of water. As it relates to prehistory research by Scott Stine, Stephen Lekson and Paul Minnis were invaluable. Recent newspaper and news articles, publications like ProPublica and a host of recent research by NASA, the Pacific Institute and UC Davis supplied important information on ground water depletion and agriculture's consumption of water.

A special thanks goes to Professor Mike Young who took time to walk me through Australia's water sharing regimen, which is a possible alternative to prior appropriation. Also, Seth Siegel, author of *Let There Be Water*, was extremely helpful in providing more specificity on the water management system in Israel. Finally, a conversation with Professor Robert Glennon was instrumental in reigning in my idealism. Although I accept that the Law of the River is ingrained into the water allocation system in the western United States, I think a change is needed. I have presented some alternatives, understanding that any changes to the existing system will require an open dialogue and the ability to compromise. If we wish to attain a sustainable water future for our grandchildren this may be necessary. I remain hopeful!

On a personal note, without Gary's support, this would still be an item on my bucket list and like many projects I have started over the years, only three-quarters complete. Fortunately, he understood my passion for the topic and continued to encourage me all along the way. I subjected him to many boring explanations in my effort to understand some new aspect on the topic and constantly pestered him with "What's another word for "allocation" or "shortage?" He also often had some excellent organizational suggestions.

Our children, Aran and Matthew, also understood my enthusiasm and gave me the time and space to finish the book. Perhaps the most patient of all was our nine-year-old golden doodle, Bailey whose brown eyes were the only indications he was disappointed when I said, "Mommy can't play right now, I have to finish this chapter first".

My brother-in-law, Tim, and good friend Nancy Karklins were brave enough to start the editing process. Their suggestions and ideas were deeply appreciated and were instrumental in determining the final structure and content of the book.

Last but not least, there is always "Stormin" Norman.

Index

A

Agricultural, 120, 162, 220, 262, 269, 274, 280, 293-295, 299, 300, 307, 322-324, 326

Alfalfa, 162, 295

Anasazi, 13, 28, 29, 36, 40, 55, 98, 147, 269

Ancient Puebloans, 13, 29, 30, 32-35, 41, 46-47, 55, 73, 242, 248, 250, 253

Arizona, v, 2, 3, 24, 29, 34, 35, 36, 37, 57, 61, 64-67, 86-91, 93-94, 101, 105, 133-144, 154-155, 161, 163, 166, 172, 174, 179, 185, 195, 198-199, 218, 229, 232, 255, 267, 269, 270-271, 279, 280, 284, 298-302

Arizona Groundwater Management Act (GMA), 134

Australia, 207, 219, 220-222, 224-227, 229, 230-235, 244, 254-256, 321-327, 330

B

Bureau of Reclamation (USBR), 15, 57, 58, 61, 68-69, 77, 81, 88, 161, 172-173, 185, 278, 280-283, 285, 287-288, 297, 299, 309, 311, 329

C

California, v, 1, 2, 3, 5-9, 13-17, 23, 24-26, 41-44, 46-47, 52-56, 58, 61-65, 68, 70, 72-73, 75-77, 83-89, 92-95, 97-98, 100-101, 104, 105, 107, 108-112, 115-128, 130-131, 135, 139, 141-144, 147, 153-155, 157, 161, 163-166, 168-169, 172-173, 175-177, 182, 185, 190, 193-194, 196, 201-202, 207, 210, 212-213, 215, 219, 229, 232-234, 236, 238-240, 242, 247, 249-251, 253, 255, 257, 259-262, 265, 266, 272, 273, 276, 278-279, 284, 286, 290, 291-300, 307-308, 314, 316, 318, 319, 327-329

California State Water Project (CSWP), 279, 291

Central Arizona Project (CAP), 65, 185, 279

Central Valley, 13, 43-45, 47, 56, 61-62, 64, 104, 108, 118-119,

122-126, 128, 130, 169, 203, 212, 233, 259, 260, 278

Central Valley Project (CVP), 61, 108

Chile, 207, 215-219, 223, 230, 232-235, 256, 321

Chumash, 24, 25, 41-44, 47, 51, 73, 272

Climate change, 185

Colorado River Basin, 8, 10, 16-17, 23, 25, 36, 53, 55, 73, 75, 77, 81-82, 86-87, 99-101, 104-105, 110, 125, 130-131, 136, 140, 144, 158, 160-161, 163-164, 166, 168-171, 176-177, 181, 185-187, 202-206, 207, 212-213, 215, 219-220, 229, 232-234, 236, 240, 247, 250, 253-254, 257-260, 262, 264- 265, 275, 281, 283, 285, 287-288, 294, 301-302, 305, 307-309, 310- 311, 329

Colorado River Compact (Compact), 85

Colorado River Storage Project, 68, 89, 186, 285

Colorado Water Plan (Plan), 176, 180-181, 184, 199, 229, 235, 251, 253, 255, 309, 313, 329, 330

Conservation, 67, 150, 170, 176, 182, 185, 261, 291, 309, 310, 312, 313, 315, 318, 327, 328, 329, 330

D

Denver, 96, 159, 160-161, 163, 174-175, 182-186, 190-192, 194, 204, 206, 212, 215, 233-234, 259, 288, 312, 315

Denver Water, 96, 159, 174-175, 182-183, 185-186, 190-192, 259, 312, 315

Desalination, 114-115, 128, 210, 293

E

Echo Park, 90-91, 116, 186, 240, 286, 327

F

Famliglietti, Jay, 1, 6, 122, 261, 329

G

Glen Canyon Dam, 90, 91, 92, 285, 309

GRACE, 122, 123, 169

Great American Desert, 9, 11, 52-54, 102, 103, 169

Great Plains, 11-13, 53, 55, 63, 103, 169, 263, 275, 282

Groundwater, 3, 4, 19, 65, 100, 118, 122-124, 128-129, 134, 141, 168, 183, 203, 261, 278, 279, 280, 296-300, 306, 308, 309, 313

Groundwater depletion, 118

H

Hetch Hetchy, 68, 70, 90, 116

Hohokam, 13, 24, 25, 36-41, 43, 47, 51, 55, 57, 64, 73, 98-99, 133, 145, 242, 248, 269-271

Hoover Dam, 4, 58, 74, 85, 88, 100, 111-112, 147, 149, 155, 156, 206

I

Imperial Valley, 15, 23, 61, 64, 88, 89, 93, 111-113, 119, 121, 162, 175, 179, 190, 200, 222, 247-248, 259, 283

Interim Guidelines for Lower Basin Shortages and Lake Mead (Guidelines), 93, 135, 287, 299

Israel, 184, 207-215, 231-233, 235, 256, 318-320

L

Lake Cahuilla, 83, 84, 283

Lake Mead, 1-4, 6, 85, 88, 92, 93, 97, 100, 109, 112, 126, 133, 139, 149-157, 166-169, 185-186, 229, 237-239, 260, 287-288, 292, 299, 302, 305, 330

Lake Powell, 2, 6, 88, 90-93, 97, 100, 126, 153, 155-156, 166-169, 185-186, 260, 287-288, 297, 299, 305, 309, 314

Las Vegas, v, 2, 23, 61, 105, 112, 141, 147-158, 161, 163, 182, 190, 200, 204, 232-233, 239, 249, 259, 292, 303-306, 314

Los Angeles, 7, 15, 23, 41, 46, 59-61, 64, 80, 85, 88, 89, 92, 97, 100, 104, 108, 110-111, 125, 126, 128, 129, 161, 163-164, 196, 201, 206, 233, 259, 260, 276, 290, 307

M

Muir, John, 68, 70, 240

N

NASA, 1, 109, 122, 169, 250, 288, 291, 296, 309

O

Ogallala Aquifer, 53, 101-102, 104, 169, 289, 309

Owens Valley, 24, 43, 45-47, 60, 80, 88, 273, 277, 290

P

Paiute, 24, 25, 45-47, 51, 59, 73, 147, 273

Price of water, 304

Q

Quantification Settlement Agreement (QSA), 92, 111, 251

R

Recharge, 19, 128-129, 297, 299, 300

Reuse, 182

S

Sacramento, 7, 44, 56, 63, 122, 194, 195, 265, 277, 290, 316, 328

Salton Sea, 84-85, 92, 111-114, 126, 283, 292

San Diego, 15, 23, 85, 92, 93, 97, 107, 108, 114-116, 125-126, 163, 206, 211, 232, 251, 286, 292-293, 297

Santa Barbara, 41, 110, 116, 117, 126, 232, 273, 293

Singapore, 184, 207, 214, 215, 232, 256, 320

Subsidies, 142, 143

W

Water banking, 138

Water sharing, 222, 224, 232

Y

Yokuts, 44, 45, 47, 73

CPSIA information can be obtained
at www.ICGtesting.com
Printed in the USA
LVHW040017030123
736284LV00026B/387

9 781535 605144